This book is different, and deserves to make an impact. Lilia Shevtsova, as a Russian expert, and Andrew Wood, a Western observer, discuss the interaction of Russia and the West since the country's emergence as an independent power. They focus on the troubling questions of whether Russia can now find its path towards renewal and benign transformation, and whether the West can regain its will to work for that surely vital objective.

The authors take the reader through some of the more controversial pathways of Russian politics. Their analysis of Western attempts to balance values and self interest is unsparing. They are not afraid to disagree. Their major contribution is in attacking the widely held myths and illusions which have for so long governed both the evolution of Russia and the ideas of Russia held by the outside world.

This is a lively book made still better by flashes of humor. You may agree with it, or dispute it. You may like some of it, and hate the rest. But read it.

—Mikhail Gorbachev
Former president of the Soviet Union, Nobel Peace Prize winner, and president of the Gorbachev Foundation

With thanks for your interest.
Andrew Wood
Lilia

LILIA SHEVTSOVA & ANDREW WOOD

CHANGE OR DECAY

RUSSIA'S DILEMMA and the WEST'S RESPONSE

CARNEGIE ENDOWMENT
FOR INTERNATIONAL PEACE
WASHINGTON DC ▪ MOSCOW ▪ BEIJING ▪ BEIRUT ▪ BRUSSELS

Carnegie Endowment for International Peace
1779 Massachusetts Avenue, N.W., Washington, D.C. 20036
202-483-7600, Fax 202-483-1840
www.ceip.org

To order, contact:
Hopkins Fulfillment Service
P.O. Box 50370, Baltimore, MD 21211-4370
1-800-537-5487 or 1-410-516-6956
Fax 1-410-516-6998

Cover design by Jocelyn Soly
Composition by Zeena Feldman
Printed by United Book Press

Library of Congress Cataloging-in-Publication Data
Shevtsova, Lilia Fedorovna.
Change or decay : Russia's dilemma and the West's response / Lilia Shevtsova and Andrew Wood.
p. cm.
Includes bibliographical references and index.
ISBN 978-0-87003-346-9 (cloth : alkaline paper) – ISBN 978-0-87003-347-6 (pbk.)
1. Russia (Federation) – Relations – Western countries. 2. Western countries – Relations – Russia (Federation) 3. Russia (Federation) – Politics and government – 1991- 4. Russia (Federation)–Foreign relations. I. Wood, Andrew, 1940- II. Title.

DK66.S52 2011
947.086'3--dc23 2011039136

16 15 14 13 12 11 1 2 3 4 5 1st Printing 2011

CONTENTS

FOREWORD

Twenty years is long enough to permit some—at least tentative—historical judgments. It is now clear that the twenty years that have elapsed since the Soviet Union imploded so suddenly have been a time of adjustment between Russia and the West without definitive outcomes.

The West was caught off-guard by the very thing that it had fought for and earnestly desired for so long: the end of communism. When it finally came—and the process of disintegration of the Soviet bloc and its attendant ideology can be measured in months rather than years—no one knew what to expect, and virtually no one had planned seriously for such an eventuality. Even now, two decades later, the West is still trying to adjust to the post-Soviet reality.

This book is an unusual series of conversations between two highly respected scholars who have not only studied these twenty years of shifting relations, but lived through them personally. Lilia Shevtsova is a distinguished Russian scholar and participant in Russian politics, and a veteran of the Carnegie Moscow Center, who has witnessed firsthand Russia's development in the postcommunist period. Andrew Wood, an associate fellow at Chatham House, served in the British Embassy in Moscow at both the beginning and the end of the Leonid Brezhnev era, as well as during the final five years of Boris Yeltsin's rule. Both have been astute observers of Russia under communism and afterward.

Their exchanges in the pages that follow are lively, vigorous, and candid. They often disagree about outcomes, values, perceptions, and meaning and yet both remain faithful to the same goal: trying to help us to understand how the Russia of Putin and Medvedev emerged from the ashes of the Soviet Union. What internal forces pushed Russia to where it is today, where no one would have guessed it would be twenty years ago—in Lilia Shevtsova's phrase—that of an "imitation democracy"? And by corollary, why did the West take the path that it took, steadily moving from Cold War confrontation to uncertain and wary accommodation? One key question they debate is whether there was anything more the West could have done to nudge Russia closer to a "liberal" Western form of government.

Shevtsova and Wood are not dogmatists. They claim no final truths. Instead, in the spirit of all the best conversations, they probe, challenge old shibboleths, and examine new sacred cows. In doing so, they successfully illuminate the relationship between Russia and the West throughout these two critical decades in a way that few others have approached.

Russia has yet to settle on its relationship with the rest of the world, and the world remains equally unsure how to handle Russia: this huge country that is neither wholly Asian nor European, neither totalitarian nor democratic, neither expansionist nor benign. For anyone interested in where the new Russia might be going, I commend these unique conversations about where it has just come from. As Winston Churchill once advised, "The farther backward you can look the farther forward you are likely to see."

—Jessica T. Mathews
President, Carnegie Endowment for International Peace

LETTER TO THE READER

What follows is a record of our exchanges from late 2010 to mid-2011 on Russia's trajectory and Western attitudes toward it.

We started our dialogue with the usual friendly catch-up. "What's new in Moscow?"; "How is the tandem doing?"; "What about the wider Russian picture?"; were the usual questions from one side. "What does the West think about the reset?"; "Don't you think Brussels is pretending it has a strategy toward Russia?"; came from the other side. Soon we began to look deeper into the trends we were discussing and zeroed in on the interaction between the Western understanding of Russian realities and the direction of events and ideas in Russia itself. As our conversations became longer and our e-mail exchanges became a regular habit, we wondered whether giving them more structure would be worthwhile. The result is the pages that follow.

The world is still coping with the geopolitical and civilizational consequences and implications of the collapse of the Soviet Union. The international system is still haunted by the ideas that governed the relationship among the major powers between the end of the Second World War and 1991. But of course one of these powers has disappeared. Or has it? Is Russia the Soviet Union on a smaller scale or a restored European power? The fact that the United States and Russia are still engaged in a bilateral nuclear dialogue suggests to us that the world still faces the challenge of building a new post–Cold War paradigm. The tension between the way that the Russian elite are adapting to outside realities without changing the rules of the game inside Russia, on the one hand, and the way that the West reacts, by accepting or rejecting Russian behavior, on the other, is a further indication that fresh approaches are needed.

Our deliberations focus not only on traditional stereotypes but also on the intellectual constraints that may have left us with so many remnants from the past. We try in this book to question established ideas and test whether deeply held assumptions stand up to questioning. We clash and we find common ground. The exercise has not always been comfortable, and the implications for the future are troubling, but we feel it worthwhile to share our thoughts and let our readers make their own judgments.

We took a deliberately long view, from the breakup of the Soviet Union to the latter part of President Dmitri Medvedev's 2008–2012 term. Our goal was to explore how the West and its values—and the expectations that follow from those values—affected Russia's evolution after the collapse of communism. We examined the link between domestic and foreign policy in Russia, and the role that Western standards and ideas about development played in Russian policymaking. We asked ourselves, in particular, whether the West has, over this time, retreated from a liberal and transformative agenda to one of working with the Russian status quo, characterized by short-term goals. Has the West become a factor in legitimizing a Russian system that is alien to its own commitment to liberal democracy? To what extent is Russia a test case for the West's ability or willingness to pursue a wider civilizational agenda?

Russia continues to be engaged in the painful experiment of trying to reconcile a yearning to modernize and prosper with a dominant and archaic tradition of one-man rule. The experiment differs this time, however, in that it hides behind a façade of an "imitation democracy," as Russia's rulers seek to persuade both the Russian elite and the wider world that all will be well. The West, for its part, has attempted to find ways to cope with the dilemmas inherent in trying to develop a constructive and sustainable relationship with a system based on different and antipathetic principles.

The conversation format allowed us to escape preaching or reaching didactic final conclusions. The context is too uncertain for that. Our goal has been to address uncertainties and to look beyond the conventional wisdom of the day. Neither of us would claim to have a clear or infallible key to the future, but we would be content if our arguments provoke others to look at the opportunities and dangers as Russia in its latest guise enters its third decade.

THE BEGINNING
WHERE HAVE ALL THE FLOWERS GONE?

LILIA: Hardly anyone could have imagined the following situation after the demise of communism: Russia imitates democracy and the West sits on the sidelines, watching patiently in a way that serves only to encourage the imitators. Russian liberals criticize the Western community, while Russian authorities, despite occasional grudges, are generally happy with it. Western politicians, meanwhile, prefer to deal with the Russian state and are irritated by the constant lamentations of Russian liberals, which stand in the way of mutual satisfaction.

How did we get here? We have to go back in time to find out. I will present here the Russian liberal view.

ANDREW: Let's agree on terms first. There are some pretty slippery ones. I would list three for Russia (though more may occur to us as we continue the discussion): Russia, the state, and liberals. The name of your country, Lilia, can be used in all sorts of senses, but in particular, it is often used in remarks like "Russia needs, or Russia wants, or Russia has such-and-such interests." This gives us a convenient way of speaking, but we should try to remember in each case whether "Russia" refers to its leaders or to some other category. This is easier said than done but worth reminding ourselves about from time to time. The same goes for "state," which is a particularly opaque category for Russia but a relatively clear one for Western countries. (Law, justice, and other such ideas fall into a similar situation. But I digress....)

The term "liberals" in the Russian context can be and has been used pejoratively to mean those who failed to impose their views in the 1990s and are now regarded by many as a divided and bitter minority. I prefer to think of liberals as those who favor a market economy—adjudicated clearly and independently—and an accountable government. This makes for a much broader group that is attached to the values the West also proclaims rather than just the narrow group of politicians dismissed as relics of the 1990s.

LILIA: Indeed, we need some clarification. The way some terms are used can be confusing. When we speak of "Russia," we should differentiate between the Russian state, the Russian political regime, and Russian society. At the moment the state and the political regime pursue the same interests. In fact, the regime now presents itself as the state. But official Russian interests and the interests of Russian society do indeed differ. That is why, when one hears, "Russia thinks…," one always has to ask, "Which Russia?"

And, yes, I agree that the Russian state is built on premises that are alien to the Western political mentality. We will discuss those premises.

Apparently, we also agree on who the "liberals" in Russia are. I personally belong to the group of "anti-systemic liberals." We believe in freedom and competition, but we also argue that the current Russian regime will never expand the "freedom area" from the top down. Society needs to fight for new rules of the game from the bottom up. "Systemic liberals," in contrast, insist that freedom and competition, while certainly good things, have to be implemented gradually and under control of the authorities where possible. "Systemic liberals" live in expectation of a "good tsar" emerging from the Kremlin who will give Russia its freedom as one gives a gift. They have waited to receive this gift from Yeltsin, then from Putin, and now, hopefully, from Medvedev.

I will name a few members of the "anti-systemic liberals": Boris Nemtsov, Andrei Illarionov, Vladimir Ryzhkov, Grigory Yavlinsky, Garry Kasparov, Georgy Satarov, Igor Klyamkin, Vladimir Milov, Andrei Piontkovsky, and Lev Gudkov. With respect to "systemic liberals," there are quite a few of them in the government or close to the government, from Anatoly Chubais and Alexei Kudrin to Igor Yurgens.

Liberals in Russia are a minority. A bitter minority? Perhaps. But the fact that the Russian leadership constantly turns to liberal slogans means that officials understand that they cannot solve Russia's problems while ignoring the ideas cherished by this bitter and oppositional minority. It also means that the Kremlin understands that this minority is the worst enemy of the existing Russian system.

ANDREW: That sketches the liberal groups well, I think. But while we are on general categories, maybe we should also look at the question "What is the West?" We all use the term a lot, and we have to for the bad but inevitable reason that it covers so much, and that explaining exactly what we mean each time we use it would be intolerable. However—and please correct me if this is wrong—its force as an *idea* is stronger for the Russians than it is for the rest of us. The emotional charge of "the West" is vastly stronger for Russians than its logical corollary, "Russia," is for either the West or the rest. There are as many books yet to be written as there are already written about how Russian history has been infected with its idea of the West and what it means for the future. Russia was traumatized—not, as was at least theoretically possible, liberated—by the collapse of the Soviet Union. Its self-preoccupation since that time, while completely understandable, has not been matched by other countries' looking to Moscow with the same, or even comparable, intensity.

The West lacks a clear self-definition, and what self-definition it does maintain is becoming less coherent over time. That goes for NATO as an alliance and for its individual member countries. Kosovo increased the West's burdens, but not its sense of purpose or cohesion; so have Iraq and Afghanistan. We shall see what changes are wrought by the events in Libya and the wider Arab world, but my sense is that, among other things, they will further erode the West's internal relationships. The European Union's "ever closer union" is not in good shape, although its effect, along with NATO's for that matter, on peaceful and constructive change in Eastern Europe has been benign; it has been benign for Russia, too, even if Moscow does not see it that way. The Atlantic looks wider than it was. The reality, which has shown itself even more clearly than it did at the turn of the century, is that Russia is dealing with a collection of different countries in shifting patterns with varying hopes and aims, rather than with the "West" that it often perceives.

LILIA: With respect to the "West," I personally use this term to mean a civilization based on liberal principles. I understand that I am simplifying reality, and that not all liberal democracies are Western in the sense of culture and tradition. Japan is a liberal democracy but not a Western country in the cultural sense.

True, from a geopolitical point of view, "the West" is a much more diverse "basket." But I assume that we mostly will be discussing the West as a community of normative powers.

You are right: "The West" is a strong point of reference for Russians. For some, "the West" is a goal and model to follow; for others, it's an enemy to confront and contain. But in both cases, the existence of this term proves that Russia is still drifting in uncertain waters. When we Russians stop using the term "the West," it will be because Russia has finished its search and has decided to transform itself.

I assume we can now proceed with our discussion. I will follow a traditional Russian pattern. When discussing what went wrong, we Russians always start with the questions "Who is guilty?" or "Who is to blame?"

My answer to both questions is "the Russian elite," which squandered a great chance to move toward new standards in 1991 when the old Soviet state started to unravel. At the same time, however, Russian liberals would stubbornly insist that, following the collapse of the USSR, the West was unprepared not only to welcome a new world order but also to help Russia along with its transformation. Moreover, liberals would argue that the Western leaders who had grown used to living in a bipolar world actually tried to prevent the Soviet Union's collapse. U.S. Secretary of State James Baker openly called on the West to do whatever it could to "strengthen the center," that is, Mikhail Gorbachev. One could conclude from this that the West won the Cold War, but "not through its own will."

The question, of course, is why was the West, which for so long had been trying to ruin and erase its main enemy, not ready for a new page when the Soviet Union vanished from the map?

I have a rather simplistic explanation, which is that the bipolar system and the paradigm of containment had become too comfortable a way of life for the Western political establishment—or at least for part of it. I remember Senator William Fulbright's great quote: "The Soviet Union has indeed been our greatest menace … because of the excuses it has provided for our failures." Isn't it convenient to have something to offer as an excuse for one's failures? The Soviet elite had the same unspoken excuse.

In any case, the Western establishment was not ready for a new world order. Moreover, the Western intellectual community appeared to be at a loss as to what model should be used in the postcommunist transformation. Zbigniew Brzezinski admitted after the collapse of the Soviet Union that "when it began," the West had no guiding concept with which to approach the task. It already had plenty of experience in transforming authoritarian capitalism into democracy, but transforming a statist system with no institutional memory of markets into a democracy was, Brzezinski argued, a more daunting challenge. Brent Scowcroft also stated that after the collapse of the Soviet Union, "We did not know what was going on and we did not think it mattered much"(!) Can you imagine what kind of world we lived in then? Then again, I have the distinct impression that we are still living in that world.

ANDREW: There is of course a great deal of truth in what you say—uncomfortable truth too. But without offering excuses for the West's mistakes, I would point out that most if not all of the actors involved were stumbling about in the dark. There were, if you like, three phases of change. It was ironic that while Ronald Reagan and Margaret Thatcher were quick to prophesy the first phase, the fall of the Berlin Wall, and were generally sneered at for doing so, Thatcher (and François Mitterrand, too) was in denial about its inevitable consequence: German reunification.

LILIA: Gorbachev later admitted that he was more prepared for German reunification than were some European leaders.

ANDREW: When I was in Moscow at the beginning of the 1980s, during the rise of Solidarnosc, I believed that Eastern Europe, the second of the three areas of change that led in the end to the emergence of an independent Russia, was the big test that the Soviet Union would eventually fail, and that the process of its failure would be violent. It was obvious at the time that radical change in the Soviet bloc posed a mortal threat to the communist system in the Soviet Union itself.

The potential dangers to the West, as well as to the Soviet Union, were in the event minimized by Gorbachev, but the dangers were real nonetheless, and thus the fears were justified. It perhaps did not necessarily follow that the loss of Eastern Europe would mean the collapse of the Soviet Union itself (this being the third area of change). I do not think many people either in Moscow or Western capitals had a proper handle on the nature and power of the nationalist forces, which were such a factor in this third area. It, too, could have been more violent. Yugoslavia was on many minds, and certainly on mine; I was in Belgrade for the second time from 1985 to 1989, and afterward in Washington from 1989 to 1992. Thus I was not surprised that the speed of Russian events and their potential for catastrophe led Western politicians to concentrate, in the first place, on settling Germany and Eastern Europe, and then to hope for the best as the new countries arising from the Soviet Union sorted themselves out. I should repeat: in the first place.

You say that the West had long been trying to "ruin and erase" its main enemy. That is an idea that still caries weight today, particularly, for understandable reasons, with Russians. But that does not make it true. The core of the problem between the Soviet Union and the West, ideological rhetoric aside, was the division of Germany and the Soviet grip on Eastern Europe. The general shape of the Soviet Union was not that different from the tsarist empire that preceded it. You rightly say that the West "won the Cold War … 'not through its own will.'" I should rather say that it was the evolving and growing weakness of the Soviet Union that was the principal mechanism, not anyone's will to win. I want to come back to the bipolarity question later, because it remains important and distorts perceptions to this day, but for now I should just point out that bipolarity, however comforting it is as an analytical framework, was eroding well before the end of the Soviet Union and would have gone on doing so even if the USSR still existed.

So Western decisionmakers may have been muddled—agreed. And others were muddled, too. But there are limits to what we could reasonably expect of them. All the actors in Moscow, and in the rest of Europe as well, managed to deal with disintegration pretty well, though perhaps with little clarity of vision about what the new Russia might be or what Yeltsin might portend. We owe a debt to Russia, and to Gorbachev, for this relatively calm passage.

LILIA. Right. The scale of change that began after Gorbachev came to power in the late 1980s was breathtaking. I agree that, as Yugoslavia's example showed, the Soviet collapse could have ended in apocalypse. But we are not fatalists. Correct? Thus one could argue that the collapse could have played out much more favorably.

ANDREW: Rewriting history is a great sport. I will not argue with your suggestion that things could have been better, but I am not at all sure that it would have been realistic to expect more than we got.

LILIA: Let us agree to disagree on this. Otherwise, we may not have issues to argue about.

Let me play an idealist here—for starters, on rewriting history. You are entirely justified in criticizing me for taking an extrahistorical approach. The past knows no alternatives: What happened can't be reversed. Meanwhile, I constantly go back to the past and think that, if we had only done this or that, perhaps events would have taken a more positive turn. I realize the flaws in this approach, but I nonetheless believe it perfectly logical to look back and replay the past, first of all, if it was our past and, second and most important, if we bear some responsibility for this past. We have every right and duty to understand whether there was at least a tiny chance that things could have been done differently, whether there were opportunities lost, and most important, whether we can keep from repeating our mistakes.

It is true that no one realized the full implications of the collapse of the Soviet Union and the "world socialist system"; neither those who began them in Moscow nor the Western leaders who watched them unfold really understood what was going on. Russian society's unpreparedness for the post-Soviet transformation was understandable, to an extent. It was hard to be prepared for anything so dramatic after living in a dictatorship for almost seventy years. But I want to draw attention to something I continue to reflect on, namely, why was the Western political community, which had tried so hard for decades to neutralize the Soviet Union, suddenly caught by surprise when the Soviet collapse began? Why were Western observers so ill-prepared for thinking about what would come next? The conceptual paralysis of the Western elite makes a rather damning statement about Sovietology, don't you think?

I have the impression that the main problem of the Western experts studying the Soviet Union was that they focused on the moment—that is, on what was unfolding before their eyes. In other words, they spent their time analyzing the Soviet press, or trying to work out what message one could discern from, say, the order in which leadership figures stood on the Lenin Mausoleum. They counted warheads and tried to evaluate the Soviet security threat. Western analytical thought was primarily concerned with describing the Soviet reality, assessing the adversary's forces and potential, and guessing who would be next at the helm in the Kremlin. They had no real incentive to forecast how the Soviet system itself might change, what would happen if it started to unravel, or how it could be transformed.

ANDREW: Well, yes, this is true, but not absolutely so. Analysts had little hard information to go on, and so it was natural for them to try to glean more from the few details available than was really warranted. No expert likes to admit that he (or of course she, though most of them were men) doesn't know that much. I cannot think of many who thought in terms of how the Soviet system might be transformed, though there were some who tried to look ahead and some who saw the dangers to the system. You had to be blind not to see the strains in Eastern Europe; the CIA reported on the failures of the Soviet energy sector; bankers knew that the USSR was borrowing heavily; the failures of Soviet agriculture were evident; and so on. I remember being in Detski Mir some time around 1980 to buy a toy tank for my son. As an assistant tossed over her shoulder all the defective toy tanks, I overheard a bystander say that he hoped the real ones worked better. That raised a laugh. It was clear to many Soviet citizens, and not just those who had some experience of the West, that the system as a whole was rotten and would very probably get worse. What was not evident was when, or even if, the building would collapse.

LILIA: You describe feelings of approaching disaster. But hardly anyone (including those who observed Soviet developments from the inside) had a complex picture of what was happening, and hardly anyone knew how to escape that blind alley, or even what to do after we hit the wall.

I don't recall any open studies from that period that proposed not a geopolitical but a civilizational forecast of the Soviet Union's development. The Sovietologists and Western political thinkers spent most of their time studying the status quo. Reagan's mark of distinction, incidentally, is that he was the first political leader to realize that the Soviet Union really was a colossus with feet of clay and to put pressure on the adversary to change the status quo. Reagan thus set in motion the first impulses that sped up the Soviet Union's demise. However, even those who realized that the Soviet Union was a dying empire didn't start thinking about what came next or how to shape that future.

I emphasize this issue not to put all the blame on the Western political community for unpreparedness. We Russians bear responsibility for not making use of the opportunity that the Soviet Union's demise gave us. I will say this again and again.

Rather, it is the West's delayed reaction that puzzles and worries me. The political class in the developed democracies just reacted to the processes under way in Eurasia and did not attempt to analyze their future trajectory. Today, too, Western political and intellectual thinkers often borrow our clichés to interpret events in Russia. Meanwhile, the gradual degeneration of the current Russian system and demoralized state of society may create new types of threats for which the West is unprepared.

I recall that Morton Abramowitz, the former head of the Carnegie Endowment for International Peace, once said to me that the Western world is still trying to adapt to the reality brought on by the Soviet demise. This is not an optimistic recollection to end on.

ANDREW: There was a popular saying at the time about the impossibility of turning bouillabaisse back into an aquarium. We found out that it could be done in Eastern Europe. But during the 1970s and 1980s, very few believed that it could be done. Analysts like the excellent Morton Abramowitz, however, did a great deal to help us understand Soviet realities. So did people like Murray Feshbach, whose study of population and health trends pointed out future weaknesses and risks. Today, to carry the point further, it is hard for the majority in the West to structure thought as to how to achieve radical change in Russia, but there is a fair amount of study of Russia's particular weaknesses and potential problems.

It would be wrong of me in any case to tip whole bookloads of analysts into the rubbish bin, when their writing has been so instructive—albeit not quite on a par with the perfection of the Recording Angel preparing for the Day of Judgment. Edward Crankshaw, Victor Zorza, Isaac Deutscher, Alec Nove, Arthur Koestler, Nadezhda Mandelstam, Sidney Hook, Alexandr Solzhenitsyn, Andrei Amalrik, Martin Malia, William Taubman, Tibor Szamuely, James Billington, Yegor Gaidar, the Marquis de Custine (of course), Richard Pipes, Robert Daniels, William Odom, Jonathan Brent, Catherine Merridale—these are just a few who have fed our minds over the years.

LILIA: Great names, indeed. Some of them are my favorite authors as well. Let me add to this list: Robert Conquest, George Kennan, Alex Dallin, Kenneth Jowitt, Robert Tucker, Archie Brown, Ralf Dahrendorf, and Alex Pravda.

But would you agree with me that the majority of the Western experts and Soviet dissidents predicting the demise of the Soviet project did not see their job as drafting a blueprint of what should come next?

And another thing: you said that ideology did not play a particular part in the conflict between the West and the Soviet Union, that the conflict had its source in the division of Germany and the Soviet grip over Eastern Europe. But would the division of Germany and the emergence of "spheres of influence" in Europe have been possible in the first place, absent the problem of ideology—that is, without civilizational and norm-based differences between the Soviet Union and the West? Geopolitics has to be based on something, after all.

I do agree that these differences were played up in a much more ideological fashion in the Soviet Union.

ANDREW: You are right to take me up on my rather cursory dismissal of ideology. I meant to imply that the West did not much mind communist ideology as such but more the imperialist urge it provoked. There were those who thought that convergence was possible. Willy Brandt's Ostpolitik was not intended, as I understood it, to bring down the Soviet Union but to persuade Moscow that it was okay to open up to the West—with, of course, the German Democratic Republic being at the heart of such a process. The thought behind this policy is familiar today as well.

LILIA: I appreciate that you reminded us about convergence theory (*Konvergentzija* in Russian). I remember Daniel Bell's famous book, *The End of Ideology*. There were quite a few Western theorists at the end of the 1960s and the beginning of the 1970s who expected that this "end of ideology" would bring a "convergence" between what they saw as softer versions of communism and welfare-state capitalism. In the 1970s and even the early 1980s, intellectuals in the Soviet Union believed in the possibility of "convergence" as well.

Ironically, Russian Foreign Minister Sergei Lavrov made a sudden and surprising attempt to return to this idea. In his 2009 remarks in Washington, he said that "we need something in between, something well balanced, something not so categorical and not so uncompromising." (!) An idea that was once meant to bring the Soviet Union closer to the West thirty years ago is today deployed by the Russian authorities for another goal: to preserve the Russian system by proving that it has elements that liberal democracy can borrow!

ANDREW: I am not so sure it was all that different back then. Quite a few Western pundits had a vested sympathy in the Soviet system. In their charitable anxiety for its humanistic evolution, they genuinely believed that there were original aspects of the Soviet system that needed to be preserved and developed, and even copied in some fashion in the West. Hence, for instance, the faith in "socialism with a human face," or Eurocommunism. Soviet analysts were more realistic about seeing such ideas as posing a threat to Soviet realities.

LILIA: At some point, "socialism with a human face" and Euro-communism seemed to stoke hopes for a revival of communism. But the crackdown on the Prague Spring in 1968 proved that they couldn't be built in a country that was a satellite of the Soviet Union. Twenty years later, Gorbachev would prove that "socialism with a human face" was unattainable. It had become clear that any liberalization threatened to unravel the whole system.

You've prompted me to think about the different repercussions the softer line had for communism versus those it currently has for the Russian system of personalized power. In the past, attempts to humanize communism accelerated its demise; today, limited liberalization can prolong one-man rule in Russia.

ANDREW: Can it? Let's come back to this later. I am not at all sure that is true, or at least that it is true for Russia now.

LILIA: Russia is moving in uncharted territory. Hybrid regimes with imitative democracy mechanisms and limited pluralism, such as Serbia and Ukraine, have opened the window. (To be sure, in Ukraine this opening has ended in a partial re-closure.) In Russia, Medvedev's liberal rhetoric and co-optation of intellectuals have given the regime renewed hopes that it can reform itself from within.

But let's return to the 1990s. This may sound naïve, but I still believe that for a brief period in the fall of 1991 the West had a genuine opportunity to influence Russia for the better. This was a moment when Russia could have chosen a pro-Western alignment and could have at least tried to accept liberal standards.

Here is what I mean: Yeltsin's team at that time looked to the West for advice and help. A collective Western strategy to aid Russia's reforms could have played an important part in achieving real transformation—and by this strategy I mean policies that would have created incentives to build Russian institutions and implement the rule of law. Instead, the West focused on preventing the proliferation of nuclear weapons and filling the role on the international stage left open by the departure of the Soviet Union. No one in the West sought to reformat the world order by aiding in Russia's restructuring. As the British prime minister of the time,

John Major, admitted in his memoirs, "Some of our European partners, for so long fearful of Russia, were less sensitive to her plight.... It was, I felt, both bad policy and graceless behavior."

Western politicians gave their unconditional support to Yeltsin's new political regime without conditioning that support on his regime's readiness to follow new rules of the game. The Western political world failed to realize that one-man rule would sooner or later set Russia back on an anti-Western track. Western leaders either did not see or did not want to see the link between Russian domestic political processes and foreign policy.

ANDREW: I understand why you say that, but I still think it is a bit sweeping. Given the ferocity of internal Russian politics, one must ask whether Western politicians could have made their support for Yeltsin conditional in the way you suggest. They would hardly have preferred Ruslan Khasbulatov (Yeltsin's opponent and chairman of the Supreme Soviet). And I think that they were indeed conscious of the link between domestic political processes and the country's foreign policy stance. I don't, however, recall any of them fearing that the presidential system would steer Russia back to an anti-Western track. Most of them saw support for Yeltsin, if I remember correctly, as a regrettable necessity; Yeltsin was certainly flawed, but his heart was in the right place.

LILIA: Looking back, we Russians doubt that Yeltsin's heart was in the right place.

I don't mean to say that the West needed to drag Russia, kicking and screaming, onto the path toward liberal democracy. But I assumed at the time and still believe today that the Western community—how to put it?—could have expanded Russia's opportunities. It's not a question of whom they should or should not have supported, but about the need to allow political competition and to let society choose its own leaders.

I hope that you don't take my criticism of the West as an attempt to mask the impotence of the Russian ruling establishment; that should be obvious.

ANDREW: We are talking about 1991–1992. You stand on solid ground in suggesting that the West could have expanded liberal opportunities for Russia, if it had mustered the confidence to do so. Gaidar, for one, certainly believed that better targeted and direct financial assistance would have had a profound effect on Russians' faith in a liberal transition and in the goodwill of the West. But in the fall of 1991, the West did not know what it was dealing with, and Gorbachev retained a legitimacy in Western eyes that Yeltsin had yet to earn. I suspect that two themes we will continually return to are the limits to Western understanding of Russia—particularly, as is only natural, among senior decision makers—as well as the time it takes for Western understanding to catch up with Russian realities. In 1991 (remember the 500 Days?) and in early 1992, there were suggestions of a new Marshall Plan, but these ideas never took concrete form—and not just because of fears that the money would disappear without doing much good, but also because the essential structures were not in place to make such a plan work. Russia was not, after all, under occupation, and its own institutions and the social assumptions that underpin any state were in flux. So while I think it quite possible that greater generosity and imagination from the West could have paid dividends in the window that opened up in 1991, I have no idea how long they would have lasted, or how effective they would have been. They could even have provoked resentment, I imagine. And I would not at all underestimate the benefits of the nonproliferation effort in stabilizing the relationship between the various states emerging from the collapse of the USSR, including Russia—though there are, of course, those who regret the result. The dangers of nuclear, biological, and even chemical weapons falling into irresponsible, fearful, and malign hands were very real.

LILIA: There was much more Russian naïveté than there was Western misunderstanding at the time. Those two factors were mutually reinforcing.

With respect to Russia, there has been and still is among some sections of society a conviction that the West "owes" Russia for the end of the Cold War and the exit of the Soviet Union. "You've saved your money on us and you should pay us for our good behavior." This has been quite a popular line in Russia. Indeed, there was widespread hope for a Russian "Marshall Plan" and frustration when it did not come.

I have to admit that my liberal colleagues and I entertained such hopes, which look so childish now. Now, we did not expect money or financial assistance from the developed democracies; we expected advice on how to build checks and balances, and we looked to the West and its representatives in Russia as role models.

But when the West readied itself to help, its help was met in Russia with criticism as well. Ironically, there is a belief in Russian society that it was the West—and the United States most of all—that forced Russia to accept the wrong model. In reality, by the time Bill Clinton became president in 1993 and made Russian reforms his priority, the Russian elite was already consolidating top-down governance. Even Russian liberals by then were in favor of returning Russia to its former role as arbiter of the former Soviet space. By the end of 1993, the window of opportunity for Russia's transformation had closed. Western support for Russian reforms in the 1990s ended up helping to build an updated version of the old Russian system based on a monopoly hold on power, the merging of power and property, and a renewed desire for superpower status.

By the way, some Western observers later admitted that there were wasted opportunities. Strobe Talbott wrote, "I think, we can only be self-critical.... We and other Russian reformers should have paid a lot more attention to the kind of structural side of what was necessary in economic reform and ensuring that there would be real rule of law." Zbigniew Brzezinski said,

> More deliberate U.S.-EU cooperation might have spilled into other strategic domains. The effort to draw Russia into a closer relationship with the Atlantic community might have been more successful if the United States and the European Union had made a joint endeavor to engage Russia.... Worse still, the Western allies never made it clear to Moscow that it risked isolation if it chose to reestablish authoritarianism.... Instead, Russia was continuously flattered as a new democracy and its leaders personally propitiated.

Let me give another Brzezinski quote. In his book *America and the World*, he said of Russia in the early 1990s, "The swarms of Western consultants appeared on the scene giving advice but also enriching themselves like crazy." For Russians, this was their first lesson about capitalism.

ANDREW: There are indeed some, perhaps many, in Russia who believe the West forced the wrong model on Russia. That is of course a consoling belief, and there were no doubt Westerners who advocated a sort of Gaullist presidency for a national savior. But you yourself remarked earlier that Western politicians gave their unequivocal support for Yeltsin's political regime without conditioning it on his readiness to build new institutions, which I think is nearer the mark. The question, however, is whether trying from the start to push a more broadly based and institutionally sophisticated model would have worked. It might have been better if the Supreme Soviet had been replaced by a more logical Duma much sooner, and it is possible, I suppose, that, if so, the traumas of the period leading up to the violence of 1993 (the confrontation between Yeltsin and the Congress of People's Deputies) might have been avoided. I am not well placed to judge, but I wonder if that would have proved practicable, given the urgent and also divisive need to deal with the economic crisis that was Yeltsin's first inheritance. As it was, October 1993 came first, and the new constitution was adopted in light of that. Russia remained divided, even bitterly divided, for the next five years. It took the crisis of 1998 to begin to force the Duma and the presidency to work together, and for the opposition to begin to accept that substantial elements of the reforms of previous years had to be made to work.

LILIA: We in Russia will continue to go back to 1993 and ask whether we could have avoided the confrontation and bloodshed, which had a tremendous impact on subsequent developments. In any case, neither of the two conflicting parties had noble intentions; both fought for a monopoly on power.

ANDREW: Of course, there is a great deal of history compressed into those suggestions, but two points seem to me to follow from them: first, the West, in choosing to work what market levers it could with the hoped-for cooperation of like-minded politicians in Russia, was making a reasonable bet, given that it did not seem that pressure in favor of a better institutional structure would have succeeded; second, while I accept that the end result has been something far closer to an updated version of the ancestral Russian system than the market democracy that liberal-minded Russians and friends of Russia would have preferred, this was not an inevitable trajectory. There were disappointments aplenty for Russia and the West in the 1990s, but I left the British Embassy in Moscow at the start of 2000 with some hope that the executive and legislative branches of Russia were beginning to cooperate rather than fight each other for supremacy; that the then-scheduled elections to replace governors whose time had expired would refresh the federal structures; and that the vigorously free, even irresponsible, media would help Russia's liberal development, too. The Russian economy recovered quickly from the 1998 crash, which gave further cause for hope. On the other hand, Russia's relations with the West were bad, in part because of Kosovo and Chechnya, and no one could be sure what the shape of post-Yeltsin Russia would be. You are, of course, entirely right to say that the institutional structure that had developed throughout the 1990s was ripe for exploitation by the Kremlin. All I really wanted to say was that Yeltsin's legacy was not entirely negative, and that he was capable to the end of a generosity of spirit, which is to be admired. The lazy and self-serving charge that the faults of the 1990s were his alone does not stick.

LILIA: You say it is not clear, "whether trying from the start to push a more broadly based and institutionally sophisticated model would have worked." I agree with you here. We really do not know if more active involvement by the Western community in Russia's transformation would have guaranteed the transition to liberal democracy. Perhaps this kind of involvement would have required what would have amounted to Western control over Russia's reforms, as it did in Eastern Europe. This would have been just as impossible in 1990s Russia as it would be today.

Would it have been possible to try to influence Russia's transformation process in a way that did not limit its sovereignty? Again, it is very difficult to know. Maybe not. But does this uncertainty justify doing nothing at all and just taking a wait-and-see position?

ANDREW: I could wriggle a bit on this hook by pointing to the extensive aid effort from the West and noting the possibility that the end result would have been better if the IMF's program had been implemented more effectively, and so on; however, that might only serve to provoke you to no useful purpose. It is true that the West concentrated on economic and administrative matters rather than the basic structures of the government of Russia, but it doesn't seem fair to me to describe this as "doing nothing at all." It is a pity that the West did not have more impact, perhaps, at the beginning. But it is also true that we were all learning as we went along, sometimes doing well, sometimes not.

LILIA: Well, I admit that I may not always be fair in my criticism. But I believe that we are bridging the gap between our differences, or at least getting closer to doing so. You conclude, "It is a pity that the West did not have more impact … at the beginning." We are now almost on the same page with respect to the "beginning."

To be sure, I have a stronger view on that beginning. I believe that the Western powers did have some opportunities to influence Yeltsin, especially at the end of 1991 and start of 1992, when the new Russia was just beginning to feel its way forward. They failed to seize these opportunities.

I am ready to make my position even more difficult to defend: I would even be willing to concede the point here and say that the chances of influencing Russia were so limited, and the window of opportunity so narrow, that the Western leaders—Bush, Kohl, Mitterrand, and Major—simply had no technical means of doing anything substantive to facilitate Russia's reforms (assuming they even knew what to do in the first place). But why, then, did these four go so far in the opposite direction? How do we explain their unconditional support for Yeltsin even when the corrupt nature of his regime had become clear? How do we explain the fact that Western leaders closed their eyes to the first Chechen war and that Clinton even tried to justify it? Was it really not clear what would happen if Western capitals and even the political class were drawn into building an oligarchic system?

ANDREW: When a historian cannot answer a question he always says, "not my period," so I can take refuge in the fact that I was not in Russia then.… But I won't leave after making that excuse. I can only point out that the economic challenge at the time was enormous, and that the task of helping a relatively liberal and still developing government, as opposed to a thoroughly reactionary opposition, seemed paramount. No one at the time thought an oligarchic structure would emerge. Had they done so, they would have had to find a way of preventing ownership of the large structures that made up the Soviet inheritance from falling into only a few hands. The only way of doing that, I suppose, would have been to break them up, which would have been impractical. It was not inevitable that the new owners would grow as powerful as they did in the later Yeltsin years.

All that said, we have, or we should have, a guilty conscience about Chechnya. And we can have that guilty conscience even though we don't know how else we would have resolved the Chechnya problem if we ourselves had had to face it. It is obvious how corrosive the effects of that war have been in the Caucasus and throughout Russia, as well.

LILIA: Well, the challenge appeared to be enormous for all.

I am pleased that you also think that what happened in Russia "was not an inevitable trajectory."

I agree with those who say that the West made a mistake by supporting market reform instead of insisting on building institutions in Russia. I am on the same page here with Alfred Stepan and Juan Linz. They were among the first Western observers who proved that one of the key reasons that Russia's transformation failed was the fact that Yeltsin ignored the need for political reform and building a new state and went with the market first. Quite a few Russian liberals would support this view.

ANDREW: Perhaps there was little choice.

LILIA: Unfortunately, political history is full of examples when one sees the choice only when it's too late.… I see the usefulness of our current exercise, the search for wasted opportunities, as being a way of alerting ourselves (and perhaps others, too) to present opportunities that we might not yet see.

You are right to remind us that the "institutional structure" at the time had not succeeded. But the numerous Western advisers working for Yeltsin and the Western leaders that he listened to could at least have tried to demonstrate to him the need to build, say, an independent judicial system and economic institutions before beginning, or even while carrying out, the process of dividing up state assets. This would have made it possible to avoid the robber-baron privatization that discredited reform in the public's eyes. Yeltsin still listened to his advisers in the early 1990s. Of course, there is still no guarantee that he would have listened to them in this, or that everything would have worked out, but at least we would now be able to say that the West had tried to persuade Yeltsin to lay down the normative foundations but that he did not listen.

Meanwhile, in the absence of independent political institutions and rule of law, the market's development in Russia produced a new fusion between power and property, helping to reproduce personalized power—only this time based on disingenuous liberal slogans.

ANDREW: I suppose that there was advice along the lines you recommend but that it got lost in the general noise. Anyway the end result was what it was.

LILIA: Let me return back to one thing you said. You've mentioned the year 2000. I remember this time well. Indeed, you are right that the executive and legislative branches finally ended their war then, but Russia went from one extreme to the other: Parliament effectively ceased to exist altogether. As current Duma Speaker Boris Gryzlov, one of the members of Putin's entourage, said, "Parliament is not the place for discussion." And so it came to pass: Russia's parliament stopped being a place for discussion.

As for assessing Yeltsin's legacy, let's agree to disagree one more time. I also disagree on this point with some of my friends among Russia's liberals: Georgy Satarov, for example, who was an adviser to Yeltsin and with whom I share the same views regarding the Putin-Medvedev regime. We differ in our assessments of Yeltsin's period and its legacy.

Yes, you are right. Yeltsin was capable of "generosity of spirit." During his time we had freedom of speech, the election of governors and political pluralism, though it was not structured. But these things were destroyed by Yeltsin's own hand-picked successor. Yeltsin therefore does bear responsibility for what happened after he stepped down. Furthermore, it was during Yeltsin's time that democratic values were discredited in people's eyes because they were used as slogans to disguise the emergence of oligarchic capitalism and a corrupt state. I think that Russian history will yet call Yeltsin to account. The fact that he looks more liberal than Putin does not make him a democrat.

But you have reasons for viewing Yeltsin in a different light. After all, it was during his years that Russia and the West had relatively good relations.

Now for other matters. Andrew, you are more familiar than I am with the debates under way in Western society at that time. Could you explain them? As I see it, the Western intellectuals and experts at the beginning of the 1990s (many of them, anyway) believed in the "end of history." They saw Russia's liberal transformation as inevitable. Many of them had blinded themselves to the signs that Russia was taking a different track. When it became clear that the reality in Russia was not what Western observers had hoped for, many of them preferred to cling to their determinism, hoping that somehow Russia would sort it out in the fullness of time.

Am I being unfair to our Western colleagues?

ANDREW: No, you are not unjust, although you are of course sweeping a lot of ideas and their proponents into one basket—or maybe trash can. The idea that in time Russia would evolve in a generally liberal direction had—and still has, for that matter—quite a purchase on Western thinking. I am biased against the "end of history" argument, which by the way seemed to me just a colorful way of suggesting that the hold of ideologies on the development of states had been weakened, rather than a suggestion that the coming of liberal justice and values was inevitable. But you can still hear plenty of people saying that the rise of a middle class in Russia will be transformative, which begs all sorts of questions but provides some reassurance, given present realities. And the fact of a new fusion between power and property is, as you say, with us now.

LILIA: The irony is that a significant part of the Russian middle class as a rule supports the statist economy and is an obstacle to its transformation.

ANDREW: There were practical reasons, however, reinforcing the desire throughout the 1990s to deal with the merely possible in the hopes that doing so would further the eventual emergence in Russia of a stable liberal order. My list of those reasons would start with the limits to the ability of Western countries and international organizations to influence developments in Russia. I have already agreed with you that the power of Western liberal ideas may have been at its highest in late 1991 or early 1992, and that, had they been more strongly urged at that time, perhaps they could have done good. But I have already suggested, too, that the most urgent problem for Yeltsin and Gaidar was survival in the face of looming economic catastrophe, followed by a need to cope with what amounted to an attempted rejection of the political order that had emerged after the August 1991 putsch. It seems clear to me that the West's ability to direct events was strictly and progressively limited, and that Russia was very largely in charge of its own fate throughout the 1990s, even though many Russians must have felt as though their country was in the grip of impersonal, implacable, and hostile forces.

LILIA: Yes, after 1993 Russia was largely in charge of its fate....

ANDREW: It was inevitable that, as Western leverage decreased, so did Western optimism and Russians' belief in the possibility of early change. We all got tired.

LILIA: Thank you for being candid. We in Russia still don't get the fact that the world is fed up with our problems.

ANDREW: And the West, at the same time, was compromised by the choices it had made, including those made in 1993 and about Chechnya. Its decision to prioritize support for the IMF program was, in my view at least, both practical and therefore to that extent also justified. The budgetary discipline that was established after the 1998 financial collapse—established, ironically, by the very people who had resisted it when in opposition—was the key to economic recovery and the beginning of a potentially benign political evolution. And the legislative reforms of the first Putin term had their origins in the IMF-backed proposals of the later Yeltsin years. I do not think that it was unreasonable for the West to try to offer consoling credit in advance (in the shape of, for instance, IMF bailouts or premature membership of the G8), in the hope or even expectation that positive results would follow. But this approach proved ill founded. Payment in advance did not work, and the West's moral authority, such as it was, decreased as Western capitals became more and more associated with a regime that could not deliver on its promises. However, to repeat myself, the attempt to use financial forces to stabilize and revitalize Russia was probably the most practical choice available to the West for Yeltsin's second term.

LILIA: Let me briefly comment on the role of IMF in Russia, about which I have mixed feelings. On the one hand, without the help of the IMF Russia would not have survived in the 1990s, as this help made up a significant portion of the Russian budget. On the other hand, I would support some Russian economists, like the late Boris Fyodorov, who spoke against the mass influx of money into Russia for destroying any incentive for reform. I would also agree with Joseph Stiglitz, then vice president of the World Bank, who argued that the mechanisms the IMF created could not succeed without the institutional environment that Russia lacked. At some point, the corrupted Russian elite used the Western financial influx to advance its anti-liberal goals.

And now on to something else: Looking back I would say that the relationship between the West and Russia in the 1990s is an excellent example of the law of unintended consequences. The West's very formula for partnership with Russia in the 1990s began to undermine that partnership. As the Russian elite saw it, partnership meant that Russia should have the same rights as Western countries but without the need to "pass any tests" of how well it was adhering to Western standards. Western leaders, for their part, failed to convince the Russian elite that complying with Western principles was a prerequisite of joining the Western club. (I wonder whether they really tried to convince them.)

Imitation partnership between Russia and the West ultimately left both sides dissatisfied. Furthermore, the "double standards" practiced by Western leaders caused Russian society to become disillusioned with the very idea of liberal democracy and allowed the elite to maintain its belief that it could manipulate the West.

Andrew, you were in the diplomatic service at the time. You are in a position to say whether the Russian liberals were wrong. They believed that the West made little effort to raise concerns about the rise of oligarchic clans, theft by Kremlin clans under the guise of privatization, and growing authoritarianism. They believed that the West looked the other way during the Kremlin's manipulations of the 1996 presidential election. The West's unbridled support for the increasingly erratic Yeltsin convinced at least part of Russian society that what the Western leaders really wanted was to see Russia stagnate and remain weak.

ANDREW: Just so. I would prefer to say "muddled standards" rather than "double standards." The West was neither sufficiently organized nor sufficiently malign to ensure that Russia remained stagnant and weak.

LILIA: Fair enough. I personally believe that the West did not have an interest in weakening Russia. The Russian statists and nationalists are the ones who would debate you on that point.

Just a quick comment on how Western experts perceived Yeltsin in those times: When I wrote *Yeltsin's Russia*, in which I gave a pretty harsh assessment of Yeltsin's leadership, some of my Western colleagues accused me of pro-communist sympathies. They were not ready to look at Yeltsin's Russia with critical eyes.

Let's sum up the outcome of Yeltsin's rule and the relationship between Russia and the West at this time. What is your assessment?

ANDREW: Mutual exhaustion would about sum up the mood prevailing as the century ended. The foundation myth of the Putin era, that the new leader brought reform and stability to replace the chaos and poverty under Yeltsin, fell on fertile soil in the West. The claim that he brought Russia up from her knees went down well in his own country, too. Neither myth has served Russian or foreign liberals well in the long run.

Let me get back to something you just said about the West's (there's that term again!) looking the other way during the Kremlin's manipulations of the 1996 elections. Different Western countries had different ideas about them at the time; some gave direct help to the Yeltsin campaign, and others did not. The OSCE report noted the media barrage against the Communist Party candidate Gennady Zyuganov but was otherwise relatively uncritical. It is interesting to speculate about whether the constitutional order would have benefited in the long run, and whether Russia would have become more liberal in due course, if Zyuganov had won. Certainly the ride could have been an exciting one, but perhaps it would have worked out like that. And perhaps more progress would have been made if Yeltsin had been in better health after the results came in.

It is certainly true that some Western countries relied more than others on cultivating personal relations with Yeltsin and so were less inclined to criticize his Kremlin. That close personal association with Yeltsin ended up, as you say, with the West getting blamed for a lot that was unwelcome or mistaken.

Several things were clear to me when I left in early 2000. First, the various guises of Russia's relationship with the West were wearing thin. Second, there was room for a fresh start as Yeltsin's successor came into office (and unlike the 2008 switch, this was a true succession). But third and last, it was clear to me that it was up to Russia to call its own shots now.

LILIA: Zyuganov's victory in 1996 would not have been an inspiring sight to behold, but the manipulation of the electoral process and the return of the sick man to the Russian presidency were the last nails in the coffin of the immature Russian democracy.

Do you mind if I offer my perception of Yeltsin's legacy? I've been thinking about it a lot, so it may sound a bit didactic.

I see Yeltsin as one of the most paradoxical political leaders in recent history. Possessing immense powers, he was nevertheless incapable of implementing his decisions. He proclaimed the building of a democracy but fostered autocracy instead. He abolished communism but survived only by exaggerating the threat of its imminent return. He was a president who won the first elections in Russia but became a screen for the cliques that hid behind him.

After Yeltsin's death in April 2007, 29 percent of poll respondents said that Yeltsin's contribution had been "mainly positive," while 40 percent insisted it had been "mainly negative." Yes, I have to admit that his tenure in office was dramatic; he was a revolutionary who paved the way for an antidemocratic restoration. By appointing former KGB lieutenant colonel Vladimir Putin as his successor and allowing for stage-managed elections, Yeltsin became the godfather of the new Russian autocracy.

However, we should mention the books of Leon Aron (*Yeltsin: A Revolutionary Life*) and Timothy Colton (*Yeltsin: A Life*), which support a more positive view of his leadership.

I will risk ending this rumination with a joke that shows what we thought about Russia and ourselves at the end of the Yeltsin epoch:

> A sick man is picked up by the ambulance. "Where are you taking me," asks the man. "To the morgue," answers the doctor. "But I am not dead!" cries the man. The doctor: "We are not there yet!"

ENTER VLADIMIR PUTIN 1999–2004

CONSOLIDATION OF THE NEW REGIME

ANDREW: I think we agree that the system that Yeltsin passed on to Putin had the potential then to become what it is now. If there is a difference between us, it is that I felt at the time that there were other options, provided that the various parts of the Russian system were allowed to continue to evolve as autonomous power centers. It rather quickly became evident that this was not going to happen, and perhaps I held on as Yeltsin gave way to Putin to the idea of benign development because I wanted to believe that the dead weight of Russia's historic political traditions had been sufficiently unloaded. The renewed campaign in Chechnya, launched in fall 1999 and much criticized in the West to little effect, was an early indication that it still burdened Russia. Putin campaigned on the "dictatorship of the law," a revealingly ambivalent phrase. Later, restrictions on the mass media and on the independent authority of the governors plus the Council of the Federation were further indications, for those who cared to see them, of the intended direction of events. The governors were paid off by being allowed to stay beyond their two-term limits, but of course they were subsequently further diminished by being reduced to the status of Kremlin appointees rather than elected politicians. The claim was that measures like this would reduce corruption and enhance stability; the reality was that the potential for renewal inherent in regional elections was neutered. If you compare the range of political options now with the range that seemed to exist in 2000, you find that today's seems dangerously narrow. Given how power has been both centralized and personalized over the decade, it is plain that Putin is the motor that has brought Russia to this point. Perhaps another leader would have been different. Yeltsin could not have done this even if he had wanted to.

LILIA: I want to endorse your belief that "the dead weight of Russia's historic political traditions had been sufficiently unloaded" during the transition to Putin. Andrew, it really had been unloaded! People voted for Putin because they thought he would be a more thoughtful modernizer who cared about them and would bring a social dimension to Kremlin policies. The majority of Russian society did not want a restoration, but that majority was not consolidated and could not prevent Putin and his team from taking Russia backwards. This was a case of hope betrayed, but the bearers of that hope did not at first notice the betrayal.

I believe that there was more continuity between Yeltsin and Putin than there was disruption. However, there are observers in both Russia and the West who view Yeltsin and Putin as antagonists.

I would argue that the fact that Putin was Yeltsin's political successor completed the process of consolidating personalized power by eradicating any doubt or ambivalence about the nature of the Russian system.

ANDREW: We might add that Putin handled the West with great skill, and that he had luck on his side. He took early steps to put the quarrel with NATO over Kosovo aside. He was a charming hit at his first G8, with Blair as an obliging second. Western leaders were disposed to think him different from Yeltsin, somehow more modern as well as younger and fitter, of course. Putin's competence at passing reforms that Yeltsin had been unable to get through the Duma, together with his continuation of responsible budgetary measures, reinforced Russia's economic recovery and growth (which was also fueled by rising oil prices). Russia paid down its international debts far sooner than most experts had expected. The West, by which I mean in this case those directing political and business affairs, preferred to see the first-term Putin as a reformer rather than as a president who was restoring centralized power. Perhaps that perception was made more likely, given the initial doubts about him as a man with

KGB stamped all over his résumé. I don't know. And possibly that was how Putin saw himself then, too. In any case, the West's leverage had been greatly diminished from the start of Putin's period in office; the IMF had been reduced to a clean-up role.

Nevertheless, I remain reluctant to see Putin as finishing Yeltsin's project, if by that you mean to imply some element of inevitability about the process. Perhaps I am too stubborn to recognize the truth, but the more one sees that progression as foreordained, the greater and more dangerous the eventual unraveling of that system will be. I hope that we can return to this issue toward the end of our discussion.

LILIA: I understand your logic. We agree here in principle: We are both against fatalism. I constantly debate with those who try to argue that Russia is destined to one scenario—usually a bad one. Thus I am reluctant to conclude that Putin's ascendancy inevitably meant the annihilation of the pluralistic trends that had existed under Yeltsin. And by the way, I appreciate your reminding us of the uncertainty of Russia's evolution.

After some deliberation, I believe I can bridge our positions on this issue in the following way: I concede that Yeltsin's "construct" could have gone either way, toward pluralism and more civilized competition or toward authoritarianism. The premises for the former scenario had already been substantially weakened by the end of Yeltsin's term, because his constitution legitimized personalized rule by endorsing the role of the president as an official who stands above the system and society. But who knows? If Yeltsin's successor had been a convinced liberal and reformer, he might have given Russia a second chance; the concrete still hadn't dried. Unfortunately, Putin chose not to keep stirring it.

Are we now closer?

ANDREW: Yes, I think we are. Personalities matter. One of Putin's expressions, which I cannot imagine Yeltsin using, is that the weak get beaten. Would Yeltsin have called himself weak? No. Thus he would not fear getting beaten.

LILIA: In our case, personalities really do matter. Putin's expressions and his constant macho gestures make one wonder if he hasn't got something to hide or compensate for. Freud might have been able to help us figure him out.

Let's go back to 1999. There were several domestic Russian factors that strengthened continuity between Yeltsin and Putin and pushed the latter in a certain direction (or justified his movement in that direction). First, when Yeltsin searched for a successor (a fact that in and of itself helps us draw a conclusion about the nature of the regime), he sought out candidates *mainly* from among the security officers in his entourage, not the liberal democrats. In short, Yeltsin and his political "family" were looking for someone who could guarantee their interests and protect their persons.

Second, the Russian political elite and oligarchs of 1996–1999 were already thinking about how to defend their positions; they loathed the idea of any change, much less reform.

Third, the Russian people had grown tired of the chaos and uncertainty of Yeltsin's time—disturbances that they linked to reform.

Fourth, as you remember, terrorists made a series of successful attacks on Russia in the summer of 1999. Apartment blocks in Moscow and several other cities were blown up. These acts were followed by the second Chechen war, which led all too many Russians to yearn for an "iron fist" and for order. Speculation still abounds in Russia that the security forces and/or their bosses perpetrated these terrorist attacks in order to return Russia to its accustomed state of cowering under a military threat.

Fifth, there is Putin's past as a KGB officer. Now, I hasten to add that there is no necessary connection between Putin's KGB past and his political present and future. For instance, former KGB general Alexei Kondaurov, a close associate of Mikhail Khodorkovsky, holds democratic views. The more important aspect of Putin's past is that he was a member of St. Petersburg mayor Anatoly Sobchak's team, which was widely accused of being both undemocratic and corrupt.

Sixth, the liberal opposition was fragmented and had lost its influence by 1999.

The seventh and final factor is that Putin was appointed successor when a system of personalized power and political manipulation—including electoral manipulation—was already in place.

All of these factors laid the foundation for the road that Russia eventually embarked on.

ANDREW: I believe that Yeltsin saw the destruction of the communists and communism as his principal legacies. I don't think Yeltsin told Putin to "look after Russia" just for show, and I don't think he did so as a kind of reminder to look out for the Yeltsin family. There were other ways he might have done those things, and it was in Putin's interests anyway to reject the idea that Yeltsin should be punished for what he did in office. Yeltsin's last commission surely meant that Putin should build on his predecessor's revolution against the Soviet system, that he should carry on what Yeltsin, however clumsily and ineffectually, had hoped would be the start of a new chapter in Russia's history. I suppose that if, say, Yevgeny Primakov had inherited the Kremlin, decent man that he was, he would have left the Yeltsin family in peace. But Primakov was, in Yeltsin's eyes, "like a tomato, red inside."

Yeltsin is said to have come to regret his choice of Putin; the quiet man turned out to be fiercer than Yeltsin had imagined. People made the same mistake about Stalin.

LILIA: If Yeltsin thought that Putin would continue his anticommunist crusade and even start a new chapter in Russian history, then he was a romantic. Yet he did not look like a romantic when he was in power.

Still, I am prepared to leave room for doubt on that particular question. What is certain, however, is that Yeltsin eventually came to regret his choice. He expressed this regret later to several people who visited him in the seclusion of retirement—Boris Nemtsov, for example.

We may agree that even in the framework of Russia's undemocratic track, different scenarios were possible. Putin initially chose the dual track of economic reform and the centralization of power. At first, many people, including many Russians, saw Putin as a reformer. But the centralization of power gradually swallowed up liberal reforms, becoming for Putin an end unto itself.

ANDREW: That was inherent in centralization.

LILIA: Like many, I've been struggling with how to define Putin's regime: electoral democracy, imitation democracy? The imitative nature of his regime is clear. Under the guise of democratic institutions, it conceals authoritarian, oligarchic, and bureaucratic tendencies. Putin's Russia is proof of Francis Fukuyama's assertion that there are "few alternative institutional arrangements that elicit any enthusiasm" aside from liberal democracy. But by the end of Putin's term as president the Russian regime could hardly even be called hybrid anymore. Under Yeltsin, mutually exclusive tendencies coexisted in an uneasy truce: there were elections (which often were fair, more or less) with nominated positions; there was political pluralism and authoritarian pressure; there was a market economy with state control. Putin, however, gradually reined in Yeltsin's awkward hybrid. Everything that ran counter to the monopoly of political power morphed into a form more virtual than real.

By 2008, when Medvedev stepped into the presidency, Russia had a kind of bureaucratic-authoritarian regime in quasidemocratic disguise. Its imitative character was so evident that only the terminally naïve or those who chose to play a game of "Let's Pretend" could call the regime democratic.

ANDREW: The game of "Let's Pretend" is a powerful and sometimes unconscious activity. Its Western practitioners had a lot of issues to play down. Quite a few of them believed that the action in 2003 against Khodorkovsky was provoked by this businessman's foolish political ambition—the implication being that his imprisonment was justified, and the incident was an isolated one. Others thought similarly about the Orange Revolution and Russia's subsequent quarrels with Ukraine. But there were nonetheless by then far fewer people who were prepared to think of Putin as a force leading toward a more democratic Russia than there had been as his first term got under way. Now, the sanguine still think that perhaps Medvedev will open up new possibilities if he is reelected: hope, as they say, springs eternal. And of course the consistently high poll ratings of both Medvedev and Putin, but especially Putin, have always been taken to confer a significant degree of legitimacy on their leadership.

LILIA: True, quite a few of my friends believed in Putin's liberal potential at the beginning. And some of his fiercest opponents today worked for him. Andrei Illarionov, Putin's former economic adviser, is one of them.

Optimistic observers began to shed their illusions about Putin toward the end of his first term in office. Some of them four years later transferred their hopes to Medvedev. You are right to say that the high poll numbers for both leaders legitimize their power in the eyes of the Russian public and the world. Western politicians can only envy approval ratings as high as 70 percent.

However, these ratings are not an indication of real support; they reflect the lack of a political alternative. The Russian people realize that their leaders are the state's fundamental load-bearing pillar when there are no other political institutions. The people withdrawing their support could lead to the state's collapse, an outcome they fear for the chaos it would engender.

Furthermore, these ratings could vanish overnight. When asked early in 2011 whom they would vote for if an election were held the following Sunday, 20 percent said they would vote for Medvedev and 27 percent for Putin. Thus Putin's real base at that time was about 27–30 percent. That is not so high.

But I am getting ahead of myself. The high approval ratings are part of the imitation that has emerged in Russia.

ANDREW: There is a herd instinct among leaders, who by their very natures must have an abnormal degree of faith in their own judgment, usually without having sufficient time to reflect on the merits of that faith. It is easy to see a fellow politician as a figure somehow like yourself. So these ratings carry political conviction at the highest level in the West. I am reminded of the political visitors to Belgrade in the late 1980s who told me I was wrong about Milosevic; he really was a reformer, because he talked the talk and looked the part. Putin, too, often does impress. And there are plenty who would like to think the best of Medvedev.

LILIA: If you don't mind my jumping to another issue, I would like us to return back to the nature of the system that has emerged in Russia during Putin's rule. We have to sort it out before moving on to concrete things.

There are other imitation democracies in the world. The Russian system of personalized power is nonetheless a unique phenomenon, making it that much harder for Russians to get rid of it. I would argue that this regime is a form of traditional Russian statism, which includes among its attributes a longing for great-power status and spheres of influence. Personalized power and great-power politics mutually reinforce each other. In fact, Russian autocracy can't exist without geopolitical ambitions. The latter help the former to survive.

ANDREW: This is a complex matter, which is not easy for Westerners to understand. A long time has passed since the days of Louis XIV. But for Russia, territorial and personalized power *still* go hand-in-hand, as they always have. The fuzziness of Russian ethnic borders complicates things, too. We heard less about such politics in the 1990s than we do now, and not just because Russia was weaker but also because the liberal strain within it was stronger, along with a struggle to determine the future course of the country's evolution. The "power vertical" espoused by the present regime and the return of great-power rhetoric go together. Putin's climb to power started with a war to reconquer Chechnya.

LILIA: Exactly! The second Chechen war legitimized the ascendance of a totally unknown personage whom the Kremlin puppeteers had taken out of the box.

Moreover, there is another key feature of the Russian system: the fusion of power and property, as evidenced by the seats that representatives of the ruling group occupy on the boards of key companies like Gazprom. To be fair, Medvedev has criticized this practice from time to time and even managed to dent it in 2011. But however this may develop, there is no question that the state's role in the economy more generally and the power of its satraps in particular has increased greatly. Thus we see the reproduction of the classical Russian matrix that includes personalized power, a great-power syndrome with imperialist or quasi-imperialist longings, and the marriage of power and property. And this "mix" hides itself behind democratic rhetoric and fake institutions. Under this regime, Russia remains antithetical to Western civilization. Who would have ever predicted that Putin, who for all the world looked like reformist leader at first, would complete the reinvention of the matrix?!

Anyway, today you advise businesses and you deal with the Russian state in the economy. What is your view of this state?

ANDREW: I will answer, but we shall have to get back to Putin's first period in due course, and this covers the last dozen years or so!

Certainly, the increasingly direct role of the state in the economy was a constant feature of the Putin years, and it has to date, rhetoric apart, remained at a high level under Medvedev. That has included the restriction of foreign direct investment in a wide range of so-called strategic areas. But this has happened without any clarity as to what the Russian state actually is. Is Gazprom private or state-controlled? Does it matter anymore? Where does bureaucratic management end and corruption begin? That matters very much of course, but my point is only that corruption has increased, according to all the measures that I have seen, as one might expect when lower orders follow the example of their higher-placed betters and arrogate to themselves the right to act as if the law does not apply to them. It is not surprising that foreign direct investment has remained anemic by comparison with Brazil, India, or China, for instance. Long-term involvement requires faith in future intentions and purposes. It is a fact that, as the system has become more centralized and authority within it more concentrated on a small ruling group, or even cabal, so, too, has corruption become endemic.

LILIA: Putin's rise to power marked the start of a new stage in relations between Russia and the West. Having consolidated Russia's imitation democracy, Putin pursued a policy that was simultaneously "with the West and against the West." One has to admit that this guy who came in with no political experience proved to be really skillful in forcing Russia to play two opposing roles: both partner and adversary to the West. If under Yeltsin the Kremlin tried to accept, albeit partially and formally, the Western rules of the game, then Putin's Kremlin attempted to force the West to accept the Russian way of doing things.

ANDREW: We are discussing a process that took two presidential terms to run its course. I don't think we need to go into detail about those eight years. We can look later at the implications for Russia and the West of what has happened since the critical year of 2008. But I'd like to make some general remarks about changing Western perceptions during Putin's first term in the presidency.

Western relief as the Putin era began and Russia's economy recovered (a recovery that in fact had begun surprisingly soon after the 1998 collapse but was credited to Putin) was accompanied by a general retreat from the early 1990s euphoria for the worldwide future of liberal, market-based democracy. The social conditions for effective markets and lasting democracy had always been clearly understood, but they began to seem more stringent to their once-hopeful supporters as the twenty-first century began. One man, one vote was not enough—especially in Russia. It was an easy step from this concession to the assumption that patience with Russian aberrations was needed. And there were numerous distractions too: Yugoslavia, Eastern Europe, internal EU questions (as ever), the 2000 U.S. presidential election, and then 9/11, Afghanistan, and Iraq, all of which got more pressing still as the decade wore on, and so on.

With Russia seeming more predictable and more stable as the new president's first term ran its course, the urgency behind Western policy formation diminished. Business ties and commercial hopes grew, and so did a whole range of personal contacts. The Russian president's swift reaction to 9/11 seemed promising. Some Western countries were more generous than others in their hopes and assumptions, with Germany being a leading and influential example.

LILIA: Yes, Germany took the lead in demonstrating optimism—or connivance.

ANDREW: The Russian administration's slow tightening of the domestic screws was usually seen as explicable and even justifiable. The brutality of the military campaign in the South Caucasus was little remarked upon. No Western leader, as far as I am aware, raised either subject in any serious way with the Kremlin.

But the tide began to turn in 2003, with the Yukos case serving as a marker of the shift. Governmental habits were slow to adjust, but the damage to Russia's public reputation was cumulative.

LILIA: Definitely. The Yukos case was a marker. In the fall of 2003 even those Russians who still believed in Putin and his liberal intentions, and who had been ready to swallow the attack on independent media, were appalled. Western observers also saw Khodorkovsky's arrest and the Yukos crackdown as troubling signs. I remember then-Secretary of State Colin Powell, before his visit to Moscow in the fall of 2003, published a piece in the Russian newspaper *Izvestia* that expressed serious concerns about Khodorkovsky's arrest. Powell was the first Western leader to openly criticize (albeit mildly) a facet of Putin's rule.

For many in Russia, Khodorkovsky's arrest became a watershed that symbolized the Kremlin's turn in the direction of a bureaucratic state with elements of repression. But still, despite the Yukos case, Putin's Kremlin had successfully pursued a quite effective foreign policy; friendly cooperation with the West continued. Or am I wrong about this? While Western leaders eventually began to suspect that something wrong was going on, their suspicions didn't affect their relationship with Moscow. I suggest we return to Khodorkovsky later.

ANDREW: I think that you are both right and wrong about the effect of the Yukos affair and the prosecution of Khodorkovsky on the relationship between Moscow and the West. The immediate response was mild shock, tempered by the supposition that this was a one-off. The long-term effects have been more serious, on both investments in Russia and the reputation of the Russian state. That has of course been part of a wider pattern of events, but the Yukos affair was for many the start of a reappraisal. I recall telling investors in 2004 that they were mistaken to take as binding Putin's assurance that Yukos would not be bankrupted. They had imagined it would not partly because the president had said it so forcefully but also because it seemed so self-evident to them that it would not be in Russia's interests to ruin such a successful enterprise. Maybe it was not in Russia's interests—but it turned out to be in *certain* Russians' interests.

LILIA: The Western reappraisal has been a long time in coming, and as it slowly arrived, it had little apparent effect on Western policy.

Let me push the ball further. I would argue that the bases for the Russian attitude toward the West were largely projections of the controversial nature of the rentier class that had come to power in Russia. Russia no longer had the kind of self-sufficiency that the Soviet Union possessed, and its transformation into a petrostate turned it into an energy supplier for Western consumers. In terms of their lifestyles and survival mechanisms, Russia's elite could not have been more pro-Western. This elite have become personally integrated into Western society, living in the West, holding accounts in Western banks, and educating their children in the West. The growing Russian community in London is but one sign of this integration.

ANDREW: It is certainly true that making comments in Russian on London buses isn't as safe as it used to be. You're much more at risk of being overheard and understood.

LILIA: To some extent, "The Russians are coming!" was a positive phenomenon, in that the vast majority of Russians were coming to live in the West for the best of reasons. But there is nevertheless another side to this phenomenon. I am talking of course about the Russian elite that prefer to exploit Russia while living in the West.

This class's dependence on, and personal incorporation into, the West proved no hindrance to the task of rebuilding an anti-Western regime in Russia. In order to keep a hold on power in Russia, this class had to close Russian society to Western influence. Anti-Western and above all anti-American slogans, the elite's dependence on the West, and imitation of liberal values all became hallmarks of the updated Russian system. This controversial survival technique became the foundation of the "Friend or Foe" foreign policy.

ANDREW: This is and always has been significant. Russia's rulers have often been suspicious of how Russians would react when exposed to foreign realities. Consider, for instance, Nicholas I after the Napoleonic Wars and Stalin in 1945. Individual Russian citizens, by no means all of them rich, have had experiences of various Western countries like my own, and not all these countries have had good political relationships with the Russian government. These experiences are a great positive factor for the long-term future. A good number of Russians have settled productively in the West and gained a different perspective on life in the rest of Europe and North America, for that matter. We need constantly to bear in mind that politics defines only one aspect of the relationship between countries. Furthermore, that fact is not just important for Moscow to remember about the West; it is also important that Western countries remember that their judge and jury are not just official Russia but a far broader set of individual Russian citizens, groups, and institutions.

LILIA: Thank you for making that correction. Yes, the Russian presence in the West can't be limited only to the ruling rentier class. This class is on my radar because it plays a crucial role in Russian domestic developments.

I would like to turn to a delicate matter, if I may. Please stop me if you think I've gone astray. For some time I've had the impression that during Putin's presidency Western leaders, disappointed with attempts to help Russia transform itself into a more democratic system, have concluded that talking about values with Russians is unproductive. They began to think that preaching democracy or even hoping for Russia's transformation only complicates their pursuit of other objectives. So instead they turned to emphasizing common interests between Russia and the West. Given the West's relations with China, Pakistan, and Saudi Arabia, working toward a cooperative relationship with Russia made a certain sense. If pragmatism worked with other nondemocratic societies, why couldn't it work with Russia, too?

Ironically, by turning toward this brand of "realism," the West opted for a policy that fit neatly into the Kremlin paradigm. There are numerous examples in which the West, by pursuing a tactical agenda, helped the Kremlin to achieve its objectives.

ANDREW: The need to balance available prizes against longer-term objectives presents a perpetual dilemma, and the more the latter seem unattainable, the greater is the temptation to get what you can, while you can. As the post-2000 system embedded itself in Russian soil, so, too, did the "get real" strategy plant deep roots in Western gardens. Nothing surprising about that. But the word "realist" is irritating and misleading, too. If you call your policy "realist," that implies that other policies are unrealistic. It also usually means that the advocate of "realism" will go on to simplify choices as much as he or she can, in a sort of macho way. Nor are "realist" policies value-free, though they perhaps strive to appear so. They may truly be blind to values, of course, but there is a price to pay for that blindness (even if it is someone else who ends up paying that price.)

LILIA: I share your irritation with realpolitik, especially in its current disguise.

ANDREW: Forgive the rant. I agree with much of what you have just said. In practical terms, though, it is quite difficult to balance looking for ways to work together—which has its uses, after all—and demonstrating attachment to one's values in such a way as to persuade others to respect them, too. Russian diplomats are past masters, as were their Soviet predecessors, at taking offense while refusing even to consider others' feelings. They are also practiced in rehearsing their grievances (real or imagined) so often that foreigners begin to take them at face value. Preaching is not much good for communications between governments, but it is sometimes essential for sending a message to a wider audience in countries like Russia. The Soviet Union, after all, was fixated on preaching, albeit without conclusive effect, I'm glad to say. But Western countries should remember that the pre-emptive cringe wins no friends either, and that the relationship with Russia is a dynamic and changing one unlike all others. (Or perhaps it only looks that way to me because of my professional focus on Russia.)

We don't have to preach, but we can hold fast to our principles and speak up for them. These tasks are particularly important when it comes to making institutions, like the World Trade Organization (WTO), which require mutual understanding in order to operate effectively. Great powers (if there are any) should understand that fact if they do not wish to be thought of as "great bullies."

LILIA: I couldn't agree more: Western leaders should "speak up for principles." The problem is, Russian leaders claim to follow the same principles! They have long since become masters of the art of demagoguery.

Allow me to offer a footnote on the shortness of political memory. All of us—Russians, Westerners, everybody—too easily forget our disappointments, thus setting ourselves up for new ones. Do you remember the euphoria that both Western leaders and Russian liberals felt from 2001 to 2003 at the prospects of Russia's impending turn toward the West? Of course you do! It was the period when Putin seemed to everyone to be choosing partnership with America. "Russia has agreed to become the junior U.S. partner," or "Putin is bringing Russia into the West," claimed observers. I myself got caught up in this narrative tide. I hoped that the rapprochement would facilitate domestic liberalization, as it had in the Soviet Union under Gorbachev.

Many in the West had the same hope. In a joint statement at the July 2002 G8 summit in Kananaskis, Canada, Western leaders sang Putin's praises:

> Russia has demonstrated its potential to play a full and meaningful role in addressing the global problems that we all face. This decision reflects the remarkable economic and democratic transformation [!] that has occurred in Russia in recent years and in particular under the leadership of President Putin.

I can only imagine how proud of himself Putin must have felt when he heard this chorus.

Under pressure from Washington, Western leaders reversed their earlier decision to forbid Russia from chairing the G8 until it had joined the World Trade Organization and met other political and economic criteria. Perhaps they thought this courtship would win for them an amenable partner in international affairs. When Western leaders visited Moscow, they refused to meet with representatives of the opposition and civil society, lest anything interfere with the construction of their "horizontal" relationships with the Kremlin. Their policy was to keep the Putin team happy in order to promote Western interests.

ANDREW: The West tends to believe that flattery works, particularly with the thin-skinned. I suppose you are right to say that the West wanted to keep the Putin team happy in order to promote its interests, but there was also the feeling, as there was with Yeltsin, that being friendly would convince Russia that the West was—as indeed it was—sincere in wishing Russia well. Thus reassured, Russia might evolve into the sort of cooperative and like-minded partner the West sought. The unspoken assumption was that Russian gratitude would be bankable.

But repaying favors is not a Russian tradition. A Moscow policeman put it well to me not long ago when he asked me how I could say I respected him if I was not afraid of him?

"RUSSIA IS RISING FROM HER KNEES"
2004–2008

ANDREW: I see the relationship between Russia and the West, meaning the individual countries to Russia's West as well as Western institutions, as a process of ups and downs, governed substantially by Russia's internal evolution and its ideas of itself.

LILIA: Let me just highlight this assumption of yours, which I share, but so few other Russia observers do.

ANDREW: The West has difficulty understanding Russia's internal development, as we know. But if this picture is a reasonable way of analyzing the issues, then I would be wary of too clearly dividing Russian history into different periods. What I see in the case of the transition between Putin 1.0 and Putin 2.0 is a gradual change, with the Yukos affair and the Orange Revolution, which roughly coincided with the end of one presidential term and the beginning of another, marking off a clear frontier. Three elements in Russia's evolutionary process combined to promote a harder Russian view of the West.

First, Putin grew more confident in himself as his first term passed. He took the measure of the leading Western politicians and found them pliable. He established within Russia a personal myth of himself as the strong man who had brought stability and prosperity. It was only natural that he began to believe himself indispensable, and from there it was only a short step (if it was indeed even a step at all) for him to believe himself wiser or, if you prefer, more reasonable and realistic than others. All leaders can fall prey to such self-regard, but the journey is even easier if you work in the Kremlin, as few contest your opinions, let alone your decisions. Now, I cannot say from personal experience that I know this is what happened to Putin; I can only say that it would be natural if it had, and that, if so, then he would be bound by his political course to present himself as standing above all other mortals.

Second, the system as Putin developed it embedded itself in Russia's foundations. Putin has had essentially the same team with him for a dozen years now. The process of centralization had already gone far enough by 2003–2004 to undermine the independence, and therefore the effectiveness, of regional structures, the Duma, and the judiciary. These institutions have been further diminished since then. The center's control over the larger enterprises and Russia's information space had also solidified by the time Putin's first term was nearing its end—and it has of course gone further since then.

Third, the energy and natural resource sectors, combined with prudent budgets, had driven the economy forward and built up Russia's financial reserves. The Kremlin must have thought that all was well, and that Russia's foundations were strong. Many outsiders thought so, too.

LILIA: Yes, by 2004, Kremlin insiders felt so cocky and even superior that they dreamed about conquering the world again—this time as the "nuclear-armed and energy-rich Great Power."

ANDREW: But there was a price to be paid; perhaps it troubled the dreams of the powerful. The structure that had seemingly produced such power and riches was rigid. There were no substantial reforms after the first wave. The leitmotif of the structure was control—control over society, over the economy, and, so far as was practicable, over the outside world. Its capacity for renewal was and is open to doubt. The claim that Russia was now a great power lacked, and still lacks, real strategic purpose, unless one counts dominance over others as such a purpose. At any rate, I cannot see that such a purpose does ordinary Russians much good. Furthermore, as a tool to achieve emotional revenge on behalf of Russia's decisionmaking elite for the trials their country suffered from the mid-1980s until the early years of this century, the delusion of great-power status is dangerous. It is understandable but ultimately foolish to blame the slights and struggles of the recent past on outside forces when the truth is that they were largely self-inflicted. And this truth would set them free from the Soviet past. Gaidar's parallel with Weimar should have struck home. Alas, populist claims to "greatness unrecognized" proved more tempting, and the rewriting of history preferred.

LILIA: We are looking at this period of Russia's development from different points of view—you from the outside and I from the inside. But different angles of observation do not change the way we see the whole picture. I hope this means that our perceptions are correct!

I agree with your view of the evolution of Putin's regime, as well as your impressions of the motives underlying the Kremlin's perceptions of domestic and foreign realities.

You are right: There were not just political motives for consolidating Putin's authoritarianism and reviving the elite's neo-imperial thinking; psychological drivers were also at work. If a leader encounters not only no resistance but not even mild objections from the elite or society, he starts to think himself the center of the universe—all the more so given Putin's successful super-centralization of power. His support and approval ratings shot up, as you mentioned, and this only further convinced him that he had found the optimum formula for governing Russia.

The Kremlin team found the means to unite a confused society that had lost confidence in itself: "Russia is rising from her knees." The humiliations of the 1990s were over, and Russia would once again be a strong and powerful country that its neighbors would fear and that the West couldn't afford to ignore. This marked a return to clichés that were still familiar to Russians. Putin didn't need to invent these ideas; he merely brought old ghosts back to life. A demoralized Russian society was ready, even eager, to march back to the past.

Why did Putin return to this paradigm after the early attempts at economic liberalization? The answer is that, for him and for the security bureaucrats he brought to power, this was the most natural way to strengthen the regime while simultaneously securing control of assets. The only way the Putin team knew how to govern was by taking all power into its hands and ruling through loyalty and submission. But they were poor students of history; they forgot that top-down rule had brought the Soviet Union to the point of collapse.

ANDREW: It is worth remembering that the economic liberalization of Putin's first term was a legacy program from the 1990s, and that it was the tightening of central control that was Putin's contribution. These two strands ran together.

LILIA: That's true. Eventually, one strand was swallowed by another.

Why did the population agree to return to the past? That is the question we Russians are racking our brains to answer.

Several factors played a part. People were weary of the chaos of the 1990s, which they associated with democracy. Many people no longer believed in the ideals of liberal democracy, which supposedly had brought nothing but deprivation and difficulties.

The thing to remember here is that the so-called "systemic liberals" played a big part in discrediting liberal democracy and the idea of reform. These people were essentially technocrats who became part of the system. They proclaimed liberal ideas, but in reality took an active role in building an authoritarian regime.

And here is the trap: The justification for returning to the old matrix was the population's supposed discontent with liberal reforms. But in reality none of these reforms were ever fully carried out. The people were deceived, however, and so they willingly agreed to return to one-man rule.

High oil prices enabled Putin to buy the public's belief in the myth that the model he had chosen was the best one. And thus the Putin consensus for stability in exchange for freedom was born.

The Kremlin suddenly seized on the idea that the world was now at its feet, and that Russia would become a new energy superpower. In 2006, Putin even called for the world to recognize Russia in this capacity!

ANDREW: Oil (and therefore gas) prices were an essential part of the story up to mid-2008. Because of them, the Russian government, while pursuing admirably sensible budgetary policies, could neglect domestic investment and the restructuring of the economy—even as it nurtured dreams of greatness. The West, as far as Moscow was concerned, could take it or leave it. European dependence on Russian gas would deepen. Central Asian gas producers could be kept subservient to Gazprom, and transit countries like Ukraine would cave in to Russian demands. It did not work out like this for long, however.

LILIA: Western energy dependence helped the Kremlin team to feel omnipotent.

Russia's return to great-power assertiveness required some additional justification. The ruling team found new pretexts for getting cocky. They allowed themselves, first, to have their feelings hurt (indeed some were looking for a pretext to get hurt, such as alleged NATO expansion, American ballistic missile defense in Europe, the Western "meddling" in the Russian area of interest). Then they complained about it and started to break the china.

Complaining and whining became hobbies for many Russian politicians and experts. For some time now, they have accused the West of a lack of sensitivity to Russia's sense of grievance, blamed it for its meddling in Russia's internal affairs, and chided it for its finger-wagging on democracy. And the bulk of the blame fell on the Bush administration for allegedly promoting the color revolutions in Ukraine and Georgia, for seeking NATO Membership Action Plans for Ukraine and Georgia, for planning to install a missile defense system in Poland and the Czech Republic, and for recognizing Kosovo as an independent state, to say nothing of the war in Iraq and withdrawal from the Anti-Ballistic Missile Treaty. Quite a few Western observers would accept this explanation.

ANDREW: I want to step back a bit to look at the fundamental idea of bipolarity, which came back into fashion in Russia with Primakov and has become even more fashionable since then. Correct me if I am wrong, but it seems to me that the idea reflects Russian nostalgia for old Cold War certainties: that Moscow's natural and balancing relationship is with Washington, and that, if there is not some sort of equivalence between them, then the world must be out of order. This idea is unrealistic now and was the more so during the 1990s. But the fact of its unreality did little to curb its appeal in Russia as faith in democratic transformation and its ability to determine the evolution of its immediate neighborhood both ebbed during that decade. Moscow found it far easier to attribute its misfortunes to Washington's ambition to establish a unipolar system than to face up to its changed standing with its neighbors and the world. The demonstrable fact that Washington was in no position to become a unipolar center did not make Moscow's sense of being cheated of its rights any less seductive to the Russian establishment. They saw NATO's acceptance of new members and its action in Kosovo as proof of its intentions to take advantage of Russian weakness. Neither action was seen in the West as directed against Russia, nor were they seen as necessarily strengthening either NATO or Washington. But that was not the point: Both showed the Moscow establishment that Russia could not make its will felt. Thus was the humiliation myth given life.

LILIA: Russian propagandists had been actively working to build this myth even during Yeltsin's time.

I think you are right to point to the "bipolarity" myth and its influence on Russian political thought. Even Russian liberals continue to view the world through a prism of bipolarity with the United States. Bipolarity is still an element of Russian statehood identity. When Americans neglect Russia or the Russian elite thinks that they have, it deeply frustrates the Russian establishment. Sometimes, I think that the Russian elite intentionally looks for reasons to feel humiliated so that they can then move back to their more familiar assertiveness. Forgive me for this crude explanation: We are dealing with political sadomasochism—a reflection of deep complexes, insecurities, and demoralization, all of which in the Russian case became systemic elements.

ANDREW: One of the ironies of the unipolar thesis, which also has its appeal for European intellectuals, is not just that the United States could not sustain such an ambition, but that those who looked at the world in this way hankered after domination themselves. The truth is that Americans have long felt that their country is doing too much, not that it should take on still more. You can see this rather clearly now. Barack Obama has been taking a back seat over the Middle East, so far as he can.

LILIA: Russian politicians will never believe that Americans are tired of the global role and overstretch. With respect to the "humiliation" myth, it helped the Kremlin to justify its assertiveness during Putin's second presidency (2004–2008).

The sad truth is that the West ignored liberal Russia's interests. As I see it from the Russian perspective, the West was more concerned with accommodating the Russian elite's interests. Look at the leadership in Brussels and in Europe's capitals. They have showed, and continue to show, a particular zeal in playing along with official Moscow. Having proclaimed in the 1990s a strategy of partnership that was supposed to facilitate Russia's integration into the European space, European leaders never managed to set conditions that would have brought Russia closer to the European Union. EU policy toward Russia has become a thin veneer of wordy declarations masking a void. One cannot help but admire the Eurocrats' zeal in creating the appearance of partnership with Russia.

Brussels did not even specify how it ought to influence the development of democratic norms and principles in Russia. The Partnership and Cooperation Agreement (1997), which regulated the European Union's relationship with Russia, referred obliquely to "the approximation of laws" and to "the integration between Russia and a wider area of cooperation in Europe." One of the leading Russian human rights activists, Sergei Kovalev, blasted the agreement: "The text of the agreement is pompous but at the same time pathetically impotent, because it lacks specificity. There is no precise formulation of obligations or mechanisms of control."

Do you think he was being too emotional?

ANDREW: I sympathize, because he hoped for more. But the Partnership and Cooperation Agreement at least gave space for discussions about particular issues, and some concrete, albeit limited, achievements.

LILIA: I think you will agree that these achievements did not prevent Russia's stagnation. My feeling is that the Brussels bureaucracy seems to have given up trying to influence events inside Russia and instead prefers to believe that everything is perfect—that Russia is adapting to EU principles at the very moment it is in fact moving in the opposite direction. Having witnessed Brussels' willingness to accommodate, Moscow has stopped taking European institutions seriously.

Do you think I am prejudiced with respect to Brussels and the European capitals?

ANDREW: As for the European Union, it is structured to be wet. Imprecision and indecision are its stocks in trade. Enlargement was a powerful force, intelligently pursued, and that might seem to contradict what I have just said. However, enlargement lost momentum as the Europeans began to absorb its costs and difficulties, and this occurred even before it might have had a serious bearing on Russia's evolution. It is conceivable that the process might resume in due course, but that is beyond the predictable future, as is shown clearly enough by the European Union's reluctance by 2010 to face the possibility of Ukraine joining at some remote stage. EU policies are necessarily those of the lowest common denominator, and they are also confused by the varying attitudes and aspirations of its member states. Russia has played very successfully on that confusion. It is a fair indication of the questionable state of a relationship when it is described as a "strategic partnership," a superbly meaningless and therefore popular phrase.

That said, it is true that there is a natural degree of mutual economic interest between Russia and the rest of Europe—far more than between Russia and the United States. The power of the European Union to set the regulatory agenda is also considerable and continues to affect Russia deeply—benignly, in my view. If Russia joins the WTO, we shall see whether the European Union will insist that Moscow obeys WTO rules, thereby opening the country up to competitive forces that will promote economic reform. And the involvement of European businesses in Russia (and Russian ones in the rest of Europe, for that matter) is a force that, in principle at least, will tend to promote a liberal agenda, broadly defined. We need to discuss that further, however, bearing in mind Khodorkovsky's remark that Russia exports two goods: hydrocarbons and corruption.

LILIA: I will come back a bit later to the idea that Western business "tends to promote a liberal agenda." I have my doubts on this issue. It is possible the "law of unintended consequences" applies also to Western businesses. But again, we would expect this to be the case when the views "from the inside" and "from the outside" differ.

I want to offer a comment on the issue of Russia and the European Union during Putin's presidency. You explain the European Union's lack of a clear policy by pointing to two facts: It has had internal problems "digesting" the recent enlargement, and it is "structured to be wet." I can't argue with either of these facts, but the remaining question, then, is why do European leaders and EU bureaucrats in particular act in accordance with the Russian regime's wishes?

It's absurd that the European Union has been implementing in Russia projects approved by the Russian authorities. This makes for a paradoxical situation indeed: Europe is attempting to promote values under the oversight of a government that rejects these values! The irony is that this didn't prevent the EU-Russia relationship from hitting a low point in 2004–2008.

ANDREW: For Ukraine and Georgia, it was Moscow more than any other factor that pushed them to try to develop closer ties with both NATO and the European Union. Official Russians will never acknowledge this publicly, however. They see NATO's willingness to keep its door open to new members as a provocation in itself. Moscow believes that former Soviet states, or even former Warsaw Pact ones, should not be allowed so much freedom as to pass through that door. Even NATO's offering to help them walk through the door is for Moscow evidence that malevolent outsiders are trampling Russia's rights. This attitude is absurd in itself. And in any case, Membership Action Plans only amount to a process by which interested countries can adapt themselves to certain criteria, such as democratic standards, that are necessary for eventual application. They are not a guarantee of eventual accession. Considering the pressure Russia put on these two countries, it was not surprising that they sought the refuge of more international support.

LILIA: Do you mind my jumping in here? You said that it was Moscow that made Ukraine (under Yushchenko) and Georgia keen to develop closer ties with NATO. This is yet another example of the law of unintended consequences at work. Indeed, the more pressure that Moscow brings to bear, the more its neighbors seek shelter elsewhere. Even authoritarian Lukashenko looked to Europe for protection from Russia—at least until his presidential election-rigging made it impossible for the West to believe that he would ever change for the better.

Perhaps realizing what their policy of intimidation leads to, the Russian ruling team has recently changed tactics, trying to envelop its neighbors in a warmer embrace. But the Kremlin is going to have a hard time convincing neighbors of this policy's sincerity after its war with Georgia.

ANDREW: The rest of the case for the prosecution is something of a soup. There is no reasonable basis for suggesting that the West meddled significantly in Russia's internal affairs—rather to the contrary, as your remarks about the West's ignoring the interests of liberal Russia indicate. Some Western finger-wagging on democracy was appropriate, but it was limited. Perhaps guilty consciences in the Kremlin were what made it seem so irritating. The Russians knew perfectly well that the proposed stationing of missile defense systems in Poland and the Czech Republic had nothing to do with Russian security. Moscow could of course interpret both the U.S. action in Iraq and its attempts to settle the Kosovo problem as proof that Washington was overmighty, but neither issue was of direct concern to Russia (besides which, one could just as easily argue that both episodes weakened the United States and its allies rather than strengthening them). To be sure, quite a few Western observers thought that the repeated Russian criticisms were justified. But that fact points less to their analytical acumen and more to their willingness to mistake repetition for sincerity, if not also Western European resentment of U.S. strength coupled with a cultural disdain for President George W. Bush.

LILIA: What a perfect paradox: The Russian elite felt humiliated by U.S. actions that weakened America and the West!!

ANDREW: The United States is in a different situation, I think, from the European Union. It has fewer direct political or economic interests with regard to Moscow. It also has an unrivaled corps of analysts of Russian affairs. Washington has obviously been of critical importance in developing overall Western policies and attitudes. That role may now be fading, but Moscow's belief that agreement with Washington will deliver the West as a whole has not faded. And of course this belief is fortified by Russia's nostalgic wish to be one of the pillars of a bipolar world. The relationship with Russia was an electoral issue in the United States in 2008, though not a major one, and we now have yet another reset. But the fact remains that Russia is not a central concern for the United States.

LILIA: Since the United States has no strong economic ties to Russia, it has a wider field for maneuver, as well as a greater flexibility in introducing the normative dimension to its engagement. However, the fact that Russia is no longer as great a priority for Washington has had another consequence, for it has weakened America's Russia expertise. One sees too few young faces in the field. What will happen when the current generation of Russia hands leaves the scene?

Getting back to the Putin-Bush era, I would like to mention that President Bush became the Russian political class's whipping boy during Putin's second presidential term; they constantly accused him of meddling in Russian affairs. This charge was another example of distortion. In reality, the younger Bush based his Russia policy on a different principle: namely, his belief that Russia was incapable of democratization. "There is something in the Russian DNA that explains centralization of power," Bush once famously said. A leader who thought that centralized power in Russia was bred in its very bones was unlikely to take a values-based approach to his dealings with that country. Bush-watchers like my Carnegie colleague Thomas Carothers have argued that the president never ventured beyond the bounds of "realism" in his policy toward Russia, intentionally "downplaying democracy concerns."

If we accept the argument that the West, and above all the United States, meddled in Russia's internal affairs and provoked Moscow with NATO enlargement and missile defense, then how is it that the Russian elite missed these threats during Putin's first term in office? The first term was a period when Moscow and the West established what could even be called a partnership. Why is it that they only remembered these "humiliations" when Putin's second term began in 2004?

ANDREW: Sneering at George W. Bush was a popular sport for sophisticated (as they thought themselves) Europeans and American Democrats, but I bet he will look better as time passes. I do not know quite what he meant by a genetic Russian disposition toward centralization, and I certainly do not take the view that such centralization is inevitable, let alone desirable, in Russia. But one must admit that it is traditional.

Nor do I think, as I have already said, that Russia's claims of being threatened and humiliated have any substance. But those protestations reflected real feelings, groundless or not, and they served notice that Russia was now a force to be reckoned with, or at least that it believed itself so. They also helped to dispel the idea that Russia itself might have been responsible for its failure to become a "pole of attraction." The only true sense in which the West provoked the Orange Revolution was its being a beacon for different ideas from those pushed so forcefully by Russia—the people's right to select their own leaders not least among them. Moscow's shock at seeing Ukraine slip away from them by means of popular resistance to electoral fraud was palpable.

LILIA: Russia has failed to become a "pole of attraction" for its neighbors, even for its authoritarian ones. However, the Russian elite won't admit that. Thus they try to persuade the world and themselves that it is the West, and America above all, that seduces or bribes away Russia's neighbors. By the way, belief in Russian "soft power" still exists even among thoughtful Russian observers. Perhaps they think that their belief can conjure it out of thin air.

Let me turn to another subject. I would argue that the period of warmth between Russia and the West during Putin's first term (2000–2004) undermines the "realpolitik" concept. This honeymoon period was based on four premises. First, Western governments refused to use values in their approach to relations with Moscow. Second, the Kremlin hoped that the West would recognize Russia's status as an energy superpower.

Third, the Kremlin expected the West to acquiesce in Russian control over the former Soviet area, and fourth, that the West would endorse a Moscow veto on European security issues. The Russian elite understood Western politicians' desire to avoid upsetting them as weakness and a pretext to up the ante.

The West evidently saw the partnership in a different way. What is your explanation for the "thaw" during Putin's first term?

ANDREW: I am not sure about this "thaw" idea. I would see it as an early "reset" coming after Putin's election in 2000. It was worn away slowly by mutual disappointment, including a dawning realization in the West that the new regime was retreating away from democratic practice and toward central control. The slowness with which this realization dawned subdued value-based criticism of that retreat, which was a pity in that it may well have encouraged a self-serving Russian belief that Western statements about principles were mere hypocrisy. But I do not think that there was a conscious decision not to press Russia on values. What we saw was more like inattention mixed with the hope that Russia would find its own path to a shared destination. If Russia supposed that the West would agree to its being an energy power, then it was wrong, not least because the meaning of "energy power" has never been clear. Nor could the West have been expected to give Moscow a veto over security questions, however much Russia might have wanted one. That too had been made clear, but maybe not clear enough.

LILIA: If, as you say, there was no conscious Western decision not to press Russia on values, then we have a problem of perception. The Russian elite and Russian leaders have begun to see Western policy as giving them carte blanche to tighten the screws at home. And there have been some cases that should force us to reconsider our own perceptions of the Western normative stance. As the media reported, French President Jacques Chirac blasted the leaders of smaller states at the EU-Russia summits when they tried to raise the issue of human rights in Russia. Can we not view this case as an example of a conscious decision on the part of some European leaders to expunge the issue of standards from the EU-Russian agenda?

As I saw it from my vantage point in Moscow in 2004, fear that the Orange Revolution virus would spread outside Ukraine gave Putin a powerful motive (to be sure, not the only one) to resort to anti-Western consolidation in Russia's domestic affairs. Looking back now, I have to admit that the Kremlin was really shocked and frightened by the Maidan Nezalezhnosti (Independence Square) events in Kiev, when hundred of thousands of Ukrainians took to the streets to protest election manipulation. For the Kremlin leader who had once thought that Ukrainians are not a nation and that Ukraine is not a state, it must have been an ominous portent: if Ukrainians can do this in Kiev, why couldn't Russians do it in Moscow?

ANDREW: What Chirac said was foolish and also counterproductive. It was certainly not supported by other EU member states, such as the United Kingdom.

LILIA: My guess is that German Chancellor Gerhard Schröder welcomed Chirac's line.

There were other factors that played a role in 2004–2008. Moscow's self-assurance, its confidence in the strength of its energy weapon, and its sense of the West's willingness to yield in the face of blackmail, on the one hand, combined with its vulnerability, its fears, and its attempts to conceal, on the other, triggered a return to an adversarial relationship.

However, there were also structural reasons forcing Moscow to play macho with the West. You reminded us about these reasons earlier when you stressed the role of domestic factors in the evolution of Russia's foreign policy. The Kremlin's return to an overcentralized state required a Western endorsement of spheres of influence. Russia's claims against NATO, missile defense, and Kosovo's independence justified its attempt to return to Soviet geopolitics. The Russian-Georgian war was an act of overt blackmail directed against the West, a proof that Moscow was ready to apply raw force to re-establish its influence. But there were still other motives as well. This by no means exhausts the list....

ANDREW: I agree.

LILIA: The system that emerged under Putin can't survive without superpower pretensions and satellites. It doesn't matter if Moscow can't control the satellites; for instance, the Kremlin was caught flatfooted by the collapse of the Bakiyev regime in Kyrgyzstan and refused to interfere when the new authorities in Bishkek asked for help. The important thing is not that the Kremlin is actually able to use its "areas of influence" (or "areas of interests" as they prefer to say now); it merely needs to pretend as though it can, or to at least try to squeeze other intruders out of the post-Soviet space. Russia's system of personalized power is expansionist by its very nature and focused on containment of Western civilization. As the developments in 2000–2004 proved, the system can soften its relationship with the West or harden it as the needs of the moment dictate.

Thus consolidation of Russia's authoritarianism, in an environment of economic growth and the elite's growing self-assurance, was bound to lead to assertiveness on the international scene. This raises a question: If Bush had refused to support Ukraine and Georgia, abandoned U.S. missile defense plans, and not pushed for independence in Kosovo, could it have prevented the crisis in U.S.-Russian relations? Possibly. It could have helped to ameliorate the tension. At times of "energy euphoria" in Russia, however, its elite would have found other splinters in America's eye. Anti-liberal and anti-American feelings during Putin's time became a very effective reserve of power, because they also represented the rejection of Yeltsin's "liberal" and "pro-Western" legacy, which had been discredited in the eyes of many Russians.

No matter how hard Western leaders tried not to irritate Moscow and Putin, no matter how hard they tried to draw them into their embrace, Moscow could never become a predictable and loyal partner for the West, due, quite simply, to systemic differences. Even the Russian elite's personal integration into Western society couldn't neutralize their anti-Western feelings, at least as long as the personalized system remained in place. This axiom has to be tested today.

ANDREW: I agree with much of what you say. Systemic differences have real meaning, and so does what I have earlier suggested is a spirit of denial and revenge on the part of the Russian leadership for the suffering of the past couple of decades or more. The West, and the United States in particular, was the natural target for those hostile emotions, though it was scarcely guilty of being their root cause. And this was all the more true as the Russian leadership began to see itself as leading not a newly constituted or liberated country but rather the legitimate successor to the Soviet Union. I have to pay tribute to the genius of Russian and Soviet diplomacy in finding and holding on to grievances until they gain purchase. Western politicians and observers also have a weakness for guilt, even when there is little or no justification for it. Russian feelings about the West, and the United States as its leading symbol, were heightened by Russian economic, and to a degree also social, success, coupled with underlying doubts about the long term.

LILIA: Your comment on the Western "weakness for guilt" explains a lot. The Russian political class, which ignores Western standards and values, nevertheless is pretty sensitive to certain features of Western psychology, and they exploit them with great success. They are well aware of other Western qualities, as well: political correctness, politeness, the desire to avoid confrontation, and the hunger for compromise, to name a few. These qualities apparently aid a regime that attempts to survive and to perpetuate itself through mimicking, pretending, manipulating, bullying, and provoking.

Western leaders, with their yearning for persuasion and compromise, gave the Russian elite reason to think that Russia could join the Western club while continuing its traditional practices at home. By thinking about how to keep the Russian elite happy and giving no thought to transformation, Western leaders prepared the way for Russian revisionism.

Relations between Russia and the West during Putin's presidency revealed two conditions. First, they displayed the Russian system's skill at mimicry and its elite's facility in using the West to advance its own interests. Second, they revealed Western leaders' lack of strategic vision regarding Russia and their inability to set a common policy. Could you comment on that?

ANDREW: You are right to say that Western leaders had a managerial approach to Russia rather than an overarching strategic vision, particularly as the latter might presuppose some concrete ideas about implementing such a vision. That was partly because their attention was not focused on Russia in the way that circumstances had earlier forced them to do—partly because their counsels were divided, and partly because they thought that they had reason to remain fairly optimistic about the long term. Western business interests reinforced belief in the idea that Russia would develop in its own way into a responsible and economically integrated member of the international community.

LILIA: My impression is that the Kremlin's hostility, as demonstrated by Putin's "Cold War" speech in Munich in 2007, which presented America as an "evil Empire," had the shock of a cold shower for many Westerners. I remember the television coverage of that event: Putin's stern expression at the podium and Western leaders in the audience hardly able to conceal their shock and discomfort.

The truth is that the relationship had already started to deteriorate in 2003–2004. Russian media coverage of the West, and especially the United States, had changed drastically. But Western analysts didn't seem to want to notice it. Or perhaps they thought that Putin was merely employing some kind of tactical device to massage the Russian nationalists and his own entourage.

The August 2008 Russian-Georgian war became the climax revealing the enormity of the political crisis between Russia and the West. The problem is that many in the West today would prefer to see this war only as a bilateral conflict without acknowledging its systemic roots. Meanwhile, the cooling off in Russian-U.S. relations and the crisis in 2007–2008 were the result of the Russian elite's attempts to strengthen the centralized state and of Putin's own attempt to guarantee the continuity of his regime during the election cycle—circumstances that demanded that the West be contained. At the same time, Moscow expected that the West would renounce any efforts to contain Russia.

The "realist" period in relations between Russia and the West ended up strengthening anti-Western feelings in Russian society. The Kremlin's anti-Western, and above all anti-American, propaganda campaign had a hand in this, of course, but of greater concern has been increasing criticism of the West and Western policy coming from liberal circles in Russia.

ANDREW: The war in Georgia was such a great shock that it has been put to one side as a sort of post-traumatic amnesia. There is some excuse for that; it came at just the moment that Russia's pretensions were about to be pricked by the collapse of oil prices, as well as the global economic crisis, which illuminated Russian weakness in a revealing light.

LILIA: The Russian-Georgian War of 2008 also says a lot about Western disarray and hesitation. Western leaders failed to anticipate and prevent the conflict, and they did not have a clue as to how to end the war. Today, they don't have any idea how to deal with its aftermath or how to deal with the changes in borders it is creating.

The Russian-Georgian war demonstrates not only that the West has problems combining "interests" and "values;" it also has trouble with regional stability and security.

I would like to mention here three names. First, the late Ronald Asmus, a brilliant analyst and a person with a mission, and author of the book, *A Little War That Shook the World: Georgia, Russia and the Future of the West*, which convincingly describes how the West, and first of all Washington, failed to prevent the war in spite of insistent warnings and appeals. When the conflict started, Bush delegated negotiations to French President Nicolas Sarkozy, and then he was "appalled" by Sarkozy's performance.

The second person I have in mind is French political scientist Pierre Hassner, who, analyzing Western behavior during and after the conflict, wrote that France, Germany, Italy, or Spain "often see Russia's neighbors as a threat to their good relations with Moscow or as a potential burden for the EU if their democratic development allows them to knock on the EU's door at a time when the European public is resisting any enlargement." What a shocking admission! Hassner acknowledges that Europe is not interested in the democratic evolution of the new independent states, first, because it does not want to undermine its relations with Moscow and, second, because it can't integrate the new states into its orbit!

The third person is Andrei Illarionov, Putin's former economic adviser. Andrei did a terrific job in collecting every possible scrap of information on the Russian-Georgian conflict that contradicts the

Russian official version and that, at the same time, is brushed aside by many Western observers.

Georgia fell victim not only to the Kremlin's neo-imperialist instincts and Putin's hatred for Georgian President Mikheil Saakashvili; it also fell victim to Western and especially American—and here I am looking for a milder word—inconsistency. (A less politically correct person would call it "hypocrisy.") Western leaders, and Bush most of all, supported Georgia's Western trajectory, creating a lot of hope among Georgians who never noticed the limited and conditional nature of this support. Soon enough, Western leaders discovered that they had no answer to the dilemma of how to pursue good relations with Moscow while simultaneously supporting Tbilisi's transformation and its Western trajectory.

ANDREW: There are all sorts of discouraging lessons to be drawn. The European Union has preferred to look at the beginning of military action, ignoring the long Russian buildup to it. There has been a massive temptation to blame Saakashvili for rash and impulsive behavior, and that temptation elides gently with the preferred Russian narrative, which states that Moscow had no choice but to respond to aggression. Western politicians underestimated Russia's determination to prevent Georgia from slipping out of its control entirely, and so I imagine it discounted Moscow's disposition to use force when sufficient reason presented itself. I do not think that was hypocrisy—more like a failure of intelligence (in both senses of the word). But on the other hand, this story is by no means over yet. Moscow's hold over the Caucasus is not at all secure, for regional reasons, with Western options playing an ancillary role. Or at least so it seems to me.

THE RUSSIAN TANDEM CHANGES ITS TACTICS

MODERNIZATION AS A WAY TO PRESERVE THE STATUS QUO FROM 2008 ON

ANDREW: The Russian belief that the West does not understand Russian realities goes far beyond the "liberal camp," however widely one understands that term. I have been struck by recent disagreements about Russia's trajectory among many, perhaps even most, Western observers, particularly in Washington and in Germany, and a wide group of Russian intellectuals, analysts, and business figures. The mood in Russia is more pessimistic than elsewhere. Russian disillusion may feed back into Western opinion in due course, but whether it does or not, the gap between attitudes reflects a difference of assumptions about the future that will endure. Western observers will continue to assume more readily than the most sanguine Russians that Russia will follow a path that, however uncertainly, will in the end direct it toward becoming a functioning civil and democratic society much like the prevailing Western model.

LILIA: It seems that Russians are traditionally more resigned to fate and more despondent than Westerners. With such a history, to be an optimist would mean being totally detached from reality.

ANDREW: There are those who might say that Russians always fall prey to gloom, but in this case that response is not good enough. There have been substantial changes over the past two or three years, starting with Dmitri Medvedev's succession to the presidency. That was not a succession in the normal meaning of the word, however. It was not the renewal that, for example, the election of a new U.S. president typically brings about. The constant questions about who is really in charge in Moscow show as much. I would go further. Uncertainties like these undermine the presidency as an institution, not just the present incumbent. They further prioritize short-term considerations over long-term ones. The existence of the tandem and in particular the predominant role of the prime minister further skew Russia's political development toward its traditions of personalized power and away from the country's constitutionally prescribed institutions. We have, moreover, the unstable paradox of a sclerotic political system coupled with shifts in the country it rules.

Two outcomes of the 2008–2009 global economic crisis had serious implications. The first was the progressive and long-term weakening of Russia's gas weapon. The European market is now more competitive, and Russia's position within it is markedly weaker than it was. It may never return to what it seemed to be in the heady days before mid-2008, even with the current turmoil in the Middle East. And the second outcome was that, while Russia paid its way through the crisis with reasonable success, it did so only at great future cost and by sustaining its Soviet-inherited infrastructure, not by economic renewal. It is at least as dependent on hydrocarbons as it ever was, but there is now greater recognition of the dangers inherent in that dependence. It is not only Medvedev who realizes that. I suppose that Putin does, too.

LILIA: Yes, the landscape in 2009 changed. You are right to mention the global financial crisis. It seriously affected Russia, forcing the Kremlin to start normalization with the West. But those who think the Russian ruling elite has had a change of heart about the Western community are mistaken. The change merely reflects the evolution of Kremlin survival mechanisms. The ruling elite came to the conclusion that Putin's assertive policies would not help Russia overcome the consequences of the economic crisis, that the Russian commodity-driven economy needs to be modernized, and that the West should be the key instrument in that modernization. The fact that Putin has softened his macho style shows that he apparently understood the need to turn to the West. One should not have any illusions, however: The aim of dialogue with the West is to facilitate the Russian system's adaptation to a changed situation without changing its principles.

ANDREW: Your conclusion is indisputable and also understandable within its own terms. One could hardly expect such an adaptation controlled by those with a compelling stake in the existing system to be otherwise. But the question is whether, or at least to what degree, the regime's preferred path of adaptation without real change is practicable. The tension between economic resurgence and political stasis is palpable. And it is the suspicion that the political status quo will win out that underlies the Russian feeling that Russia may enter a cul de sac, or that indeed it already has. I do not detect any confidence that an injection of Western technology will do anything significant to alter that prospect. That has after all been tried many times before.

LILIA: Agreed. There were two times in Russia's history when the rulers attempted to breathe new life into its traditional personalized power system by drawing on Western means. The first "modernization campaign" came under Peter the Great, and the second one came under Stalin. They brought some energy into the economy, but the country soon plunged back into stagnation. Why do we constantly forget history's lessons?

Today the Russian elite is desperately trying not only to find a means to revive an obsolescent economy; it is also trying to justify the prolongation of personalized power into the twenty-first century. Within recent memory, its key representatives were declaring the end of Western civilization. In June 2008, Foreign Minister Sergei Lavrov, who had already proved his facility at wielding the "Russia is getting off her knees" rhetoric, announced that "a stage of world development in which European civilization was dominant has ended." The world, said Lavrov, faced a dilemma: either it could "accept Western values and become the Big West," or it could take "another approach, which we promote." Moscow, in other words, planned to turn Russia into an alternative to the West. As to what norms Russia was ready to offer the world, it remained silent.

In 2009–2010, the Russian ruling tandem suddenly changed its reading of world history. From that point on, Medvedev and Putin never missed an opportunity to assert that Russia had committed itself to the same values that underpin the West. "We are no different from you," they repeated. "We espouse the same values as you in the West," Medvedev assured us. "I see no big differences when it comes to human rights and freedoms. Is there anything dividing us? Nothing," he reiterated to Western audiences whose members all nodded approvingly.

ANDREW: There have always been, and probably will always be, mixed messages coming out of Moscow. The Lavrov view is certainly not dead. Russia's leaders have cast around for various models to follow: Chinese, Korean, Singaporean. But the appeal of a special Russian path remains powerful, even dominant, I would say. That path entails being different from the West, or otherwise it means nothing. But it would be fair to add that Russia is not the only country to have sought a special way.

LILIA: Well, the Kremlin will most likely return to the "Russian special path" again. It will happen at the moment when Russia and the West fall back into a pattern of mutual frustration, which, I think, is unavoidable. The Kremlin continues to hold this idea up its sleeve. And even as it chants about democracy, the Russian elite adds in parentheses that they're talking about "Russian-style" democracy. Thus "the special way" has never been taken off the table entirely.

To be sure, there is a lot of confusion within the Russian ruling group. However, we would underestimate Lavrov and other representatives of the Russian authorities if we doubted their commitment to tough-minded pragmatism in pursuing their corporate interests. If we assume that they do understand what they are doing (we shouldn't make the mistake of faulting their intelligence), we may call a spade a spade.

Look at Medvedev. He is a perfect example of what I have in mind. Medvedev has made democracy his credo. He never tires of saying that only "free people" can modernize. He also asserts that "Russia is without doubt a democracy." But on the basis of what criteria does he draw this conclusion? What kind of a democratic regime has political censorship, liquidation of any political opposition, and prohibition of freedom of expression? For many Western observers the Kremlin's liberal statements are sufficient evidence to conclude that the Russian president is sincere about democratization. If they would only listen more carefully, they would find that he always adds that "democracy standards can't be forced on us." Taken together, these lines mean that he does not think that Russian political reality is in need of any serious transformation.

ANDREW: It is not always easy to work out what the president (and others, for that matter) really mean, but it isn't altogether discouraging to note that they feel that they have some sort of case to answer. Maybe their gyrations around this issue will widen debate in Russia—as it seems to have done in a way that it had not before—about what sort of country it should become. But that said, the West, or some in the West at least, read too much into the talk and see Medvedev as clearly of a different stamp from Putin. They are different people, and personality certainly matters, but I have seen no evidence that would point to any intention on Medvedev's part to change the current system of government. I commend in this regard Isaiah 32:8, which in the King James version reads: "But the liberal deviseth liberal things; and by liberal things shall he stand." Of course Isaiah was a long time before John Stuart Mill but the point is rather relevant, anyway.

LILIA: I'll bet Isaiah, together with John Stuart Mill, are not Medvedev's heroes.

Medvedev and Putin constitute a ruling tandem that is desperately (indeed one can feel their desperation) trying to preserve the status quo. They and their respective teams, engaged in an imitation of effective governance, are unlikely to have any illusions about what they are doing, which is to say that they are indeed in their right minds. They definitely feel that Putin's previous consolidation efforts are no longer enough. They realize that the old consensus built during Putin's presidency is falling apart among society and among the elite. They therefore need to look for new mechanisms to ensure support for the regime. They try to appeal not only to their traditional base, the pensioners and budget workers, but also to the discontented and most dynamic section of society: people who want more freedom. They know that they can no longer ignore these people if they really want to seem sincere in their desire to modernize.

The authorities are quite frank about their objective. They say that they need to prevent the Putin regime's collapse through "gradual" democratization. This means making a promise to consider a measure of liberalization in the future, when the people are "mature" enough. But they warn that the people are not ready for full democracy yet, so the authorities have to decide on their behalf which policies to implement.

When will this promised future come? Will it ever come? This is the typical Soviet practice of postponing a solution for an unspecified later date: Communism will most certainly come, but no one knows when. Democracy will come, but you have to be patient!

ANDREW: St. Augustine, as we all know, prayed to the Lord to make him chaste, but not yet. He eventually changed his mind, so maybe one day some ruler of Russia will recognize that democracy is not a gift from above but a growth from below, for which those in power should work, lest it work its mischief on them.

LILIA: At the moment, Russian leaders are distancing themselves from the chastened St. Augustine. They are returning to the old arguments in order to justify the status quo. The authorities say, "It is not the reality, but how people perceive the reality, that matters." Thus, there is no need to worry about democratic institutions. What matters is not the existence of these institutions but the people's sense of freedom. And you can do two things: convince people that they are "free," or deprive them of the ability to talk about their lack of freedom.

Look at what Medvedev says: "Freedom and justice are the most important human feelings." He does not talk, however, of the need to guarantee freedom and justice. He says these things even as the authorities manipulate election results, forbid the opposition from taking part in elections, and use the police to break up demonstrations in defense of freedom of speech and justice and to arrest their organizers.

It is doubtful that Medvedev's liberal leitmotif convinces anyone in Russia today. In 2009 and even at the start of 2010 some liberals called for Russians to support Medvedev as a reformer. Nearly all those optimists have fallen silent now. They have opened their eyes to the Kremlin's games with democracy.

Russian audiences understand what is being said when the authorities declare that they will continue to develop "Russian-style" democracy. The real intended audience of the democracy mantra is the West. And the mantra works!

ANDREW: Democracy is of course a wonderfully fluid word. It is nonetheless just to acknowledge that there is far more individual freedom in Russia now than there has been at many times in the past, including the freedom to travel abroad, which is significant. The freedom of Russian citizens to act together independently of the authorities is a different matter, of course. One must also recognize that an effective working democracy has to be underpinned by a clear set of societal understandings and social conventions that take time and experience to develop. One essential condition is that the rulers and their agents should themselves be bound by these parameters. In Russia they are not.

LILIA: You've raised an important issue: "Working democracy has to be underpinned by a clear set of social conventions." I think you would agree that those conventions and experience will never come about if the population is denied elementary political rights—if the people can't elect their authorities and control them.

ANDREW: Absolutely. I would have added the September 2010 dismissal of Luzhkov to your cautionary list. The reason given for the dismissal was that he had forfeited the president's trust. There was not a word about the views of the people of Moscow, who had repeatedly endorsed their mayor in the past. Luzhkov's replacement, Sergei Sobyanin, was chosen not because he had earned popular backing but because of his close ties to Putin.

LILIA: Correct! Luzhkov's dismissal says a lot about the nature of Russian "democracy," as well as Medvedev's and Putin's respect for the views of Muscovites.

Andrew, I think we need to add a footnote. We are discussing now mainly leadership and Putin-Medvedev policies. The reason we are doing so is apparent: The Russian political landscape has turned into a political desert. To be sure, there are still influential groups, clan interests, and a lot of conflicts behind the scenes. Moreover, the Kremlin leaders to some extent are hostages of these informal interests. We acknowledge all of this. However, in our discussions we have decided to limit ourselves to the most important element of Russian politics—namely, the actions of the ruling tandem and the characteristics of this political regime, a rather unusual one for Russia. Later we will turn to Russian society, what ordinary Russians are thinking, and what we can expect from them.

ANDREW: You are right. I should be more disciplined. The spaghetti style of analysis is difficult to avoid, however, when you find that wherever you stick your fork in and begin turning it, the whole plate-load ends up on the end of it. That is all too easy to do with Russia, where the "power vertical" is not so much a system as an attempt to ring-fence the near anarchy that lies beneath its flimsy structure.

But back to our immediate purpose. The wider question arising from your account is whether the regime could manage change if that is what it decided was right. Is the regime right to be afraid of the people? If Moscow had been allowed to elect a successor to Luzhkov—and surely if any polity in the Russian Federation is mature enough to do so, it would be that of the capital—then I suppose it would be hard to deny the same privilege to other elements of the Federation, particularly given the fact that they have had it before without disaster occurring. But of course if one decides that elections are mature only if they produce the "right" result, then it is safer and more efficient just to appoint the "right" candidate. And thus there is talk not of nurturing popular experience of democracy but of abolishing still more of it, in the form of mayoral elections, because some of those electorates are proving awkward.

LILIA: What the Kremlin has already done here has left people with only one possibility for expressing their views: taking to the streets.

ANDREW: It is not clear to me how Medvedev or even Putin can close the circle between maintaining the "power vertical" and the need to adjust to pressures from below. Such pressures have had political repercussions in a variety of cases. Kaliningrad in effect dismissed its governor in 2010 because it had lost trust in him. The president took care in this instance of the formalities. There have been plenty of other examples recently of the center having to take account of local feeling. This is not an easy one. But the instinct of the tandem is to confine the agenda to technologically based tinkering wherever it can.

LILIA: The Kaliningrad case, in which the Kremlin bowed to pressure from the bottom and fired Governor Georgi Boos, proves that the Kremlin is afraid of mass protest. But this fear does not force them to open the window—quite the contrary. They try to prevent any mass protest by inventing new gimmicks, including dividing and harassing or, alternatively, co-opting the opposition and bribing disgruntled voters. Repressive policies have their limits, however. The early 2010 Kaliningrad rally demonstrated these limits. The Kremlin can crack down on a rally of 1,000–2,000 people, but it is afraid to use force when 10,000 angry citizens take to the streets.

In any case, the authorities are not ready to lose power. The modernization the tandem offers is meant to guarantee the status quo by importing Western technology as a kind of Viagra to re-energize an impotent system.

ANDREW: Viagra reportedly helps to manage dysfunction but does not cure it. Technology imported from the West may help at the margin, but that is all it can do. And money, whether Western or Russian, will surely not come in sufficient quantity nor be effective on its own without deep-rooted structural reform. Russia's investment needs are daunting. But deep change would be destructive of existing assets. The record so far suggests that the ruling elite is dedicated to preserving such assets, the obsolescent or obsolete along with the rest. Genuine modernization would disturb a significant majority of the population, as well as threaten the bureaucracy and the current rentier class.

This is a very serious long-term problem for Russia. The dilemma for the current, and therefore future, leadership is acute, and it will become harder to resolve as time passes. It is understandable that the leadership would prefer to wish it away or to tinker with it at the edges.

But Russia really is falling behind, and Medvedev was right to raise the alarm about that. He is not the first to do so, and he will not be the last now that Russia has awoken from the enchanted dreams of hydrocarbons solving all problems. Those Russians who argue that economic renewal is impossible without political renewal are surely right. But political renewal threatens existing insiders.

LILIA: That is why the ruling team, including Medvedev, hopes it can pull off the trick of re-energizing the economy without introducing real (as opposed to imitation) political competition and freedom.

ANDREW: To be fair to the Russian government and the Kremlin, the authorities would not be the first ones to duck the turmoil inherent in true modernization. I enjoyed reading in Tony Blair's memoirs (chapter 10) the other day:

> My boundless, at times rather manic lust for modernization could occasionally be misdirected, but I was sure the basic thrust was correct.... I hadn't by any means worked out all the right policy answers.... We had to divest power away from the dominant interest groups.

Blair made little substantive progress. But the aspiration is worthy, and the word "modernization" rolls off the tongue easily. (You never hear a politician crying, "Forward to Decay!") Giving content to modernization is a different matter.

LILIA: With respect to change in Russia, it will inevitably be more disruptive than in any developed democracy. In the case of the United Kingdom or other liberal democracies, "change" means a change of government, and usually a change of political course or economic agenda; in the Russian case, real change will inevitably bring collapse or an unraveling of the system of personalized power. That is why the Russian authorities try to limit change to its merely imitative forms. But if the West has to help the Kremlin with its controlled, top-down modernization, then the Kremlin has to present an attractive image of Russia to the outside world.

Russia's leaders have started a "charm offensive" against the West. They want to be friends with their Western counterparts and their neighbors. Thus they have normalized Russia's relations with countries with which relations have been tense (Poland, Lithuania, and Latvia, for example) or with countries with which Russia had unresolved issues (Norway). Having decided to modernize Russia's economy using Western money and knowledge, the Russian elite now have to thaw out the suspicions that froze over during Putin's later years in power. Finally, a reset with the United States has to persuade the West that Russia has changed its trajectory.

ANDREW: We should be glad that tensions have eased, and that particular problems have been handled sensibly. But you are right, of course, to ask if Russia has changed its trajectory. The political modernization question is critical here. So is the future relationship between Russia and its ex-Soviet neighbors (to which we should perhaps turn later). This relationship will prove whether Russia has really changed, for what it says about the nature of the regime is decisive.

LILIA: Sure! We should be glad that tensions have been dissolved, even if only for the time being. But we have to remind ourselves how fragile the basis for the rapprochement is. (Or is it still détente, as many Russian observers prefer to interpret the process that started in 2009?)

Now let us return to how Russians view Medvedev's modernization slogan. Few in Russia believe that top-down reform will succeed. Only 11 percent of Russians are ready to believe in Medvedev's modernization. They remember that Putin undertook even more radical economic reform in 2000–2001, and that failed. So far, Medvedev has been re-running a failed experiment, mostly rhetorically.

ANDREW: I would not go so far as to say that the reforms Putin signed off on in his early years failed, but they were not enough to allow the Russian economy to grow in the way that the country deserves. Medvedev has spoken as though he understood the need for further reform, and he has spoken in almost apocalyptic terms about it, too. But it is difficult to tell what exactly he has in mind, which is one reason his rhetoric has yet to catch the imagination of the Russian public, or intellectuals and power brokers, for that matter. It is hard to know what he would do if he had sole power. The ghost of Gorbachev presumably haunts him just as it does Putin. Perhaps they should think of Brezhnev's ghost, too?

The essential tenets of a successful market economy are widely accepted, and are fundamental to a liberal society, too. Perfection in putting them into effect is rare, of course, but Russia is unusually far from achieving these benchmarks: equality before the law, independently adjudicated; separation of powers between the legislative, executive, and judicial branches; and secure property rights. No vertical of power, however well intentioned, can fabricate these. Such a structure is inevitably interfering, not enabling. It is also, inevitably, inefficient.

LILIA: Gorbachev's destiny definitely haunts the current ruling team. As to Brezhnev's ghost? I wonder.... It seems that if the Kremlin team really thought about the Brezhnev experience, they would have reminded themselves of how Brezhnev's stagnation ended. It was after all the prelude to the collapse of the USSR. I don't believe their imagination goes that far. Otherwise they would think about damage control in following Brezhnev's path.

The Russian "modernizers" have been engaged in a campaign to persuade the world and Russia that modernization "from the top" is the only way to proceed and that Medvedev is a reformer. Do they themselves believe this? Hardly. It is more likely that they understand such claims as justifying their presence within the system. To support Putin would mean propping up a corrupt and authoritarian regime, whereas being associated with Medvedev permits them to hold on to their reputations—at least for now.

ANDREW: I have some sympathy for those who want to work within the system, and I have respect for some of their achievements. I am not at all sure how I would have chosen if I were in their position. I think it perfectly respectable to hope that you can contribute to a better outcome by being inside rather than outside, holding your nose when you have to. But as Br'er Rabbit found out, if you play with the Tar Baby, some of it sticks to your fingers.

LILIA: Andrew, I am sure that if you were magically transferred to Russia and became a Russian citizen you would choose to work outside that system. You've already given such a devastating analysis of it!

Here are some of the arguments of Medvedev's supporters (not numerous, I admit) as presented by Igor Yurgens, head of the Institute for Contemporary Development, which operates under the president's patronage. I list them with my comments:

"Medvedev's modernization has not worked yet because an archaic society has not supported it." But has Medvedev proposed anything more concrete than vague slogans?

"We have the Skolkovo project." This project creates the conditions "for free thinking." But why not give the whole country the possibility for "free thinking"?

"There is the Presidential Council for Civil Society.... It meets, forms its agenda, expresses criticism, and presents its conclusions once every three months to the president." But what change does this council bring for freedom in Russia?

"More than 60 percent of people in our society think in paternalist terms and have a village mentality. A minimal role for the state and full freedom of the individual are idealistic notions in this situation." But what kind of modernization can one even talk about then? Who will decide when the population is ready for greater freedom? How will the population learn to live in freedom if never given the chance to try? How can you learn to swim if there is no water in the swimming pool?

These are some of the arguments of one of Medvedev's most enlightened supporters. I sometimes wonder, do they believe their own words?

I took the trouble to list these arguments because I hear them so often from very intelligent observers in Western capitals.

I think it is useful to analyze these arguments, because holding them up against real life can at last dispel the illusions of the reform-minded nature of the team running Russia today.

ANDREW: I suppose that there is a difference between top-down reform and top-down prevention of reform. If reform is to mean anything, it has to mean devolving responsibility, not relying on a sort of militarized system of high command remote from business realities. That is one end of the spectrum. "A minimal role for the state and full freedom of the individual" is another end. The point is to travel toward the latter and let accountability and independently adjudicated responsibility work their magic—on the rulers as well as the ruled. I have every reason to suppose that those trying to persuade Medvedev of the need to modernize in the full sense of the word have very much taken this lesson to heart.

LILIA: Even if they have, we have never seen the results of their good intentions. I think we have to mention the debates going on in Russia over the true nature of Medvedev's modernization idea. One could view these debates as reflections of the conspiratorial mentality or even of cynicism. However, reality proves that we have to take seriously suspicions of the Kremlin's modernization agenda.

ANDREW: There are no doubt those who would like to exploit "modernization" and pro-Western rhetoric to privatize state property for themselves, if possible with the help of the West and in hopes of securing the legitimacy that that help would bring. I would not see that as modernization in the full sense of the word, but perhaps those are the sorts of people that you have in mind in urging us to look carefully at what in fact emerges?

LILIA: Exactly. Quite a few serious Russian experts argue that the Russian elite need this "opening" not for the country but in order to guarantee their escape from Russia and comfortable resettlement in the West. Putin's époque, they say, was the time of grandiose asset grabbing and property redistribution. The team of *siloviki* and the groups close to it that arrived at the Kremlin took over huge amounts of property, in many cases nationalizing it or putting it under their direct control.

ANDREW: There has indeed been such a process. It took place indirectly at first as state representatives or sometimes relatives of senior apparatchiks took high-level positions in companies.

LILIA: Today the Russian authorities understand the fragility of this situation. No doubt about that. They feel that bureaucratic capitalism can't exist forever because it becomes either ineffective or legally vulnerable. Moreover, the situation in the country is turning out to be more and more uncertain, which is why the time has come to privatize the property they control and prepare escape routes. How to make this process legitimate? Of course, with the help and funding of Western partners. Actually, the Russian rentier class doesn't even need the money for investment; they need partnership and share swaps that will make their property and their fortunes legitimate in the eyes of the civilized world. The slogans of "modernization" and "reset" appear to be a perfect cover for legalizing property acquired in gangster fashion.

ANDREW: Evgeny Gontmakher was one of the first who explained the nature of the "evacuation project." I remember he wrote that the goal of the current Russian elite is "to interconnect 'their' business with foreign business," which means having to attract foreign investors to Russia and then investing the Russian money they control into various businesses and property outside of Russia. He explained the motives behind the Kremlin's inviting foreign experts and businesspeople to Russia and offering them ridiculous salaries and possibilities for enrichment (usually at the Russian state's expense). The goal is the same: legitimation in the developed democracies of those representatives of the Russian elite who host Western partners, using them as the friendly lobbyists.

LILIA: In fact, this "project" works—not in attracting Western investment to Russia, but in helping Russian rentiers to make themselves comfortable in the West. I wonder how long the Russian elite will succeed at this game.

ANDREW: There is legitimate Russian investment in the West, too, as well as Western investment in Russia, of course. But there is a problem stemming from the uncertainty of property rights in Russia, and the fear of property holders there for the security of their tenure, which washes over into the West.

LILIA: For all the skepticism over Medvedev's modernization, Russia nonetheless has enjoyed the West's support. "I think he [Medvedev] understands the necessity of modernizing not just the Russian economy, but the Russian political system as well," said Hillary Clinton. She must know something about Medvedev's plans that Russians do not.

ANDREW: One of our former prime ministers, Harold Macmillan, once remarked that "a Foreign Secretary is forever poised between a cliché and an indiscretion," so I suppose that Secretary Clinton was reaching for a flattering formulation when she talked of Medvedev's realizing the need for political as well as economic modernization. And she could have found quotations from him, too, that would have backed that up. Whether she really believes it, I cannot say.

LILIA: Let's call it a "pragmatic approach"! Quite a few Western pundits, it seems, are sincerely charmed by Medvedev. Some of my Western friends can't bear my criticism of Medvedev. They view it as a typical example of Russian "*nieverije*"—the habit of seeing everything in a gloom-and-doom way.

I recently came across a well-known Western pundit who wrote, "Medvedev carefully implements the ideas announced in his key speeches." I wanted to call him and ask him, "Where do you see the implementation of these ideas?"

"Power in Russia is taking on a more human face," writes another Western expert. "Russia is becoming less authoritarian," says still another. "Russia is turning toward the West," declares a third. Listening to this chorus, small wonder that Western politicians have also begun to buy into the idea that Russia is liberalizing.

Another, even more sophisticated analyst wrote that Medvedev wants Russia to join the West and even "to measure up." I understood from my conversation with this colleague that he did not think much of Medvedev's current actions, but he thought that continued expressions of hope in Medvedev's liberal agenda from Westerners would keep Russia from backsliding.

What a curious means of influence! The future will, of course, tell us how justified our colleagues' predictions are. But for the time being I regretfully have to point out that their hopes have become players in a show put on by the Russian authorities. These authorities, seeing the benevolent Western reactions to their meaningless words, have come to the conclusion that the West is ready to play their game.

ANDREW: I suppose the encouragement argument has some rather forlorn basis. But I just don't see how anyone can have that much confidence in Medvedev's ability or even willingness to deliver. He may or may not be a more charming dinner guest than Putin, but he is in the same trap as his predecessor, for change would threaten him at least as much as Putin, and it would threaten the ruling structures too. So all anyone can offer are small adjustments. And what really happened to the four national projects that Medvedev was to administer in the run-up to his presidency? What happened to the four "I"s he spoke of when he campaigned? Does anyone even remember what they were? Is Russia less legally nihilistic after almost three years of the Medvedev presidency? These are of course rhetorical questions.

LILIA: Medvedev could respond to your rhetorical question the way Putin responded once to Larry King's question about the Russian submarine *Kursk*: "She sank." Medvedev can say exactly the same: "Those projects have failed!"

ANDREW: I bet he wouldn't say it like that, though. But your mention of Larry King reminds me of Putin's latest interview with him, in December 2010. Perhaps King did not want to upset the "reset." King scarcely pressed the Russian prime minister, allowing him to insist for instance that Russia is a democracy, and one that could teach the United States a thing or two. He repeated that he and Medvedev would decide between them who would run in 2012 so that their achievements as a tandem would not be jeopardized. The scarcely democratic implication was clear that this would amount to their nominating the next president. Putin also said that Bill Gates was "profoundly wrong" to declare that Russia "is being run by the security services." Putin was clear about that: "Our country is run by the people of the Russian Federation.... No one should have doubts on that score."

Perhaps you, too, have enjoyed that Internet video of the Russian prime minister's performance of "Blueberry Hill" before an audience of notably obsequious Hollywood stars? His rendering of the line "all of those vows we made, were never to be" was particularly affecting. I hope he was not referring to the money that was said to have been raised for charity at the event. It is a bit of a mystery what happened to that.

LILIA: Money in Russia always tends to disappear. Larry King's interview with Putin, despite King's failure to debate with his subject (by the way, why was he so soft on him?) demonstrated the cynicism of the Russian "national leader," as well as his apparent belief that the American audience would accept his arguments, including those about "Russian democracy" and the allegedly undemocratic U.S. system. Putin evidently did not care if these arguments sounded persuasive. He even seemed to stifle a chuckle when he said, "Russia is run by the people."

Oh, my! With respect to Putin's "Blueberry Hill" performance, we in Russia enjoyed watching the Western celebrities in the audience who couldn't conceal their admiration for the Russian national leader. As I watched, I noted how easily Putin can bowl you over with his primitive theatrics, even despite your knowing the nasty stuff he is doing.

ANDREW: Yeltsin's public performances were rather more endearing, though they shamed many Russians. Putin as a bare-chested macho is less appealing to the Western public. Celebrities are a group apart, of course.

LILIA: Those who believe in the reformist potential of the current Russian ruling team should have attended Mikhail Khodorkovsky's trials. Those were more serious farces. The first time, Khodorkovsky and his friend and co-defendant, Platon Lebedev, were accused of and indicted for not paying taxes. The second time, they were tried for stealing every drop of oil that they had not allegedly paid taxes for—a charge that was obviously implausible. The absurdity of the accusations and the fact that they made a mockery of the courts did not bother the legally trained President Medvedev in the slightest! Khodorkovsky and Lebedev were found guilty at their second trial of embezzlement and money laundering and sentenced to remain in prison until 2017, to absolutely no one's surprise. These verdicts could be seen as an indicator of the direction the Kremlin is heading. The reduction of their sentence on appeal by one year in May 2011 made no difference to that.

ANDREW: In his interview for Bloomberg TV before his address to the World Economic Forum at Davos in January 2011, Medvedev said that the accusations against Khodorkovsky and Lebedev "did not provoke doubt for anyone." As Putin had before him, he compared Khodorkovsky and Lebedev to Bernard Madoff. Had he compared them to the Sergei Mavrodi case, which was also about a pyramid scheme like Madoff's, he might have been nearer the mark, but then he would have drawn attention to the fact that the sentence eventually passed on Mavrodi was so mild that he was soon back at it, trying to set up yet another scheme. Madoff and Khodorkovsky/Lebedev, meanwhile, have absolutely nothing to do with each other.

LILIA: In this way Medvedev proved that there are no differences between him and Putin.

Engaged in nonstop "reformist" chatter, the Russian ruling tandem has not a single successful reform to boast of. Medvedev has been playing, with evident relish, the part of the "liberal face" of Russian power. He has been talking about modernization for several years now, but there is no link to be seen between his rhetoric and any sort of reality. He has blasted corruption, the ineffectiveness of the state, the lack of political competition, the weakness of the judicial system, and the institutions that "constrain" modernization. An outsider thus might view Medvedev as a radical reformer. His constant chattering, however, has had no impact on real life—other than, perhaps, the occasional hilarious things he has said. For instance, explaining why Russian law enforcement organs hadn't investigated the bribes that Daimler had paid to high Russian officials, Medvedev said, "The Russian side did not get the names of the officials who could have been involved in the deals." As if Daimler were the one who had responsibility for conducting the Kremlin's investigation!

What the tandem can legitimately boast of is its success in improving Russia's image in the West, thanks to the Western readiness to believe in myths.

I can't resist concluding that some Western politicians understand (at least, I want to believe that they understand) that Medvedev's economic "miracle" will fail just as Putin's did. But the "modernization" mantra gives the West a pretext to return to the familiar "realist" toolbox and "pragmatic" policies.

Here is what I can't understand when I listen to the energetic Western "Medvedevites": Do they really believe in Medvedev's modernization and the Kremlin's pro-Western turn?

ANDREW: There is a standing temptation for political leaders to hope for more than they should from their colleagues, and to believe that saying nice things about them will encourage them to cooperate. In the present case, there is also just now the supposition that a third, and then fourth, Putin term would be more alarming than a second Medvedev one, so why not help Medvedev by treating him as weighty and the man of the future? You can also argue that by pinpointing particular parts of his discourse you are supporting the principles underlying them. But the record of success for this approach is not that encouraging. We had after all "ol' Boris" for Clinton, and "Putin's soul" for Bush, with rival claims from European leaders for special relationships with these presidents, but without much lasting effect in any of these cases. It is Russia's own historic development that will count, not the rhetoric of foreigners, and Russia is in a self-absorbed condition. Outside influence seems to me to be limited, at best.

The ideas of analysts of foreign affairs affect domestic opinion in their own countries, and they contribute to the formulation of policy in those countries and in the international organizations that include their governments. But analysts, too, are subject to fashion and to professional rivalries. I would not want to pay undue attention to particular examples. There are others that readily contradict them.

LILIA: You've offered a sober diagnosis of the West's reaction to Medvedev's impotence. I have nothing to add. Only one footnote, if I may: hope on the part of Western leaders that their support and embrace will strengthen liberal elements in Medvedev's psyche produce precisely the opposite result: they persuade the Kremlin that it can go on pretending. We need to alert politicians about this "unintended consequence."

There is another issue that I hate to raise because although it is much debated, its real substance is questionable. But apparently, we need to state our views on the argument that has been going on for several years now inside and outside Russia: Who's the boss in Russia, Medvedev or Putin? As one of the Western ambassadors in Moscow told me, they spend 80 percent of their time trying to find an answer to this question. This is what their respective ministries of foreign affairs demand from them. The Russian pundits also love to speculate on this question, which only serves to demonstrate the lack of real politics in Russia.

In 2009, one could hazard a guess either way. Today, however, the answer is clear: Putin remains the leader in control of all power resources. I would like to quote Saakashvili. When asked whether he talked to the Russian authorities, he said, "Yes. In 2008, I called Medvedev. Twice. But both times Putin responded." "Why so?" asked the journalist. "Because it is Putin who solves the issues," he said. And he was right.

Medvedev is a junior partner who has a definite, two-part agenda. In short, he offers a legitimate cover that helps guarantee the continuity of Putin's regime in a more civilized way, and he has created a more "human" face for the Russian leadership. He has been pretty successful in performing both functions. One could even say he has been brilliant in changing Russia's image, as we could conclude from Western reaction to his presidency.

Putin does nothing to conceal the fact that he is preparing to take back the presidency. "I have two options," he said in September 2010. "To sit on the river bank and watch how the water moves, how something collapses and falls apart, or interfere. I prefer to interfere." He was clear about his intentions, don't you think?

ANDREW: Looks that way. But for now there is no need for the West to place bets on either Putin or Medvedev, and no concrete reason to construct optimistic ideas as to substantially different programs that would flow from the appointment of either one of them. Various persons are working on various programs for the transformation of the Russian economy after the 2012 elections, Vladimir Mau and Yaroslav

Kuzminov for Putin with the help of Igor Shuvalov and others working on the Russian scenarios for 2020 and Putin's newly created Institute for Strategic Initiatives under Nikolai Fedorov, INSOR (the Institute for Contemporary Development) for Medvedev, and the government Center for Strategic Decisions for anyone who cares about reforms. These are useful in highlighting Russia's problems, and the link between solving them and political liberalization. That is surely important. Unfortunately, from what I have seen of them, their suggestions are also so wide-ranging as to be daunting, even revolutionary.

LILIA: I don't expect that, if Medvedev stays longer, which is to say if he is "reelected" with Putin's consent, he will suddenly turn into a real reformer. When the shell is empty, it remains empty.

Regarding "reform programs" offered by the aforementioned expert groups that are close to the authorities, I would like to make two points. First, their key messages are that the status quo can't be preserved and that Russia is moving toward disaster if that is attempted. This is a new rhetoric for groups close to the authorities. Second, their authors seek salvation in "the political will" of a leader who will impose the reforms from the top. But Russian history proves that all Russian reformist leaders have been trying to pursue reforms that would re-energize personalized power. Russia has never had a kamikaze leader who has intentionally desired to dismantle that power structure!

Let's look at it from a different angle. When Western colleagues, especially European colleagues, try to explain their attitude and their governments' policies toward Russia, they almost always mention Western business interests as exerting a key influence. My impressions of Western business in Russia are mixed. Representatives of the Western business community often say that little has changed in Russia and that no modernization is taking place, but that they need to do business here because the Russian market is safer and more promising than many other markets.

There are some who actively defend the situation in Russia and want to demonstrate their loyalty to the authorities. Perhaps they believe that this is the only way business can be conducted in Russia. At a conference sponsored by Deutsche Bank in Berlin, the audience, which consisted mostly of German businesspeople, greeted my critical remarks about Russia's political regime with stony silence. The moment I finished speaking, the German entrepreneurs began getting up one after the other to tell me that I do not understand Russia. I felt like a real Russophobe in their midst.

Gleb Pavlovsky, who then held a Kremlin position, spoke next. He criticized me harshly, and the audience greeted his words with enthusiasm. Even Russian businesspeople were not accustomed to putting on such overt displays of support for the Kremlin as did that German audience.

Of course, it would be wrong to think that it is just German business that is so "loyal to the Kremlin." Any Western business that wants to do business in Russia tries to parrot a loyalist line back to the authorities.

I remember talking about this issue with Dutch newspaper *Handelsblad's* Moscow correspondent, Michel Kriliars. (The Netherlands, incidentally, ranks ahead of Germany in terms of trade with Russia.) I asked how Dutch business in Russia mixes the drive for economic benefit with the principles of Protestant morality. The correspondent answered, "Profit has long since cast aside our Protestant traditions."

Based on your own experience of working with business, how do you think it perceives the new Kremlin course? Can we expect to see Western business come to Russia on a large scale and take part in the Kremlin's modernization projects—first of all, Skolkovo?

ANDREW: That's two questions, so I shall take the easier one first, about Skolkovo. We need to explain first what this project is. Skolkovo, advertised as Russia's Silicon Valley, is the symbol of the new Russian modernization. It is supposed to become an "innovation city" of 30,000–40,000 of the brightest and most talented people from all corners of the world. By 2015, they need to create cutting-edge technologies that will generate up to $7 billion of annual income.

Some will come, partly to suck it and see, and partly to please the Russian authorities. But I should be surprised if anyone now believes that Skolkovo will make for a real breakthrough, whatever they may say in the inaugural speeches. I cannot help remarking here that the Americans have better manners than the British and are given to more extravagant rhetoric, too. This is not a snide remark, just an observation from an admirer of the United States (and the husband of a U.S. citizen, for that matter).

The Skolkovo project, whatever the foreigners do, will be hobbled by a dearth of qualified Russians, as well as by Russia's management mind-set. This is a truth little remarked upon in polite society, where it is more fashionable, as well as more pleasant, to celebrate Russia's educational standards and its scientific and technological inheritance. With all due and considerable respect to those, Russia's record in science and innovation has grown worse and worse over the past decade and more. If you look at any of the indicators like patents registered or papers published, the decline is all too clear, not just in comparison with the other BRICs but also with countries like Turkey. Russia is well behind, and the Russian scientific community is all too aware of this.

It was quite striking that when the list of the world's top 200 universities included no Russian universities for the first time in 2010, Russia's official reaction was to call for a list to be managed by Russians rather than to see what might be going wrong.

I noted, too, that the two Russians who won the Nobel Prize for physics in 2010 were both at Manchester University in the United Kingdom (where else?), and that neither of them, according to the press, intends to return to Russia in the foreseeable future. Their reported reason was, in part at least, that research in Russia is not much fun. Now, maybe what follows is a stretch too far, but, if this account is right, doesn't it say something about the dominance of a top-down approach in Russian universities? If the seniors and the established call the shots, what does that do to innovation? Is there a wider lesson here for Russia? I think there is. At any rate many of the best and brightest Russians are leaving their country.

LILIA: Let me first comment on Skolkovo. You are absolutely right: No one in his sober mind in Russia would believe that a gated city for foreigners will be a breakthrough that will help Russian modernization. There are no illusions with respect to that. But Skolkovo could be a successful project in achieving a different agenda: for some participants it will be a means to form cozy relationships with the Kremlin; for others it will be a way to line their pockets.

Skolkovo has already triggered a lively competition among Russians for the best demonstration of sarcasm. Here is one of the popular jokes: "No one knows how Medvedev's modernization will end, but you can be certain either way that Skolkovo's mayor will make the *Forbes* billionaires' list."

The real attraction of the Kremlin's Innovation City, Russian observers believe, lies not in what it will accomplish for innovation but in how much it will allow corrupt Russian officials to steal. Yevgeny Yasin, a prominent liberal economist, has said that "the principal question is whether we can do something effective and reminiscent of a Silicon Valley in a country with an authoritarian regime."

Ironically, Putin, by creating in May 2011 his own Agency for Strategic Initiatives, not only proved that he is in charge but that Medvedev's Skolkovo is simply a joke!

Indeed, the Skolkovo project *also* demonstrates the dire state of Russian education and science, in that the authorities decided to invite foreigners to do innovation rather than investing in Russian universities and the Academy of Science. Meanwhile, the Russian education system is collapsing, and we are losing intellectual and scientific potential. Talented scientists have either already left Russia or are planning to leave. We are losing the opportunity to educate our younger generation.

ANDREW: This is an increasing worry for many prominent Russians and a major focus of the INSOR paper I just referred to, which was published in March of 2011. In places its tone verges on despair.

LILIA: Do you think this problem is not understood "at the top"? They understand it all too well, but the current Russian ruling team does not need an educated young generation that could create problems for the state. They would prefer to have an uneducated youth that is easy to manipulate and to brainwash. This policy, of course, contradicts any modernization trajectory.

ANDREW: As to the bigger question, I think it most unlikely that Western business will come to Russia on a big scale anytime soon. There are many better-placed rivals for investment. Investors have their own values and will prefer safe havens with long-term prospects. I think that Western businesses nonetheless have a creditable record in improving Russian business practices, and that this has been important in cooperation with independent Russian business in developing Russian commercial governance. It would be stupid to claim that these efforts have been entirely successful, or that they have been as effective with those parts of the Russian economy dominated by the state as they have with the private sector, but they are nonetheless real and worth acknowledging.

German firms have been particularly active in Russia, of course, including with Gazprom, for instance. Gazprom is one of the least transparent companies in the world, with a remarkable number of subsidiary companies in various jurisdictions with opaque ownership structures. German companies have interests beyond that, and have established an impressive system of engaging with each other and the government in Berlin.

It would be a mistake to generalize too much about business in Russia, given the differences between the various sectors of the Russian economy. The United Kingdom, for example, has had problems in the energy sector, and the political relationship between London and Moscow has often been rather cool. But British financial, auditing, and legal firms have become well established, and British firms are well represented in the Foreign Investors Advisory Council, which has improved aspects of the Russian business climate. Maybe the modernization logo will help to carry that sort of effort forward. But my bet is that Russian entry into the WTO would have more influence, provided that Russia was ready to accept and to implement the common rules that make that organization effective.

LILIA: I apologize for being stubborn. I would like to continue on the role of Western business in Russia. Russia needs it without a doubt, and for a number of reasons. First, Western business brings investment and jobs. Second, it also brings new technology. Third, it helps the Russian market adapt to new rules of the game.

This last expectation has not been fulfilled, however—at least in my view. Instead of encouraging growing transparency and supremacy of the law, Western companies have often adopted Russian non-transparent rules. I'll give you just a few examples: Siemens and Daimler paid huge bribes to the Russian authorities. Incidentally, after a thorough U.S. investigation of the Daimler corruption scandal, the Russian prosecutor's office reluctantly opened an investigation into bribery of Russian officials. But of course we all know that investigation will go nowhere....

Even employees of IKEA, a Scandinavian paragon of clean business practices, gave in and tried to solve problems by means of bribes. These kinds of cases are only natural in Russia, where government and assets, power and property have merged, and it is practically impossible to do business without appealing to, and doing deals with, the authorities. Seldom can any Western businessperson expect to survive in Russia without concluding a "pact" with local or federal authorities. These deals vary in their nature—from direct bribes of Russian officials to the creation of "social" and other kinds of funds that fall under the authorities' direct control.

What is the result? Not only does such corruption discredit the West; it also discredits the liberal principles associated with the West, including market mechanisms.

ANDREW: There are dangers for foreign firms and businesspeople, and a considerable number of Russians view them with suspicion. That is in part a communist legacy, which inculcated the idea that "capitalism" is evil. That idea is quite prevalent in the West, too, which is going through its own acute phase of ignorant banker-bashing. But in fact the idea of capitalism is almost as slippery in definition as the idea of democracy. We aren't discussing that issue, so better to let it pass. All I need say now is that, while there are poor instances, the overall record of foreign firms is not shameful, and that if foreigners start dealing corruptly even in small things they are foolish, because they will find themselves being pulled into the swamp. The line to be respected is also getting tougher with the growth of regulations from Western governments, too. The U.S. Foreign Corrupt Practices Act is fearsome, as Siemens, Daimler, and Panalpina, among others, now know. European countries have parallel laws. The British one to be brought into play, I believe later in 2012, will be especially stringent. But of course it is the case, I agree, that foreign investors need to keep alongside the government as best they can, so there are reputational questions to be addressed beyond the questions raised by straight-out bribery.

LILIA: Let us hope that the Western regulations you are mentioning will help business, including Russian business, avoid the Russian corruption "virus."

There is another angle to this story: I have the impression that Western business has more of a negative influence on Western policy toward Russia. Business is forcing Western leaders to close their eyes to Russia's internal problems and be friends with the Russian regime, thus legitimizing it. It seems that business influence is a decisive factor in shaping an accommodationist policy toward Russia in Germany, France, Italy, the Netherlands, and other countries. I doubt that, for instance, Chancellor Angela Merkel has any illusions regarding the Kremlin and the Russian political regime. But German business interests are a significant factor (though not the only factor, it seems) forcing her to withhold criticism of what is going on in Russia.

There is a story I should tell you here that says a lot about how Western business pursues its interests, and at what price. We and other Russia observers have argued that Khodorkovsky's case in particular and the dismal situation with the rule of law in general bode ill for Western investment in Russia. One could mention quite a few arbitrary laws and the state's and corrupt politicians' habit of grabbing assets that do not belong to them. In 2006, Royal Dutch Shell had to cede majority ownership to Gazprom. BP had visa and other problems for several years. Its chief executive, Robert Dudley, was forced to flee Russia and go into hiding, but this did not prevent BP from trying to make a deal with Rosneft that would legitimize its possession of Yukos assets stolen by the government. One could surmise that, in the light of the disastrous oil spill in the Gulf of Mexico, BP no longer has anything to lose by making a deal with a corrupt Russian company and regime.

However, this "happy marriage" has met a few bumps in the road. The Stockholm Arbitration Court has confirmed the interest of the Russian government and Rosneft, which is under its control, in the expropriation of Yukos property. Moreover, the arbitration courts in The Hague and Stockholm ruled unanimously that the Russian government had indeed stolen Yukos's assets. There was yet another "bump" in the BP deal when the Stockholm Arbitration Court ruled that the BP-Rosneft deal contradicted the previous BP-TNK agreement. In the end, the deal collapsed! What a story....

ANDREW: Businesses prefer to stay out of politics, and so businesspeople are often rather naïve when it comes to its machinations. You are of course right that the dangers and difficulties of doing business in Russia are considerable. It may be that many in Russia suppose that Western business is corrupt, having bought into the values and assumptions of the governing elite. I would still maintain that it is better for Western business to be there than for it not to be there. Western businesses have a moral role to play insofar as they improve Russian business practices, and I believe that they have had measurable success in this regard. Should we expect business to do more than that? Probably not.

Potential investors who have so far stayed out of Russia have, if you like, cast an absentee ballot against present-day Russia, and this includes the many Russian citizens who prefer to send their capital abroad.

In brief, therefore, I do not think that business has been fully co-opted by the Russian regime—though there are differences within the business community, which is not the same thing. Gas dependence can create tensions, and countries vary according to the degree of involvement between business and politics. But in the end it will be investment flows that count. Russia would have done far better in attracting funds if it had followed the path of liberal market reform instead of growing state involvement and central political control, with all that has gone with them.

LILIA: I at least hope for one thing: that Western business will try to persuade us—the skeptics—that they are doing more good than bad. That is, if they cared what liberals think of them; apparently, they don't.

ANDREW: I would like to add some statistics to my absent investors point. According to the World Bank's *Doing Business 2011* report, Russia ranks in 123rd place in having user-friendly investment processes, whether for foreigners or for Russians, down from 116th place in 2009. There are

183 countries on the list. A small- or medium-sized business operating in Moscow goes through 53 procedures over the course of 540 days at the cost of 4,141 times the average income to obtain all the necessary approvals to build a simple commercial warehouse and connect it to basic utility services. Russia ranked 162nd in trading across borders. Cross-border trade with Russia can be a nightmare, and corruption in the Russian Customs service is notorious. Russian businesspeople must process eight documents over 36 days and spend $1,850 on average to export goods across the borders.

LILIA: I can add that, according to the Bloomberg Global Poll, only 10 percent of foreign investors are ready to put their money into the Russian economy. The report surveyed 1,030 investors, analysts, and traders. That means that the Kremlin's innovative agenda still needs a lot of work to improve the country's investment record. In any case, the business community is not rushing to take part in the Kremlin's modernization. And Russian capital flight has risen to alarming levels, reaching more than $40 billion in 2010 and continuing at around $35 billion during the first five months of 2011, according to official figures. There are those who argue that the real total is higher.

ANDREW: The Russian Economic Development Ministry and its head, Elvira Nabiullina, have recently joined the pack of critics of administrative barriers to direct investment.

LILIA: Thank you for reminding me about Nabiullina's comments. At the end of 2010, she admitted that FDI before the economic crisis accounted for 10 percent of all investments in basic capital. Before the year's end, it accounted for only 5 percent.

ANDREW: Major Russian business figures like Peter Aven (AlfaBank) have become increasingly critical. In November 2010, he called the Russian financial system and the 2011 budget reminiscent of the budget before the collapse of the Soviet Union: When Gorbachev came to power, the USSR had huge reserves, a low level of debt, and the advantage of high oil prices. In three or four years, the money had vanished and been replaced by an enormous load of debt. "Groups connected with the state restrain competition, and the increase of state expenditures creates a threat to the budget," Aven concluded.

LILIA: Aven, one of the most successful Russian oligarchs and quite loyal to the authorities, is right. The fact that a figure such as he has started to openly criticize the official policy says that even the regime's base has started to worry.

With respect to foreign investors, as you know, they can always come back. Some of them have come back. The dramatic fate of Khodorkovsky and even the unhappy plight of some Western investors seems not to prevent others who believe they know how to deal with the authorities (we've mentioned BP already) from maintaining and even strengthening their involvement in Russia. Anatoly Chubais said, "Investors are special creatures who always want to invest like the animals who always want to eat."

The question is: What kind of investors are we talking about? Those who rush in to reap the benefits and run away, those do not care about any stain on their reputation, or those who invest in infrastructure. For the latter to come, Russia will have to change its rules.

I want to raise another subject that worries me very much, one that I should have raised before. Here it is: Medvedev's liberal talk has been followed by an authoritarian clampdown. Violations against democracy and attacks against defenders of human rights continue, and in some cases have escalated. The authorities have created mechanisms to crack down on any possibility of dissent: they control the main media outlets; they make it impossible to register opposition parties; they forbid opposition politicians from taking part in elections; they fiddle with election results and commit outright election fraud; they make it impossible to raise funds for opposition activity; they broaden secret service powers to keep watch over and persecute opposition political figures.

We see in Russia signs of an increasingly open and aggressive authoritarianism. This trend began during Putin's time in office, when the authorities began implementing policies that increased the state's control over society. This was quite overt in many cases, without any attempts to mask what was going on. The argument that Russia had to follow its "own road" of "sovereign democracy" served as the justification for this growing authoritarianism. Russia under "liberal" Medvedev is moving toward a new version of the police state, in which the authorities try to prevent any independent social and political activity by new regulations and restrictions. This is Medvedev's contribution to Putin's "dictatorship of the law."

ANDREW: The record speaks for itself, and from time to time, it speaks loudly enough to be heard—even by those who would prefer to be deaf.

LILIA: I hope it is heard! Here is what going on. The Russian authorities are introducing new laws all the time, reducing the people's already limited freedoms. The decision to give the FSB (the successor to the KGB) broader powers is just one example. This was done on Medvedev's initiative, as he proudly proclaimed to the world. Laws that would restrict freedom on the Internet are being drafted. Bills making it more difficult to organize public demonstrations against the authorities have been rushed into law. These laws illustrate the authorities' blatant mockery. The deputy head of the presidential administration (the president's staff), Vladislav Surkov, declared with a smile that the opposition will be allowed to hold meetings at sites of its choosing, on Moscow's *Triumfalnaya Ploshchad*, for example (although the constitution allows meetings to take place if local authorities are notified). But then it turns out that the opposition is not permitted to bring more than, say, 800 or 1,500 people into the street. If 801 or 1,501 people attend a meeting, it is brutally broken up. And how will they count the participants?

The new laws on public access to information that came into force in 2010 are also illustrative. They essentially block ordinary people's access to official information that would enable them to follow the decisionmaking process.

The "reformer" president has hastened to send to the Duma a bill that essentially makes the Constitutional Court dependent on the executive authorities and limits ordinary people's ability to turn to it with complaints against anticonstitutional actions by the executive authorities.

Thus this confirms that the authorities are tightening control over society with the help of "the law." They are closing off all opportunities for legal manifestations of public discontent. Any unsanctioned activity can be suppressed on legal grounds. Thus we see the boundless "innovation" of the Russian tandem.

Clampdowns on political pluralism and freedoms via rules rubber-stamped by parliament are occurring alongside a Russian effort to warm up the relationship with the West.

These steps are evidence of another paradox in the behavior of the authorities: they are losing confidence but getting more shameless, more defiant, at the same time.

ANDREW: To be fair, Medvedev has reacted to some signs of public anger, whether over environmental issues or scandals like the death of Sergei Magnitsky in police custody. But I am not sure to what real effect.

The new Moscow mayor, Sergei Sobyanin, has allowed some anti-Putin rallies, and St. Petersburg governor Valentina Matviyenko has even suggested that representatives of the opposition join the local government. There are inconsistencies here.

LILIA: Thank you for bringing these facts to our attention. They only confirm that the Russian authorities are engaged in a never-ending search for ways to survive in power. They've been extremely effective in riding two horses in opposite directions. On the one hand, they play soft melodies, pleasing to the liberal and Western ear; on the other, they strengthen repressive mechanisms and prepare internal troops to combat future turmoil.

The Kremlin apparently believes that letting off a bit of steam can lower the pressure in a hermetically sealed system. All of this is part of a damage-limitation mechanism. The authorities will never allow real political struggle that can endanger their position. They have just endorsed newer, tougher rules regulating rallies and opposition activity, but even if those rules had been softened, the authorities would always have the freedom to interpret them as they see fit.

Look at what Governor Valentina Matviyenko offered the opposition—the office of the deputy head of the commission on historical monuments (!)—that hardly constituted giving the opposition an effective role in local government. But it does allow the authorities to say: "We are democratizing Russia!"

One has to listen to the real boss when it comes to these issues. I will quote Putin, who continues to control the key buttons. "If you take part in a rally without permission, you'll get whacked with a truncheon. That's it!" He repeated this warning twice, showing evident satisfaction both times. It almost goes without saying that it's essentially impossible to get the authorities' permission for a true mass rally.

ANDREW: The position is certainly odd, at best. If you took some of the things Medvedev has said as serious calls to action, you would expect radical changes. He repeated in one of his blogs toward the end of November 2010 that Russia faced mounting problems, including the "stagnation" of its political system. That word in Russian (*zastoi*) is a loaded one—a very loaded one—because it is used to describe the fate of the Soviet Union as the Brezhnev regime sputtered toward the eventual disintegration of the USSR. The hopeful in the West, and maybe even some optimists in Russia (or at least those who suppose that talking Medvedev up will prove beneficial), hailed his utterance of this word as a strong signal. As usual, everything ended the way it always does, as Chernomyrdin might have put it. The annual Presidential Address to the National Assembly on November 30 could not have been less exciting, let alone reform-minded in tone or content.

LILIA: Indeed. The mountain gave birth to a mouse. One has the impression from time to time that Medvedev wakes up every day and racks his brain for something new to say to bolster his fading image as a "reformer." No matter what he says, he is always late; the train left the station long ago. Thus Medvedev was being too optimistic when he described the Russian situation as stagnation. We had *zastoi* already during the Putin years, but it was difficult to recognize under the cover of oil money. Today, Russia finds itself in the midst of deep degradation (or perhaps "degeneration" is the better term).

Medvedev has suggested a cure for Russia's political "stagnation." He promised that representatives of the opposition (but only systemic opposition—that is, from registered parties) will have the right to one or two seats in the regional parliaments. This is not "liberalization;" it is an insult, a joke! First of all, regional legislatures are rubber stamps of the executive branch, and second, one or two opposition figures can't make a difference in those bodies.

ANDREW: Medvedev ordered senior government officials to be removed from the boards of more than 100 companies.

LILIA: That is right. But will the state control of these companies be weakened if their replacements are selected by the same Putin team?

We have to admit that the flurry of interviews that both leaders gave could create the impression of a growing rift between them.

ANDREW: Putin and Medvedev assess corruption differently, and describe the state of the Russian economy differently, too, with Medvedev usually applying darker colors. Putin plays down the gravity of the economic situation. He is more critical of the West.

LILIA: Indeed. They could pretend that they differ or they really differ on certain issues. But as Medvedev himself explained—they differ on tactical issues. It is natural for their respective teams to each tug the rope its own way. In April 2011, 55 percent of Russians did not believe that there was a rift between the two. What is important, there is no evidence that any real power has started to move Medvedev's way.

Anyway, Medvedev will have to justify his role somehow, and he will be forced to continue undertaking "reformist" rhetorical exercises that do not respond in any meaningful way to society's needs or desires. Both leaders, each in his own way, are trying to save personalized power, whose cracks are growing wider and harder to fill by the day.

ANDREW: I hear what you say, with accustomed sadness. I do not think you should underestimate how much all of these things have affected Western public opinion or government policies and investment decisions. Russian attempts to counter the damage to the country's reputation have had little effect. But there will naturally be experts who try to paint a shinier gloss over things than others, and they will look for the chance to do so in the run-up to the presidential elections in 2012, arguing that if Medvedev returns to the Kremlin, he will be free at last to act as he would like. "Who is this that darkeneth counsel by words without knowledge?" (Job 38: 2).

LILIA: I know that you care deeply about Russia. That's why you are sad.

Before we continue, we need to clarify our attitudes toward the Russian parliamentary and presidential elections. We are having this conversation as Russia enters a new election campaign. Soon this campaign will become the key item on the menu for the Russian media and political life (if one can call the current political desert thus). This new and heightened level of activity may create an impression among outsiders that elections in Russia really do matter, and that the new elections could signify that change, or at least a hope for change, is in the offing.

The reality is much more boring and pathetic. The elections in 2011–2012, just like the elections in 2003–2004 and in 2007–2008, will be a new sham that will inevitably guarantee the same ruling group's hold on power. Who will symbolize the group and who will be its "face" are not that important. The question of who would rule was still a significant one in 1999–2000, when the system was still soft and Jell-O like. But today the Russian system has consolidated, and the political establishment is desperate to defend its position and property. That is why future elections have no chance of changing Russia's course. Unless, of course, the Russian population decides it's time to wake up from its slumber. Thus we should look at the elections not as an instrument of change but as the means to preserve the status quo. We also should keep in mind what can bring down this house of cards: masses of people taking to the street.

The opposition can play two roles in future Potemkin elections: if it participates without a chance of winning, it will legitimize the sham; if it outsmarts the Kremlin, it can use the elections to appeal directly to society and demand free elections as Ukrainians did in 2004. The latter is theoretically possible, but hardly feasible if current trends continue through 2012.

ANDREW: You must be right to point out that the ruling cabal has no interest in seeing the 2011 Duma and 2012 presidential elections change the current setup. Otherwise, how could it be that the choice of winner is to be made by that group even before the electorate is asked to ratify the result? I would only add that the law of unintended consequences that you have cited from time to time applies to them, too. Putin currently has no fresh ideas to bring to bear. Medvedev has shown himself able enough at suggesting a great many things, but helpless when it comes to implementing anything notable. Why would we expect them to do any better in the future? The strains of the coming longer terms for both the Duma and the president will in all likelihood be even more considerable. The more that elections are manipulated, and the candidates presented for anointment, not free popular choice, the less the legitimacy of the result. Quite a few citizens would be needed to ensure a managed result, and that makes them directly complicit in the corruption of the process.

LILIA: We have to keep in mind the unpredictability of a system based on an intention to guarantee results for the authorities in advance.

We are analyzing a snapshot of the Russian situation and political agenda at a certain historical moment. Two years from now, today's worries and today's struggle, myths, and manipulations will possibly be seen as irrelevant or unimportant. But we still have to discuss it as if this were one of the crucial issues on the Kremlin's agenda, even if it only serves to distract attention from other issues that are important for Russia.

With respect to the 2012 presidential elections, some Russian commentators, having grown weary of Putin, have tried to convince their audience that Medvedev is on the rise, apparently believing that mere hope and talk about his gathering strength will prompt him to take the helm. This logic reminds me of a conversation I had with a former European foreign minister, an attentive and intelligent observer, who, explaining why he is optimistic about Medvedev, said, "If you believe in something enough it will happen for sure."

Other Western observers have taken this same tack, casting about for proof that Medvedev is taking power into his own hands and that he is Russia's best hope in 2012.

You are no doubt keeping abreast of the latest political forecasts of Russia's future. Let me quote several well-known Western experts. Here is the key line of a leading American expert: Medvedev's re-election, even if Putin stayed on as prime minister,

> ... would offer the promise of more rapid progress in opening up the political system, encouraging individual initiative, and fostering good relations with the United States and Europe. A new Medvedev presidency, with or without the tandem, ultimately leads to a different place than a Putin presidency. And to one that is likely more in tune with American interests.

I am not going to get into what is or is not in American interests. It's up to Americans to decide that. But I am left wondering why Medvedev's next presidency will "[open] up the political system," especially when Medvedev's first presidency led Russia in the opposite direction?

ANDREW: I can't see why anyone would put money on that result. Medvedev, like Putin, albeit perhaps more so, is part of a group in power, not someone who has real freedom of action. If he had another six years, maybe that would change as circumstances permitted or compelled. But he would be no more able than he is now, it seems to me, to impose his will if that affected the interests of the rest of the group (as it certainly would, if he really wanted to open up Russia).

You could argue that Medvedev's inconsistencies, which are pretty notable, might unintentionally create difficulties in what may well be an uncertain situation, and that that could become a motor for change, in that it would be an accident waiting to happen. But again, and with due regard to the American expert you quoted, that is not much of a basis for prediction. Better to admit that we don't know what will happen.

LILIA: Let me try your patience a bit longer. Let's look at a well-known British pundit's forecasts for Russia's future. Medvedev's statements and his youth, he argues, make the following scenario possible:

> ... a natural and positive historical progression from a Putin generation dedicated to the restoration of order and state authority as the basis for economic progress to a Medvedev generation anxious to use the new order as the basis for the development of a law-based state and economy—a Rechtstaat.

Here we have a couple of arguments that merit a response. First, both Putin and Medvedev admitted that Putin's "restoration of order and state authority" did not bring "economic progress." That is why the tandem decided to undertake modernization. Second, where does this expert find the evidence that Medvedev is anxious to build a law-based state? Perhaps we could say that his generation hopes to move in that direction, but Medvedev himself is presiding over a corrupt court system that is, among other things, apparently trying to keep Khodorkovsky in jail forever. Undermining the Russian Constitution does not make one look like a staunch supporter of a *Rechtstaat.* "Historical progression" is possible, I hope, but only after Putin and Medvedev have left the Russian scene and Russians have come to the conclusion that top-down modernization can't work. I must admit, certain well-respected experts never fail to amuse me!

ANDREW: Pundits love theories and neat formulations. The premise for the theory that Putin restored order as the basis for economic progress is highly disputable, and the nature of centralized rule by a tight-knit cabal is not changed by calling it a Rechtstaat. Nor for that matter is life in the Kremlin likely to make anyone particularly representative of any generation. What experience has Medvedev gained except experience in how to work the existing system? How did he earn his position, by fighting for it or by waiting for it? I am reminded of what a Soviet wife said to me in the early 1980s. She explained that she loved her husband because he was "so naïve. You see, he was brought up in the Kremlin."

LILIA: Isn't it hilarious? Medvedev was brought up by his own "Kremlin" gang that still obeys its chief puppeteer, and Medvedev had no chance to see a real political struggle or prove that he deserves his post. To be sure, he has learned how to work the system.

Let me add another thing. I feel that Western pundits and politicians who dream of Medvedev as the next president do so for one reason: the outwardly mild and smiling Medvedev at the helm would legitimize the West's policy of a reset in relations with Russia. It is rather awkward, after all, to reset relations with Putin's regime, which is perceived as openly anti-Western and authoritarian.

ANDREW: I think you are a bit too cynical here, and that the optimists genuinely hope that Medvedev would indeed move in a more liberal direction than Putin. I do not think that they are just looking for cover for a reset exercise.

LILIA: I wonder how Western leaders will justify their soft approach to personalized power if Putin returns to the Kremlin, which is at present the most feasible outcome.

What, in your view, would constitute signs that the Kremlin is serious about political reform? In Gorbachev's time, the sign was his rejection of the Communist Party's monopoly and his opening of Russia to political pluralism. By the way, quite a few observers compare Medvedev to Gorbachev and find the former to be more liberal. Nothing could be further from the truth. Gorbachev was the first Russian leader to open Russia up to political freedom. Medvedev, apparently remembering how Gorbachev's tenure ended, has done everything in his power not to resemble him.

There are several concrete things Medvedev could do that would show that Russia is on the verge of a new epoch: If Medvedev were to open all national television channels to opposition voices; if he were to guarantee that all oppositional parties could register; or if he at least pledged that in 2011–2012 Russia would have free elections that both he and Putin would sit out. However, all current signs in Russia point in the opposite direction: The authorities do everything in their power to prevent political competition from threatening their grip on power.

ANDREW: You have chosen some of the tougher options. Letting Khodorkovsky out of prison, abandoning United Russia to a well-earned period of decay, changing the team around the tandem, allowing fairer regional elections, enlarging the freedom of the media, softening the pressure on Georgia, bringing some light into Gazprom might all be initial options. But the trouble would be knowing when and how to stop.

LILIA: If one starts an "apertura," one can do little to stop dehermitization until the entire construct unravels at the seams. Closed systems can't survive when they start to open up.

ANDREW: Your speaking of Gorbachev reminds me that, as I should have mentioned before, one of the critical changes from Yeltsin to Putin was the transition to a regime dominated by security service personnel. As a group, security service personnel had not prospered during the 1990s. People in that line of work in any country tend to be inward looking, attach a high value to mutual loyalty, and treat those outside their circle with suspicion. I do not at all mean to imply that they are stupid, rather to the contrary. However, if they are not tied to a superior political layer, as they formerly were in Russia, their innate tendency is to revert to the sort of characteristics I have just sketched out, and to keep their decision making to themselves, as though they were conspirators. Such a mind-set would be all too aware of the risks of any process of devolution getting out of hand.

There is another point I should make. Corruption was endemic to the Soviet Union, without question. And no one would claim that the 1990s were pure. The arrival of the *siloviki* to the seat of power in 2000 gave corruption a different dynamic, however. In Soviet times, the Communist Party was supreme, and the security organs were subordinate to it. That subordination did not mean perfect control, but there was sufficient control. Yeltsin then came along and split up the security apparatus and downgraded it. Putin's arrival meant the liberation of that apparatus from effective control, and allowed its members, as well as the wider bureaucracy, to abuse their positions to make money. Increasing numbers of them turned from being protectors to becoming predators. I say "increasing" because I am referring to a process, a habit that feeds on itself. The result has been twofold: growing public contempt for those responsible for securing law and order in Russia; and declining effectiveness of the security organs, to say nothing of the wider bureaucracy. This is a dangerous trend.

LILIA: I agree with your analysis of the *siloviki* group and its mentality. Moreover, as one former KGB general who turned into a democrat (this can happen!) explained: "The worst and the weakest, pathetic failures came to power in Russia!" Apparently, this fact also plays a role in the way the Russian *siloviki* operate and how they sort out their complexes. One would argue that their constant attempts to look macho and their excessive longing for power and its attributes, arrogance, and open impertinence conceal their feelings of inferiority or previous failures.

Now let me turn to a broader issue. The Russian elite, including the *siloviki*, are gradually changing their self-preservation tactics. Medvedev's arrival in the Kremlin chanting a liberal mantra has led to more emphasis on an approach that we could term "gradualism." This approach is nothing new. It has simply become more popular of late. Its essence is that change cannot be forced in Russia; it has to be made slowly and step by step. Look at what Medvedev says: "Change can be only gradual so as not to destroy the fragile balance that we have today."

The Kremlin propagandists repeat over and over the warning that "radicalism" will lead Russia into bloody revolution. But the fact is that revolutions in Russia have always been the consequence of insufficient change. One can attempt to undertake gradual change by stepping up the fight against corruption in the economy, for example. But without the introduction of new principles—the rule of law, an independent media, and an independent parliament—this struggle turns into yet another form of imitation. Putin already tried to do this during his first term in office and achieved no real results. Medvedev's struggles to win respect for the law and fight corruption have resulted in even greater legal nihilism.

Medvedev attempted to bring order to other areas, too. He began by undertaking what he thought of as the liberalization of the political system, giving the opposition one or two seats in local parliaments (something we have mentioned already) and reforming the military. But can these steps really change anything? What can a couple of opposition deputies achieve in parliaments controlled by the pro-Kremlin United Russia party? In fact, all they can really do is discredit the opposition. How can Medvedev's attempts to create an effective and honest police force ever work if that force remains outside public control and if its repressive powers are increasing all the time?

Attempts to partially improve the system under Putin and Medvedev have only proved that the gradualism that keeps the system's main principles intact (the chief principle being a single group's monopoly on power) inevitably ends up discrediting the very idea of change. Meanwhile, I can't think of any concrete examples of step-by-step measures to improve the rule of law, free and competitive elections, or freedom of the press.

ANDREW: Gradualism without a program for further evolution is both meaningless and, in its own way, provocative. It shows all too clearly that those to whom one is in one's wisdom granting rights or privileges are inferior beings. There are bound to be those who test the boundaries.

LILIA: I would mention two axioms that today's Russia demonstrates. First, the "step-by-step" changes Medvedev is advocating will only prolong the life of the Russian system of personalized power. Second, elimination of monopoly power in Russia will most certainly unravel the whole system based on this monopoly. Many in Russia and in the West are afraid of what this unraveling will bring.

ANDREW: The West would not at all want Russia to dissolve into chaos, either because central control was relaxed haphazardly or because it was maintained for too long. Nor would Russia's neighbors want this to happen. Some of them have even greater problems than Russia in transitioning from a frozen status quo dependent on the coherence of a small ruling group.

LILIA: That means that, if we have two options, then the West prefers Russia's stagnation.

ANDREW: That may well be true for the short term. In the recent past it has been so, for instance, in North Africa. But the trouble is that the risks of unpredictable change, even violent change, increase the longer one puts off efforts to address the underlying tensions.

LILIA: Andrew, do you think we are ready to move from the domestic front to foreign policy?

ANDREW: Let's do that. But I should not want to let it be assumed from our ending this part of the conversation here that stagnation is an enduring or even a long-lasting option.

LILIA: Fair comment. I agree with you.

Now we are turning to the most difficult page of this book. There have not been many attempts to examine Russia's foreign policy that have also kept in mind domestic developments and normative criteria.

I believe we should begin our efforts with an assessment of how the West is coping with the broader challenges it faces. I wonder how you will react to some quotes I've chosen that give an impression of what Western experts think about the West. Walter Laqueur: "America is passing through a crisis of its own, not just an economic or financial crisis, but a crisis of both confidence and governance." Richard Burt: "The European project is in deep crisis. 'Malaise' … now seems the most apt description of the EU mood." Pierre Hassner: "Hesitation and bickering driven by conflicting interests took pride of place [in Europe]."

I will also share with you how I view the West. I believe that, after thirty years of victorious expansion, liberalism and democracy are in retreat. Western society now prefers to look inward and to pursue short-term goals. Having failed to combine values and interests in its relations with the outside world, the powerful forces in Western society have returned to a pre-Helsinki view of international policy. Meanwhile, the world today is more controversial, multilayered, and turbulent than ever, requiring a new mentality and new policies to replace the old, which in many cases are now obstacles to responding to new challenges. Western society needs to reflect on how to update its principles.

It is in the interests of all countries trapped in a historical time lag, Russia above all, that the West sorts out its problems as soon as possible. It is possible that the lack of a civilizational alternative to the West makes it harder for liberal democracy to improve itself. I would argue that a civilization that thinks only about itself and replaces its principles with pragmatism in its dealings with the world has little chance of successfully resolving its internal crisis.

The West's ability to hold to its principles in its dealings with Russia could therefore become one of the criteria of the renewal of its civilization.

Anyway, what do you think?

ANDREW: I would not take the idea that the West, or the United States, the United Kingdom, or whatever face a defining crisis any more seriously than the previous claims that the West and its values had triumphed. We all love a good moan; distinguished commentators thrive on them. But there have nonetheless been significant changes. I have two in particular in mind.

If we look back to the late 1990s, the doctrine of liberal intervention, grandiloquently but in my view foolishly articulated by Tony Blair in April 1999 in Chicago, was in full flower as NATO forces intervened in the former Yugoslavia. The attacks on Afghanistan and Iraq in 2003 and 2004 were, of course, justified in part by 9/11, but they were also part of the same mind-set. There was pressure to solve the Darfur tragedy by Western intervention, citing also the UN "Right to Protect" doctrine. The results have been enough to discourage individual Western countries, let alone NATO as a whole, from attempting any more "liberal interventions." We have not been good at nation building. I believe that NATO, in becoming more modest and in my view realistic in its outlook, will be a more comfortable neighbor for Russia. The attempt in March 2011 to establish a no-fly zone over Libya and Putin's attack on it as being undertaken by crusaders might seem to run counter to that prediction. It certainly illustrates the Russian prime minister's visceral dislike of the West. There is also an obvious risk of Western powers getting sucked in further than they intend. But Western leaders have been eager to put limits on their policies, and to seek clear UN sanction. So, for my part at least, I hope that we are not returning to full-blooded ideas of liberal intervention.

The second change, in my view, is that the European Union has lost its ability to act with strategic intent beyond its present borders—or at least, to put it less emotively, it has abandoned enlargement for the time being. I think the first change better than the second, but that both are here to stay for the predictable future.

LILIA: What you say prompts me to conclude that these two changes place an effective limit on Western strategic thinking and the West's desire to think about its global mission. Too bad....

ANDREW: No, I did not really mean to imply that. Just that the West has a more realistic view of what it can achieve; that it has to act in accordance with cultural and other realities rather than to seek to impose its own nation-building program; and that the European Union is going through what looks like a deepening crisis that has undermined its faith in itself and its attractive power to others—not destroyed, but undermined.

We might perhaps now discuss the U.S. "reset" and EU policies toward Russia with these changes in mind?

THE U.S.-RUSSIAN RESET
HOW SUSTAINABLE IS IT?

LILIA: If you don't mind, I will sum up my rough thoughts. Three years on, the reset appears to have produced notable successes. Barack Obama and Dmitri Medvedev signed the New START treaty, and after a pretty tough struggle in Congress the treaty was ratified by both parliaments. They also reached an agreement on cooperation on Afghanistan (by May 2011 it resulted in the transit through Russian airspace of more than 170,000 U.S. personnel on over 1,000 flights); bridged positions in dealing with the Iranian nuclear program; and created an infrastructure for cooperation—the Bilateral Presidential Commission, consisting of sixteen working groups. U.S.-Russian relations withstood the test of a spy scandal in July 2010 and other unpleasant situations that were successfully downplayed by both sides.

Obama called Medvedev his "friend and partner," and Medvedev declared that "Russian-American relations have immense potential." This marks a clear change of rhetoric compared to the Bush-Putin period!

The warming atmosphere has weakened popular Russian anti-Americanism. In 2007, only 43 percent of respondents viewed the United States positively, and 47 percent had a negative view. In 2010, 60 percent of respondents expressed a positive opinion of the United States, and only 27 percent had a negative view. The Obama administration deserves credit as the initiator of this "reset."

Have I missed other positive results?

ANDREW: You are clearly right to go into the practical details of what has been achieved. There have undoubtedly been successes, the results of an improvement in the U.S.-Russian atmosphere. It has been worthwhile to pocket those, for both Moscow and Washington.

LILIA: The reset has successfully allowed both sides to pursue some of their tactical goals, but more optimistic conclusions than that are premature. The U.S.-Russian relationship only proves that appearances can be deceiving. The very term "reset" inserted inflated expectations into a situation that offers no civilizational or economic basis for a breakthrough. America and Russia rest on different principles and values, and their elites do not share the same view of the world.

The key premises underlying the "reset" make for a fragile foundation. Belief in the existence of "mutual interests" (that which is good for Russia and good for the United States at the same time) has, as we have discussed, shaky foundations. As for the attempt to avoid "linkage" between domestic developments and foreign policy, you have already argued that that is a trap.

There is one more premise for reset on the American side. This is Medvedev, who, in many American observers' view, "being the face of Russia, made it easier for the Obama administration to reset relations with Russia." But a policy based on a belief that Medvedev has potential would become unsustainable if it were proven that that potential is illusory.

ANDREW: I suppose that policymakers can have doubts as well as hopes, and that they may nonetheless think that the potential gains are worth the risk. That would be particularly true of a new administration, in the United States or anywhere else. New administrations naturally desire to look for new avenues, regardless of the discouraging information reaching them, as revealed by some of the documents in the WikiLeaks splurges—or by the press, for that matter.

LILIA: Your mention of WikiLeaks is very timely!

We all knew about the nature of the Russian political regime, but some of us believed that Western governments, and first and foremost the

Obama administration, had an inadequate grasp of Russia's political landscape or maintained illusions about the Russian leadership. The WikiLeaks dump has proved that Western leaders understand full well what is going on in Russia behind the demagoguery curtain. But this only proves that the "reset" is based on a simple foundation: "We know what you are. We pretend that we trust you in order to get what we need from you." This is vintage pragmatism, without serious thought of what it might bring.

ANDREW: The WikiLeaks cables are certainly vivid and professional, but they are only one element in Washington's decisionmaking processes. It would be wrong to draw too strong a conclusion from these leaks alone. In particular, as we have discussed, there is the question of how the Americans suppose that Russia will evolve and what they can do to help it to do so in a constructive manner. This is not just a matter of pretending to be trusting for Machiavellian purposes. One positive thing the cables reveal is that they offer no evidence for conspiracy theorists who believe that Washington nurtures cunning plots to plunge Russia into chaos. On the contrary, they contain pretty much what you would expect—or ought to expect, at least.

LILIA: These leaks prove that U.S. policy toward Russia is the result of their conclusion that they don't expect Russia to evolve in a positive direction.

I suggest that we take one example of reset-based cooperation and see how successful it can be. Let's start with Iran. Russia and the United States have really bridged their positions on Iran. But will the trend hold after our dialogue is published?

Russia's readiness to support the U.S. position on Iran is limited for three reasons. First, even a nuclear-armed Iran is not a priority threat for either the Russian elite or Russian society. Second, Russia has its reasons for making sure that Iran continues to restrain itself in the post-Soviet space and the northern Caucasus. Third, Russia's independent approach to Iran is proof of its geopolitical role. That is why the Russian elite will always be limited in its ability to accept Washington's position on Iran. But even among Russian liberals who do not think much about Iran, U.S. toughness after the Iraqi drama poses many questions.

ANDREW: We have to distinguish between what is being or may be done now and what can be expected over the long term. That will depend, critically, it seems to me, on what will happen in Russia over the next decade or so; it will depend far less on what may happen in the United States or the rest of the Western world. Our earlier discussion of modernization has shown how uncertain, even discouraging, those prospects are. Are we even confident about who will be in charge in Russia in a couple of years' time, let alone confident of what difference, if any, that will make? The United States has, as you say, put something of a bet on Medvedev.

I think that we should be careful, as well, to distinguish between what the U.S. administration has to say and the spin put on it by some of the more enthusiastic interpreters of its policies. The word "reset" itself encourages perhaps more expectation than is justified, and even American officials can look more optimistic than perhaps they really are in the hope of building up momentum on the Russian side. But there is also a section of the U.S. commentariat inclined to extrapolate from the achieved, or perhaps achievable, to a permanent and even determining relationship between Washington and Moscow, which is surely not in the cards.

Iran is a case in point. I am not sure how much influence Russia really has on Iran. Its interests, crudely described, are conflicted. On the one hand, Russia has its commercial hopes for the country, Iran has influence in the Caspian that may be useful to Moscow, it will one day become once more a significant energy player, and so on. On the other hand, Iran is a neuralgic issue for the United States, its possession of nuclear weapons would be destabilizing, and its fundamentalist Shiite allegiances are not at all to Moscow's liking. Washington's courtship of Moscow is flattering, and the Chinese can block things in the UN without Russia's help, so why not be both accommodating and restraining toward the United States at the same time? Moscow sees no need to take a lead on this issue, especially because the foreign ministry probably supposes that Iran will get its weapons in the end, despite Western efforts. A classic case of tactical positioning, not long-term alignment.

LILIA: You are suggesting that we distinguish tactical success of the reset from ungrounded expectations, correct?

ANDREW: Correct.

LILIA: There is one more premise of the reset—"dual-track engagement"—that may have controversial implications (to put it mildly). I have to admit that several years ago I myself liked the idea of dual-track engagement. I understood it as a simultaneous dialogue between two authorities and two civil societies. In practice, however, the American sides have fallen into a trap. The Americans, after all, have agreed to conduct dialogue with Russian society under Kremlin supervision. The co-chairman of the working group organizing this dialogue is none other than Deputy Chief of Staff of the Presidential Administration Vladislav Surkov, who is responsible for clearing the Russian political stage of any opposition. I think Washington made a mistake when they agreed to Surkov's candidacy. This undermined the whole concept. By agreeing to discuss civil society with a person responsible for the annihilation of civil society, the American side has demonstrated a readiness to pretend that only serves to undermine the integrity of the Obama administration.

ANDREW: I may be wrong, but it seems to me that Surkov was at one stage paying court to Medvedev, which would have helped reinforce, by coincidence or design, the U.S. calculation that the Russian president was a coming man. I am not sure this is still the case. Sorry to interrupt—just thought I'd throw that in.

LILIA: You may be right: Surkov has definitely been spreading his eggs around all useful baskets. But this does not change his role in the U.S.-Russian dialogue. With respect to Washington's attitude to Medvedev, I have the same feeling.

Washington made another concession to the Kremlin by agreeing to conduct the dialogue in a "sharing-best-practices" format (!)—that is, the parties discussed their experiences in various areas of civil society. What could America possibly learn from Russia about fighting corruption, juvenile justice reform, prison reform, and migration? Perhaps Russia meant to share the secrets behind its bureaucracy's personal enrichment schemes, or to show America how to turn migrants into people with no rights at all. And what could Moscow hope to learn from America's anti-corruption experience when Russia has renounced independent courts and independent media?

I understand that Washington has limited room for maneuver. If Obama wants to succeed on the issues of Afghanistan, Iran, or proliferation, then he must not press Russia on democracy and civil society issues. But even these concerns shouldn't force the United States to be so accommodating on these issues.

ANDREW: Maybe the hope is that some ideas get through and do good in the end. I suppose that there is also the thought that holding Moscow to discussions of these sorts of questions may act as a restraint on bad behavior. At least it gives both sides an excuse to comment on these matters. But mainly it is all for form's sake, surely. It would surprise me if anyone took it as more than that.

LILIA: Washington had plenty of time to discover that "society-to-society dialogue" controlled by the authorities does not do anything to restrain the Russian side. Apparently, Moscow's "bad behavior" inside the country is not Washington's key headache, or even a headache at all. Here is my take: Washington, together with the other Western capitals, came to the conclusion that Russia is no longer a threat. They may even believe that Russia is moving toward the West because the Russian elite has adopted a Western lifestyle and can't risk confrontation with the West. This assumption leads to another one: Western dialogue with Moscow will gradually civilize the Russian elite.

This is an example of typical Western reasoning. For the time being, this dialogue only serves for the Russian elite to encourage them to continue the same policies—policies that may permit Russia's decay to proceed unchecked, to disastrous geopolitical implications. A rotting nuclear power: not an encouraging scenario!

By the way, the Russian anti-systemic opposition demanded that Medvedev fire Surkov, whom they blame for "the atmosphere of hatred and intolerance with regard to whoever has the temerity to disagree with Putin." Let me quote the leaders of the Russian liberal opposition, Boris

Nemtsov, Vladimir Ryzhkov, and Vladimir Milov (the leaders of the new People's Freedom Party and the Coalition for Russia Without Lawlessness and Corruption movement):

> It is Surkov who steers extremist organizations like the *Nashi* (Ours) movement, financed by the Kremlin.... It is Surkov we owe censorship to. It is Surkov who is to be blamed for the organization of the so-called elections and for the campaigns against independent journalists and opposition leaders.

I can only imagine that it is an uncomfortable situation for the Obama administration to continue to cooperate with a person who has come under such fire from the liberal opposition in Russia.

ANDREW: It is hard to see this getting anywhere at all, but sometimes a bit of hypocrisy can be tempting. Maybe it was supposed to show U.S. diplomatic respect for Russian ideas? Perhaps it will be an opportunity to achieve something at some margin? I do not know, but I am glad I don't sit on the working group.

Of course, things would be different if "modernization" began to achieve substantive goals, since that would mean, as I think we have agreed, devolution and change within Russia. I hate to be like the cuckoo in the clock, repeating myself at regular intervals, but the message is worth driving home: The evolution of Russia itself will determine whether there is change or degradation. I have yet to hear a U.S. spokesman or an apologist for the reset say where they think Russia's internal politics and conception of itself are headed. If one thinks of the reset as a strategy rather than a useful tactic, then these are surely key omissions.

LILIA: In any case, the "de-linking" of foreign policy and domestic developments, combined with engagement on points of agreement with the Kremlin, is a formula one could hardly call strategically oriented.

To be sure, beginning in the fall of 2010 the Obama administration, apparently understanding the brittle nature of its reset, started to make certain gestures that it hoped its domestic and foreign critics would accept as proving that it was not appeasing Russia.

Each time the Kremlin brutally cracked down on political freedoms or Russian journalists were beaten or killed, the White House reiterated "the importance of embracing and protecting universal values, including freedoms of expression and assembly, enshrined in the Russian Constitution as well as in international agreements which Russia has signed." But the Kremlin, as a rule, has ignored Washington.

I recall that, after yet another Russian journalist had been brutally attacked and Medvedev had again declared that "the criminals must be punished," the *Washington Post* wrote, "Neither the Obama administration nor any other Western government has held the Russian president accountable for failure to deliver. That's probably one reason the crimes continue."

Of course, that's not the only reason the crimes continued, but the *Post*'s editorialists were right to point out that the Obama administration has failed to find a way to make the Kremlin listen to its concerns.

ANDREW: Western politicians as a group have been reluctant to speak up. Their silence risks making them look complicit in wrongdoing. Let me cite the Italian newspaper *La Repubblica* to illustrate the reputational risks of failing to speak up. The paper recently published an investigative report that concluded that economic and political decisions taken by Silvio Berlusconi and Putin might reflect their "joint private investments." The newspaper quoted an Italian comment that "Berlusconi and people from his close entourage have dividends from energy agreements with Russia." The point here is not whether these accusations are true, but that the mere possibility of their being true is damaging.

LILIA: Berlusconi is the perfect example of a leader who is draining Western policies of any moral foundation. Thank God that neither Obama nor any other U.S. president is suspected of having gone that far.

But by the end of 2010, one could get the impression that the Russian authorities were beginning deliberately to put the Americans into awkward situations, as if to tell them, "We will do as we please and won't take orders from you." You of course remember Lev Ponomaryov, the prominent human rights activist. The police detained him and held him in a cell for "stepping on a policeman's toes" just before he was scheduled to take part in a meeting between Russian human rights activists, Deputy Secretary of State Bill Burns, and Obama's Russia adviser, Michael McFaul. The American side had to express their regret at the jailing, yet the Russian authorities had nonetheless demonstrated their right to ignore Washington and use repressive measures against the opposition and human rights activists.

Russian observers claimed that America and Russia had struck a deal stipulating that Russia would not react to American statements. My Carnegie colleague Dmitri Trenin asserted this in an interview in *Kommersant*.

ANDREW: This sounds like an odd deal. You could argue that in preferring to remain silent in the face of American criticism the Russians were accepting the U.S. right to express it, but then official Russia does not do shame so that is not too convincing. Other Russians may hear the broader message about just behavior, though it is equally possible that irritation at American criticism is a more general reaction. It depends on the circumstances.

LILIA: I had several discussions with State Department representatives who were actively involved in the reset, people who know and understand Russia. In response to my criticism of the U.S.-Russian "civil society" group co-chaired by Surkov, they usually said: "You're wrong. We are conducting dialogue at the civil society level, and Russian rights activists are happy with this"; "Statements by State Department and Administration representatives decrying the use of heavy-handed measures against the opposition irritate the Kremlin, which proves that they've gotten at least some kind of reaction." They also added, "Our task is to engage Russia in the hope that, through rapprochement with the West, it will gradually become more liberal."

In reply, I would always ask them, "Where are the practical results of this engagement? Has it led to a real expansion of political freedom? Do State Department expressions of 'concern' keep Russian riot police from beating dissidents? And why should civil society representatives have to meet with your people under the supervision of Kremlin officials?"

In most cases, I received no satisfactory response.

I must confess that the American officials were a lot more comfortable listening to those of my Russian colleagues who adopted a soothing, accommodating line, saying, in effect,

> Yes, there are problems in Russia, but things are not so bad! Russia has come a long way since the end of the Cold War. Russian society is not ready yet for liberal democracy, but it will get there one day. The reset will help Russia to become more civilized. Dialogue between civil societies, even under the Kremlin's supervision, will help us to resolve some of our problems.

These arguments may make U.S. officials feel more confident in asserting that the reset is both justified and sustainable, but, to be frank, they look to me like self-delusion, whether conscious or unconscious. No, I am not calling for a return to the Cold War. We Russian liberals would be the first victims of such cold winds. Nevertheless, there should be a way for a liberal democracy to avoid coddling a repressive regime!

ANDREW: I want to raise an issue over and above the mainly bilateral issues we have discussed so far: the meaning of the reset for the ex-Soviet space beyond Russia. This is a question that both Washington and Moscow would rather ignore, but it will very probably threaten their future relationship—and, of course, the relationship between Moscow and many European capitals, too. Silence, or virtual silence, after the "reset" implies some degree of Western acceptance, or at least understanding, of Moscow's claim to have a sphere of special interests. Authoritative Russians have made it clear, with considerable satisfaction, that this is how they see it. The West, on the other hand, ought to care that Ukraine is regressing toward present Russian political structures, not because we want to play some sort of power game in Central Europe, but because that eventuality would be bad for Ukraine, and in the end bad for Russia, too. Belarus, too, seems after the presidential elections in December 2010 and the economic crisis that followed them to be falling increasingly under Russian dominance.

I said earlier that we should distinguish between the message that the U.S. administration wanted to convey and the spin that some of the commentariat put on that message. Tom Graham, for instance, was only making it clear what the reset implies when he recently argued that it is in Russia's interests to be a great power and to be accepted as such. Nonsense, but let that pass. Graham recommended that Washington and Moscow should work together to ensure that Ukraine and other such states do not create problems for them:

> What is needed now is a far-reaching bilateral discussion of the former Soviet space—and other fundamental conflicts of interests—so that each side understands the other's perspective and the two sides can work together in developing acceptable rules of the road to diminish the risks of a major U.S.-Russian standoff that would upset the relationship as a whole.

LILIA: The former Soviet space and the Kremlin ambition to preserve its "areas of interest" will certainly present a formidable test for the reset. I have the impression that some politicians (I would guess more in Europe than in the United States, but I could be wrong) are content to allow Ukraine to regress and move closer to Russia even as it becomes more authoritarian and to allow Belarus to lean toward Russia again as well. There could be a simple explanation for this stance, that it would mean they don't have to rack their brains to figure out how to support Ukrainian reforms or the Belarusian opposition. It would also strike one more point of contention with Russia off the list.

ANDREW: That may be true of the short term but there is also the question of how a greater Russian stake in former Soviet countries will affect Russia's own development. My bet is that it will make it still more authoritarian.

LILIA: With respect to Tom Graham, I believe that you are interpreting him correctly. As far as I understand it after reading his pieces, he believes in a kind of U.S.-Russian tandem in the former Soviet space. Here is an important question: What is the basis of this cooperation: transformation of the area, or preservation of it as a "gray zone"? In the article published in Russia, he clearly states that Russia will be built on the basis of "authoritarian and statist rules of the game," and that Russia's "presence in this area supports a balance of forces and serves U.S. interests." I want to emphasize here Graham's point that authoritarian Russia's role as arbiter in the former Soviet space "serves U.S. interests." If this is true, then we have returned to the nineteenth century, and there is thus no hope for America's agenda. But in this case, the interests of Russian and other societies in the newly independent states contradict America's interests. Why should they want to stay in the past??

ANDREW: Graham is not alone in his opinion, and I only quoted him as an example of a way of thinking that classes independent small countries as irritants that must be taught to behave properly by their betters—which of course they will not and ought not to do. If he only meant to say that Western countries should talk to Moscow about the former Soviet states, then I agree with him, even if the Russians would not be very eager to listen.

LILIA: There are several other "reset" premises that raise questions, in my view. One of them was Washington's return to the START treaty talks, a gesture intended to build trust and lay the foundations for renewed cooperation. On the one hand, the START negotiations and subsequent agreement really helped to thaw relations. On the other hand, the negotiations provided more evidence that Russia and the United States are still locked into their mutual deterrence regime, within which there are still big unresolved issues (above all the anti-ballistic missile issue). Moreover, the return to Cold War–era mechanisms is an unusual way of building trust. I would have thought that nonproliferation talks were rather a sign of mistrust!

ANDREW: The New START agreement is useful, but not unambiguously so. In any case, it may end up being held hostage to the anti-ballistic missile issue for emotional reasons rather than for any real threat present or even conceivable Western plans would pose to Russia's ability to chuck bombs at the United States. The trouble is that this sort of unreal problem lies at the heart of the philosophy behind New START. Its great drawback is that it encourages Moscow in the delusion that it is some sort of natural partner to Washington, as the Soviet Union was before it.

It is plain that Russia is not now and will never be such a partner to Washington. I recently had a conversation with a senior Russian diplomat who informed me out of the blue that Russia did not have an identity crisis. I said I was surprised to hear that, because most of us did, which I thought tactful. But it is obvious that Russia does have questions about what it really is and where it is going, and I believe that it is proper, even necessary, that it should have such questions. The delusion that it has the right and the ability to be a "great power" is a dangerous security blanket. Russian nuclear weapons are the last real gauge of its ambitions to be of a different order of power than the rest of us, and an illusory one, too.

LILIA: The Russian political class still has this security blanket pulled up over its head.

Here is another Russian illusion as well. From the very beginning, the Russian side has viewed the "reset" as a way for the Americans to respond to its grudges. It has plainly regarded concessions from the United States as payment for further Russian cooperation. "Obama, who has no foreign policy achievements, now owes the Kremlin." This has been a typical take on the "reset" in the Russian media, even among liberal outlets.

The official Kremlin approach—"We have nothing to reset"—already contains the seeds of future frustration for both sides. In a September 2010 interview with *Kommersant*, Putin, discussing the relationship with the United States, said (and not without some cockiness) that he continues to believe that nothing much has changed since his "Cold War" speech in Munich in 2007, and that "there is not much reset" in the relationship. Such is the reality for Russia's "national leader," not the proclaimed reset breakthrough.

ANDREW: The Russian prime minister spoke true. Medvedev's warm words about his "friend Obama" can't change the fact that the true Russian leader is mistrustful of Washington.

LILIA: Ironically, we are both in agreement about Putin's diagnosis.

U.S. observers have also become more cautious. Discussing the achievements of the reset, Stephen Sestanovich has said that there are "serious points of disagreement that could complicate the cooperation that the two sides have established so far." Robert Legvold has concluded, "A series of very significant factors will continue to constrain how far and fast the U.S.-Russian relationship will move."

Official U.S. statements, in contrast, have been full of optimism. Indeed, one couldn't help but notice that the United States has started to borrow language from Soviet times. A 2010 U.S.-Russia "Reset Fact Sheet" published by the State Department trumpeted the facts that "dozens of delegations have traveled to each country, video conferences have been held, and numerous new bilateral activities and programs have emerged to pursue projects of mutual benefit to the American and Russian people."

The administration would argue that Russian attitudes toward the United States have grown more favorable. But the Russian attitude toward America was very favorable in the early 1990s and then reached historic lows under Putin. What guarantee is there that the same thing will not happen again? The Kremlin has learned the art of using its control of television to manipulate the public mood.

ANDREW: The May 2011 Joint Report by the Coordinators of the U.S.-Russia Bilateral Presidential Commission was even more positive. It stressed that the joint efforts "are contributing to the growing economic prosperity of both our countries" and emphasized the American participation in the Skolkovo project. I am surely not alone in finding these assertions strained.

LILIA: Apparently, they had in mind the prosperity of the Russian upper class. As for Skolkovo, maybe the American side does not know that they are taking part in a joke? Or they know but think that this is an inevitable price for entering the Russian market?

ANDREW: Both sides claim credit for "collaborating to monitor corruption and establish new best practices in corporate governance."

LILIA: If the U.S. side is "monitoring" Russian corruption, then they must also accept some responsibility for its irresistible growth.... I see that there is also U.S.-Russian cooperation in preserving the population of Russia's Amur tiger ... Putin's pet project.

ANDREW: Official statements—and I speak as a former government official—always put the best gloss on things. Their authors love to list goals achieved, preferably ones selected in advance for their ease of achievement and then later ticked off as proof of progress.

LILIA: Even seemingly practical ways of Russia and the United States working together can prove counterproductive. Congress endorsed the 123 Agreement on civil nuclear cooperation, which would give a green light to storing waste from American nuclear power stations and American-supplied reactors around the world in Russia. Many Russians, who do not want to see their country turned into a nuclear dump, oppose these plans.

ANDREW: The Soviet (and now Russian) safety record is suspect here. I suppose that the Americans would try to ensure that nuclear material would be properly handled, but the fact remains that no one in Russia would have any confidence that promised safety measures would be followed. This could turn into an emotional and divisive issue. The Germans have taken a far more cautious line: Environment Minister Norbert Rottgen has declared that Germany will not send its nuclear spent fuel to Russia because Russia can't guarantee its safety. Public concerns about nuclear power after the March 2011 earthquake and tsunami in Japan are on the rise in Russia as in other countries. These concerns may or may not be well founded, but they are without doubt strong.

LILIA: There are serious commentators in Washington who have criticized the reset from the beginning. The most thoughtful critic has been David Kramer. I totally sympathize with his normative view of the reset. He asks, "What will it take for higher levels of the Obama administration to unequivocally condemn arrests of activists, violence against protesters, pressure on journalists and murders of government critics?" He concludes that "a growing values gap will reduce areas of common interests between our governments."

ANDREW: David is an acute observer. President Obama will have to pay more attention to the opposition in Congress now, after the mid-term elections, than he did during his first two years. I would have thought that one result of this change would be a lessened temptation to turn a blind eye to abuses abroad.

LILIA: That's true. At any rate, by early 2011 one could feel the growing frustration of U.S. officials with the reset. My hunch is that members of the Obama team have started to wonder if their hopes of Medvedev and his presumed pro-Western attitudes and liberalism were justified. The Americans accomplished their tactical agenda, but the ground for further steps is shaky, which undoubtedly worries them. The Obama administration is also aware of the approaching 2012 elections and may feel constrained to temper its claims about a revived relationship or its sustainability in light of them.

ANDREW: Vice President Joseph Biden had some pretty strong things to say about democracy and human rights when he was in Moscow in March 2011, certainly by comparison with earlier top-level approaches to these sorts of issues. And according to Garry Kasparov's report in his blog, Biden told attendees at his meeting with opposition figures that he, the U.S. vice president, had advised the Russian prime minister that he should not run for president again, and that Russia was tired of him. If so, then that was extremely blunt. Rude, in fact. I wonder what the U.S. reaction would have been if Putin had said anything like that about the United States or its elected leaders?

LILIA: This is one of the difficulties of unduly personalized relationships between nations. Some people are quick to take offense and slow to forget a slight. Nevertheless, I would argue that no matter how hard the U.S. administration tries to avoid ruffling Moscow's feathers, the Russian elite is highly unlikely to be willing to help Obama accomplish his objectives. Russia will only accept an expansion of cooperation with the United States if this cooperation helps the Russian political system to survive.

This naturally raises the question, does cooperation help transformation, or does it cement the status quo?

ANDREW: I believe the Arab revolutions necessarily influence Obama's foreign policy approach, including his attitude to the interests versus values balance. He started at the realist end of the policy spectrum. He spoke of "strategy no longer driven by ideology and politics but one that is based on a realistic assessment...." His credo downgraded by comparison with that of his Republican predecessor the ideas of promoting democracy and protecting human rights. This was reflected in his reset policy.

LILIA: Looks like Obama believed that the age of ideology was over. But his speech on May 19, 2011, about the Middle East, and what he said during his subsequent visit to London represented an attempt to find a new balance between his "non-ideological" approach and a normative dimension. Look what he said on May 19: "The status quo is not sustainable. Societies held together by fear and repression may offer the illusion of stability for a time, but they are built upon fault lines that will eventually tear asunder." He was talking about the Middle East, not Russia. But what he said would by extension apply to Russia, too.

If, after the Arab Spring, the Obama administration continues to pursue the same type of reset, it would mean either double standards or a misunderstanding of Russian reality.

EUROPE AND THE RUSSIAN SYSTEM
ACQUIESCENCE OR INFLUENCE?

ANDREW: The rest of Europe is as I have said before more closely bound up with Russia than is the United States. The European Union is, in principle, well placed to exercise influence on Moscow. Russia's ability to put energy (that is, gas) pressure on Brussels and on a range of individual EU countries has diminished in the past few years. However, the main reason for the Russians to take Europe seriously is its ability to attract other European countries to its standards and the prospect of eventual membership in the European Union. This influence has in recent years been undermined and Moscow has long been able to divide EU member countries.

The European Union has declared an interest in a Modernization Partnership with Russia. It is hard to see what this could possibly mean in terms of a real transformation of the Russian economy. EU money can fund particular projects, and implementing these can have useful effects at the local level and provide for some transfers of technological and managerial skills. These are not to be sniffed at and will benefit individual EU firms, too. However, these measures are more like aid than projects aimed at joint modernization. And even more to the point, investors will not go wherever governments wish just because it suits current political moods. Is there a rush to go to Skolkovo, for instance? Why should there be? It seems to me that foreign investors' current mood is to wait and see what happens with modernization, particularly given that no one knows quite what modernization is supposed to mean.

I see no reason to expect this well-meaning but insubstantial pattern to change, Lisbon Treaty or not. The European Union will continue to punch below its weight. The June 2011 EU-Russia Summit was preoccupied by the emergence of a virulent form of the *E. coli* bacterium around Hamburg allegedly caused by Spanish cucumbers. This gave Putin the chance to take a populist stand by forbidding the import into Russia of all fresh vegetables from the EU, which he claimed was done to protect the people of Russia. His move also pandered to protectionist feelings in his country. Putin added in reply to criticism from the EU Mission in Moscow that the "spirit" of the WTO negotiations for Russian entry had nothing to do with the case. This was typical of his dismissive public comments about the WTO when agreements reached in the course of Russia's entry negotiations conflict with Putin's immediate desires.

LILIA: Unfortunately, this is what we see looking at the European Union from outside. We've already discussed the European Union and Russia during Putin's presidency. Nothing much has changed from that time to the era of Medvedev-Putin tandem rule.

The European Union is the world's only normative power. However, EU policy and the policies of its individual members toward Russia raise questions about their values-based approach to foreign policy. Here is what I have in mind: European politicians and even former European leaders sit on the boards of Russian state corporations (as former German chancellor Gerhard Schröder does). This would be fine, if not for the fact that these corporations are the pillars of the corrupted state and extreme examples of non-transparency. Western businesses are being drawn into behind-the-scenes deals and murky activities on the part of Russian authorities. We have already discussed this fact.

European think tanks have also been quite willing to take sponsorship funds from Russian businesses subservient to the Russian authorities. The result is that quite a few European (and Western) think tanks are reluctant to criticize anything the Russian state does. Participation by European intellectuals and politicians in Kremlin-staged propaganda events (for example, the Valdai Club or the Yaroslavl Forum), as well as the European elite's general eagerness to be chummy with the Russian authorities, amount to legitimating Russia's personalized power system.

My question is: Why are so many in the normative community reluctant to back their own values when it comes to relations with Russia? Is it out of a desire to settle matters of more immediate concern? Or do individual European politicians have a personal interest in maintaining good relations with the Kremlin? Or is political Europe simply weary of Russia's unpredictability and assertiveness, and therefore seeks mainly not to irritate the authorities in Moscow?

ANDREW: I wouldn't attach much importance to the possibility of Western politicians taking retirement jobs in Russia. Nor does it seem to me that there is any consistent EU policy of avoiding giving offense to Moscow in order to resolve particular matters of immediate concern. It's more of a general muddle really, with basic attitudes settled at the country level.

LILIA: This muddle, however, has certain political implications. In the case of Russia, the "muddle" helps to preserve things as they are.

Germany is the key player on the European scene. In its relations with Russia, Berlin openly and unequivocally pursues an accommodating line. We can put down its "realism" in part to German business's desire for friendly ties. However, my guess is that this isn't the only explanation.

When I asked German historian Wolfgang Eichwede about the reasons behind German pragmatism, he said that the Germans still feel a certain amount of historical responsibility for invading the Soviet Union during World War II. Here is the irony: Conscious of their responsibility for the past and their desire not to repeat it, the Germans are pursuing a policy that makes it more difficult for Russia to escape its own past. And this is all the more tragic and ironic in that EU policy toward Russia is unlikely to change unless Germany takes the lead.

ANDREW: Germany is, as you say, the decisive country within the European Union when it comes to Russia. I do not see it taking a lead to change anything—rather to the contrary. We discussed some of the factors underlying this reality earlier. I should have mentioned then the success of Ostpolitik as a formative influence. Softly-softly is now remembered as what worked back then.

LILIA: Current German Ostpolitik, I'm afraid, has had the opposite result. It has helped the Russian elite to close Russia off and to move it away from Europe, rather than the reverse.

There is another influential member of the European Union: France. Now, I am not an attentive observer of Russian-French relations, but from what I see on the surface, Sarkozy appears to be continuing the traditional French policy toward Russia that Chirac pursued. I see how Sarkozy is trying to forget the way that the Kremlin humiliated him in 2008 after the Georgian war, and the aftermath of that, too. The Kremlin still refuses to fulfill the terms of the Medvedev-Sarkozy settlement of that conflict. Its troops are still on Georgian territory. Withdrawal is unlikely to happen now that Russia has recognized the former separatist enclaves' independence and refuses to let European observers onto their territory. Sarkozy prefers to ignore all this, and to try instead to become a preferred partner for the Russian ruling tandem.

ANDREW: Vincent Jauvert from *Le Nouvel Observateur* wrote revealing articles about Paris's behavior during the Russian-Georgian war.

LILIA: Oh, yes. It was Jauvert who reported the famous conversation between Putin and Sarkozy: "I will hang Saakashvili by his balls!" said Putin. "Will you hang…?" asked Sarkozy, shocked almost speechless. "Why not?!" responded Putin.

ANDREW: Jauvert quoted an influential French politician, Herve Mariton, who said of the French mediation in the Russian-Georgian conflict: "We looked a caricature of ourselves. France has betrayed its principles." He also quoted an official Russian representative who said, "Sarkozy did exactly what we hoped for: He in fact endorsed the annexation of Abkhazia and Ossetia."

LILIA: I found it interesting how Sarkozy tried to gain Putin's trust and turn France into Russia's "privileged partner" at the cost of almost the last remaining drop of his dignity. He constantly praised Putin: "Vladimir is very smart. He understands everything. He is pretty open…." I talked to Jauvert about the reasons behind Paris's connivance regarding

Russia. Here is his explanation: "There is no naïveté. The French leader and his advisers understand that the Russian regime is corrupt and undemocratic. This is pure realpolitik." That is, Paris is trying to pursue economic, security, and geopolitical interests with Moscow, just as other Western leaders are doing. But Jauvert points to an interesting difference in Sarkozy's case: He "thought he could be the Thatcher of the 'liberal' Medvedev and could gain from it."

ANDREW: To adapt the words of another politician in another country, we knew Gorbachev, and Medvedev is no Gorbachev—or, we knew Thatcher, and Sarkozy is no Thatcher.

LILIA: When I talked to other French experts about French policy, they all mentioned two factors: the first is business interests (not at all original), and the second is vestiges of Gaullism in French thinking. In other words, despite Sarkozy's own transatlantic-oriented views, France retains its somewhat dissenting attitude with regard to the United States and therefore tries to use its partnership with Russia as a counterweight to excessive American presence on the continent. What do you say about this?

ANDREW: I am not an expert here either, but apart from the factors you mention, there is also France's desire to keep alongside Germany and its wish thereby to retain the image of being a co-leader in the European Union.

LILIA: Jauvert mentioned that Sarkozy had ambitions "to topple Berlin as the first European partner of Russia, and to a certain degree he succeeded." The Kremlin must feel like the belle of the ball, looking on as the guys fight among each other for her attention....

ANDREW: Surrounded as she is by the towers of her virtue.

LILIA: Western leaders demonstrate that leadership for them means pragmatism. I've always thought that being a leader without a mission undermines leadership.

I would like to make one more comment. Some of my French colleagues have spoken of a so-called "Beijing consensus" with regard to Russia. The idea is for the West to take a pragmatic approach toward Russia as it did toward China. Unlike China, however, Russia is a member of the Council of Europe.

ANDREW: China and Russia are clearly different things. The parallel here is false.

LILIA: In any case, the impression these days is that Paris is trying to build relations with Russia that leave the normative dimension out of the picture.

To be sure, there are some exceptions that give grounds for hope. Among Russia pundits, Marie Mendras is notable, and among experts with a broader profile, Thérèse Delpech stands out. Let me quote Mendras' piece on the Khodorkovsky affair and what it says about the Russian system. "A system that can eliminate an inconvenient entrepreneur is a regime which has established the absence of accountability and the impunity of the ruling groups as a principle of government." There is nothing more I could add to this statement.

I have not heard of a "Russian lobby" in other Western capitals, but both Russian observers and the French themselves talk of its existence in Paris. I remember a June 14, 2010, article in the Russian magazine, the *New Times*, on the "Russian trio" in Paris. This was the name given to Sarkozy's and Fillon's three key Russia advisers: Jean de Boissue, Igor Mitrofanoff, and Jean-David Levitte. All three have Russian roots and, according to the media, were involved in one way or another in concluding trade deals with Russia, from Renault's deal with Avtovaz, to Sarkozy's decision to sell French Mistrals to Russia.

In principle, it should make me happy as a Russian citizen to think that there are people lobbying for Russia's interests in an influential Western country. But it matters to me which Russian interests they are lobbying for: the interests of Putin's Russia or the interest of ordinary Russians in having a normal democratic state? I have no evidence that the Russian lobby in Paris, if it does exist, is acting in the interest of achieving a democratic and open Russia.

ANDREW: Sarkozy should have learned from his experiences in promoting the Georgia cease-fire that posturing is no substitute for concrete activity.

LILIA: It seems to me that the whole pattern of French-Russian "partnership" today is based on only a vague understanding of what is going on in Russia and on the complicated network of interests around the Kremlin. For instance, there is the French sale of Mistral amphibious assault ships to Russia. The deal was advertised in Paris as a commercial and political coup by Sarkozy. As it turned out, Russian oligarch Sergei Pugachev, who is living in France and who is suspected of murky activity in Russia, had before been lobbying heavily in favor of such a deal.

ANDREW: Pugachev now seems to be having problems of his own in Russia. And not everyone in the Russian Defense Ministry supports the Mistral deal.

LILIA: Correct. Anyway, the deal was completed, and as far as I understand it was concluded on terms other than those Sarkozy had hoped for. The Kremlin gang has perfected the art of pursuing its own interests. This is the price the French have to pay for relying on informal networks and for not knowing exactly what's happening inside Russia. Or perhaps the French authorities know exactly what goes on in Russia but find it not so repulsive as to endanger their long-desired friendship with Russia's leaders.

Let's turn to British policy on Russia, if you have no objections. You implemented this policy while in Moscow. Today you cannot help but reflect on the relations between our two countries. I think my job here is to formulate some questions for you. How do you assess London's policy toward Russia over the last two decades, and what part has the normative dimension played in it? What could London have done but failed to do, or what did London do, but not as well as you would have liked?

What are the reasons for intergovernmental relations being for the most part rather cool? What line can we expect to see the present British government take toward Russia?

I will also make a couple of comments of my own, and then I would like to hear your reaction to them. In the spring of 2010, the news came out that the British Council, which had had its activities suspended in two Russian cities, had agreed to take part in the Seliger Forum, organized by the Kremlin for pro-Kremlin youth movements. But it was *Nashi*, one of these movements, that had organized the provocative actions against British Ambassador Anthony Brenton a few years back. I witnessed these events myself.

True, the British Council soon reconsidered, but the very fact that this organization, which had been put under pressure, even considered supporting pro-Kremlin movements aroused mixed feelings in me. I note also that various foreign businesses are reported to have supported the Seliger Forum, for instance Cisco and Mercedes-Benz, in sufficient degree for them to have been claimed by *Nashi* as sponsors.

I recently read an interview with your foreign minister, William Hague, in which he said what seemed to be the right things. He spoke of the need to "support our values." But sometimes rhetoric like this plays just a ritual role. How would you react to this?

ANDREW: British policy has, of course, always been absolutely splendid, and particularly when I was ambassador. But then we have rarely had warm or close relations with official Moscow. I did not and do not think that this was of prime importance.

London has never been inclined, in my view at least, to pursue good bilateral relations just for the sake of them. The United Kingdom has been a convenient substitute for the United States when the Kremlin needs someone to beat up on. London's influence in Brussels is not that great. We are less prone than some others to make general rhetorical statements. On the other hand, the United Kingdom has considerable investments in Russia, a large Russian expatriate community, a significant cultural role, and is for Russia a financial center of great weight. We presently come under the Russian truncheon for our refusal to extradite a number of Russian citizens accused by Moscow of various crimes, coupled naturally with our refusal simply to waive the right to try in London people accused of brutal murders or other crimes in our country. But I believe, and I certainly hope, that our attachment to the law commands respect in Russia. In general, the British attitude toward Russia's present regime is more reserved than many of those on the Continent. We are, if you like, honorary Nordics here.

Nothing that happened during or after the Hague visit in 2010 leads me to think otherwise. Nor do I suppose that our prime minister's September 2011 visit will change the fundamentals, though if smiles are still in fashion by then, he will no doubt come with some in his baggage. Of course we shall want to work with Russia where we usefully and properly can, but "reset" is not a very British word, and David Cameron has been rather forthright in his support for those in the Arab world who have opposed their local tyrants.

LILIA: British respect for the law and British reservations with regard to the Russian regime really do command respect.

I would like to mention the "duality" in the Russian elite's attitude toward the United Kingdom. The Kremlin is annoyed and irritated by London, no doubt about that. At the same time, numerous Russian oligarchs and officials happily live in the United Kingdom. Moreover, they have learned to live there while abiding by British laws, which means that we are not a totally hopeless nation! Our task is now to teach our officials and businesspeople to do the same in Russia.

I suggest we move to the East now. The "new" Europe—that is, the former communist states in Central and Eastern Europe and the Baltic republics—until recently played an important part in forcing Brussels and other European capitals to think about values with respect to Russia. This was especially true of Poland, Lithuania, and the other Baltic states. But the Kremlin's adroit efforts over the past two years to give Russia a new image and its success in repairing relations, first of all with Warsaw, have paid off, effectively neutralizing criticism by the "new Europeans."

Normalization with Poland was crucial for the Kremlin. Two factors played a big part here: first, the spring 2010 plane crash that killed Polish President Lech Kaczynski and a large number of the Polish elite near Smolensk, along with Moscow's reaction to this tragedy; and second, Moscow's decision to settle the Katyn issue—that is, the case of the more than 20,000 Polish officers, prisoners of war, killed by the Stalin regime in 1940. President Kaczynski and the others had been on their way to a commemoration of the anniversary of the Katyn executions—what a strange and tragic twist of fate! Putin and Medvedev managed to find the right words of condolence after the crash. This touched many people in

Poland and opened the way toward warmer relations. As an aside, what does it say about the Russian authorities and Russia when even words of ordinary human feeling on their part are treated as an extraordinary event?

ANDREW: Your striking aside speaks for itself. It reminds me of Putin's rapid call to Bush after 9/11. Much was made of that, too.

LILIA: As for the Katyn tragedy, the Kremlin took a clever line. Putin, though not without reservations, admitted Stalin's responsibility for these executions. Medvedev, for his part, called for de-Stalinization and the need to recognize the past and put it behind us. The Russian elite had clearly decided to let go of Stalin, at least in Russia's relations with other countries. This step made it possible for Warsaw to engineer a reset of its own.

ANDREW: This is a positive development. At the end of 2010, the Russian Duma issued a declaration condemning the Katyn massacre and for the first time blamed Stalin for the execution of the Polish officers. "We strongly condemn that regime, which despised people's rights and lives, and offer friendship to the Polish people and hope for a new era in our mutual relations," the resolution said. This was a long-awaited step. But I believe that Russian school textbooks still call Stalin an "effective manager" and credit him with victory in the Great Fatherland War. There is a long way to go before we can truly speak of de-Stalinization.

LILIA: You touched on a serious issue that has controversial implications. The Duma did indeed condemn the Katyn massacre, and this really could have been a positive development. But … with the Russian leaders, there is always a hidden "but." The resolution itself had a diplomatic purpose and was intended to create a positive atmosphere for Medvedev's visit to Poland in December 2010. More generally it was intended to help the Kremlin create a positive image for Russia in Europe. It would not be an exaggeration to say that Poland became the Kremlin's key to opening European hearts. However, the Russian side, having talked the talk, refused to walk the walk—that is, it refused to declassify the archives relating to the Katyn massacre, which are still under seal, by order of the general prosecutor. One can't help but conclude that the Russian authorities always want to stop short of modifying their long-standing attitudes.

True, Medvedev went further than Putin in denouncing Stalin's crimes. But this denunciation hasn't led to a policy of complete de-Stalinization of Russian political life. I would even argue that Medvedev was more cautious in addressing the crimes of Stalin's era than Khrushchev, Gorbachev, or Yeltsin. Medvedev has not admitted (yet) the need for condemnation of Stalin's crimes in a court of law or the need to make re-Stalinization a crime. That is why there are hardly any serious grounds to compare the Russian-Polish reconciliation process to the German-French and German-Polish reconciliation process. Those latter two acquired a strong basis in fact because all the states involved abide by a common set of standards.

ANDREW: This is a deeply painful and important subject. True de-Stalinization is not a mere matter of using the right words to describe Katyn. It would involve the Russian population as a whole facing up to the realities of what was done in their name over the years, and the emptiness of the ideals that persuaded so many of them to make such huge sacrifices and enact such cruelties. The present authorities have no serious inclination to ask any such thing of them. There is nothing surprising in that. There was a time for a more open approach, but that time has passed now. Russia has been encouraged to see itself as the heir to the Soviet Union, not a newly liberated state. Those in the West who claim to see the official rhetoric about Katyn as the beginning of a true accounting are likely to be disappointed. It would be wrong to oversell it.

LILIA: I think so, too. Stalin's total condemnation would undermine the system of personalized power that still does exist and the Russian elite is not ready for this. If you denounce Stalin completely—that is, using judicial means—then you have to go further and start asking questions about current personalized power. Thus ambiguity on Stalin and his rule remains.

Anyway, I had a number of debates with my Polish friends about the nature of a "turnaround" in our respective countries' relations. My Polish colleagues interpreted the Kremlin's steps as a sign that the Russian regime was liberalizing and reconciliation with Poland was the first step in this process. I argued that this was no more than a change of tactics and of image in the Kremlin's policies toward its neighbors; in reality there has been no real de-Stalinization in Russia.

I maintained that it was good to see positive changes in Russian-Polish relations, but this progress did not signify change in the Russian domestic and foreign policy paradigm itself.

ANDREW: It is natural that there should be changes of mood and pace from time to time, and the previous Polish government had a generally shorter fuse than the one we have now. Of course, if it turns out that Russia has taken a decisive and lasting step toward liberalization, as your friends believe, then we can expect that Poland, along with other Western powers, will find it easier to work with Moscow, whatever the traumas of the past. But we aren't securely there yet.

Besides, the results of the investigation of the plane crash, which were made public by the Russian authorities in January 2011 and which put all the blame on the Poles, inevitably eroded the good faith between Moscow and Warsaw. The Moscow report made Polish Prime Minister Donald Tusk and all those in the Polish government who were actively engaged in normalization with Russia look a bit too trusting in the eyes of many of their fellow countrymen.

LILIA: This report demonstrated that Russia still follows the old Soviet principle that Moscow can't be wrong. If Moscow were ever wrong, it would never admit it. Moreover, there is another axiom this sad story has proved, which is that all Western leaders who engage closely with the Kremlin put both their reputations and their public approval at risk. Look at what happened to Schröder and Chirac, and look what is happening now to Berlusconi and Sarkozy. The same thing could happen to Tusk.

Both "old" and "new" Europe are united in their desire to "reset" relations with Moscow. That might have been positive in and of itself.

But again, there is a big "if": if only this European ambition were not limited to naked realpolitik coupled with a desire to avoid rubbing Moscow the wrong way. One could understand why Europe, bogged down in its own problems, doesn't feel ready to pressure Russia on ethical standards. This, however, does not explain why Europeans take such an active part in the Russian elite's "massage" sessions. If they just stuck to a restrained "realism," I would not object. But "Realism Plus" is too much for me to swallow.

The European Union, acting under Germany's influence, has initiated a "Partnership for Modernization" with Russia (a program you've mentioned already) that appears to be even more pathetic than the previous Partnership and Cooperation Agreement. It's pathetic not only because it has no implementation mechanism; it's also flawed because partnership in pursuit of a chimera will yield exactly zero results.

Anyway, Europe's involvement in the efforts to "renew" Russia without using strong conditionality will amount to nothing more than another session of the game "Let's Pretend."

Does a policy of connivance even have a chance of achieving EU interests? Charles Grant once observed, "Russia presents a test case for the EU's ambition to run a coherent and effective foreign policy, and it is a test that the EU is failing." Even I must admit that, with respect to individual European countries' short-term interests in areas like energy and security, a policy of accommodation could pay some dividends. If we are talking about strategic issues, however, it is unsustainable, because it will only serve to block the incentives that could make Russia a true European state.

ANDREW: Russians are not fools and have a highly sensitive nose for hypocrisy. So Moscow will be quick to see through any attempt by the European Union to collect dividends through a policy of "Let's Pretend." The only way that European companies or investors will put a notable portion of their money in Russia is if in so doing they will get a better return than they would if they put it elsewhere. No gilded words of partnership or modernization can change that calculus. Foreigners may well be wrong about Russia or slow to catch on to the truth, but I believe they will get there in the end.

I agree with Charles Grant's conclusion about Russia being a test that the European Union is failing. I would only add that there are other tests that the European Union is having trouble passing, because they are too ambitious to be realistic. In the case of Russia, I can't quite see what a coherent and effective EU policy would be at present; there are too many crosscurrents. However, I would not go on from there to deny that there may be particular aspects where EU coordination can and does work—for instance, on energy security. The trouble with the European Union is that it is too keen to rush ahead to its own vision of a "bright future" to recognize the value of practical steps. Oliver Cromwell wisely said that a man goes never so far as when he knows not where he is going (or something very like that anyway).

LILIA: You've mentioned energy security. It remains contentious.

ANDREW: Absolutely! Moscow wants to opt out of the EU agenda of liberalizing European energy markets. Gazprom will fight hard to prevent it....

LILIA: That will be a moment of truth for Europe! By the way, quite a few representatives of the Baltic states have a critical view of EU policy toward Russia. I've recently been discussing European policy toward Russia with Marko Mihkelson, the former head of the Estonian delegation to the Parliamentary Assembly of the Council of Europe (PACE). "The ghost of Yalta is haunting Europe. There is a view among the big states that small states could be left in the Russian area of influence," he told me bitterly. Marko told me the story of his confrontation with former PACE chairman Rene van der Linden, whom Estonians accused of having "special" commercial interests in Russia. According to discussions in the media and on the Internet several years ago, van der Linden might have owned interests in a real estate project in the Vladimir region in Russia (V-park) worth 500 million euros. This fact allegedly accounted for his extremely warm attitude toward Moscow. Van der Linden strongly denied that he had any commercial interests in Russia. Regardless of its veracity, the story at a minimum proves that policy toward Russia remains a controversial issue in Europe. And regrettably, conflicts of interest among representatives of the European elite are not an unimaginable thing.

ANDREW: Your sense of humor has not deserted you … "not unimaginable." I'll say!

But of course the Baltic states have been exposed to pressure from Moscow over the years. In any case, I'm sure that debate about Russia will remain lively in the European Union and in the West in general.

LILIA: There is an optimistic trend, too. European civil society and nongovernmental organizations are increasingly concerned about what is happening in Russia. In 2009, PACE prepared a report on the judicial systems of various countries that focused mainly on the problem of the rule of law in Russia and the Russian courts' dependence on the executive branch. The European Court has heard several appeals by Mikhail Khodorkovsky of rulings against him by Russian courts. It also accepted a multibillion-dollar lawsuit brought by the former managers of his company, Yukos, which was essentially seized by the government after his conviction. Furthermore, the Parliamentary Assembly of the OSCE passed a resolution in July 2009 calling both Nazism and Stalinism totalitarian regimes. And the OSCE proclaimed August 23, the anniversary of the signing of the Molotov-Ribbentrop Pact, as an international day of remembrance for the victims of Stalinism and Nazism. The OSCE proclamation was followed later that year by the German parliament's near-unanimous passage of a resolution in support of Khodorkovsky—a measure I applaud because it demonstrated that not all Germans have caught either the "guilt" virus or the "accommodation" virus.

ANDREW: The European Court plays a vital role. The number of appeals it has received regarding rulings from Russian courts is a standing tribute to that, as well as a rebuke to Russia. I have seen reports that the chairman of the Russian Constitutional Court, Valery Zorkin, is arguing based on a strained precedent from the German Constitutional Court that Russian appeals ought to be restricted. I cannot wish him well in that.

LILIA: That is true. Zorkin even threatened that Russian law would have precedence over international and European law. If this is so, I wonder how Russia could ever expect to be a member of international and European institutions?

I would like to mention another German initiative. I've been so critical of the official German position on Russia that I should definitely balance that out by mentioning positive signs. Andreas Schockenhoff, the coordinator of German-Russian intersocietal cooperation, has begun forming the grounds for closer cooperation between European (not just German) civil society groups and their Russian counterparts. His idea is to create real cooperation between them without state control or any kind of supervision. This would differentiate it from the U.S.-Russian civil society dialogues, which have fallen under the control of American and Russian officials. Schockenhoff is ready to make a critical review of existing EU programs and funding mechanisms, and he is ready to listen to what representatives of Russian civil society are saying.

ANDREW: The European Parliament strongly criticized the second guilty verdict on Khodorkovsky and Lebedev. Jerzy Buzek, president of the European Parliament, said, "The trials of Mikhail Khodorkovsky were the litmus test of how the rule of law and human rights are treated in today's Russia." The European Parliament's subcommittee on human rights called for sanctions against the Russian officials responsible for the trial. Even the European Commission condemned the trial this time. High Representative of the European Union for Foreign Affairs and Security Policy Catherine Ashton said that the

> ... independence of courts and every citizen's right to a fair trial specified by the European Convention on Human Rights signed by Russia bear decisive importance for the strategic partnership between the European Union and Russia. Supremacy of the law is the cornerstone of the Partnership for Modernization program.

By and large, these words constitute a warning to Russia from the European Union. They indicate that there can be no strategic partnership as long as Russia lacks truly independent courts. U.S. State Department spokesman Mark Toner made an analogous statement. American media outlets quoted an unidentified representative of the Obama administration who said that the sentence in question would complicate the process of Russia's entry into the World Trade Organization.

That, of course, was then, not now.

LILIA: We should mention the extremely vital role that some European deputies have played—first of all, the chair of the subcommittee on human rights, Heidi Hautala; the members of the Alliance of Liberals and Democrats for Europe (ALDE), headed by Guy Verhofstadt, Annemie Neyts, and Kristiina Ojuland; and the European Greens. All of these groups have been playing a crucial role in persuading the European Parliament to address issues of human rights and democracy in Russia. Thanks to them, these issues are on the European agenda in a way that the Euro-bureaucrats have trouble ignoring.

Hautala has said, "There is no way to trust all talks of modernization in a country where the judiciary is so political that the law is openly defied," Hautala added. Ojuland, joined by a group of European parliamentarians, called on the Parliament to consider visa restrictions and economic sanctions against Russian state functionaries involved in the unfair verdict. "Sanctions are the only way to make the Russian authorities respect the law.... I believe that the Russians deserve better than that. Like the Europeans, they are entitled to life in a country where human rights are respected and where there is but one law for all," she said.

ANDREW: In June 2011, the European Parliament adopted a resolution calling on the Russian authorities to guarantee fair and free elections to the Duma in December 2011 and the presidency in March 2012.

LILIA: There are forces in Europe that want to strengthen its normative power. Even if Europe's political leadership have not yet disavowed their "pragmatism" they have at least been made to feel uncomfortable about it.

REALPOLITIK VERSUS CONSTRUCTIVE REALISM

ANDREW: We should not forget that the changing balance between Asia and the rest of the world will also affect the relationship between Russia and the West. I do not, however, think that the changes in Asia will make Russia less important as a question for the West—probably the reverse: The rise of China is disturbing for an already insecure country. Russia likes to think of itself as a Eurasian power, and so it is, geographically. But it is a minor power for Asia, and not one that can call on China, for obvious reasons, as a counterbalance to the West, leaving aside tactical maneuvers. Thus we have been right to concentrate on the trans-European and transatlantic relationship. What do you think, Lilia, about the weight Moscow assigns to Russian-Western interdependence?

LILIA: There are two ways I could respond to this question. One is to follow the geopolitical route and say that, of course, the threat of a rising China, an uncertain Central Asia, an aggressive Iran, and an unstable Pakistan may push Russia toward Europe and the West. At the moment, Moscow is still trying to play the role of arbiter in the former Soviet space, or rather it is trying to mime this role, pretending not to notice that it is becoming a junior partner to China. Zbigniew Brzezinski's prophecy about Russia ending in China's shadow is coming true. In the end the Russian elite will be forced to make security arrangements with the West.

ANDREW: I do not think we can be sure about that. It depends how Russia develops in the meantime.

LILIA: Dialogues, even alliances, forged on the basis of security concerns are always fragile. The Soviet Union's alliance with various Western states during World War II did not prevent the Cold War.

Another approach is to look at the Russian/Western relationship from the normative angle. We have to take into account the geopolitical aspect, of course, when looking on from this angle. But this vantage point also gives us enough elevation to look farther ahead to Russia's trajectory. If Russia limits its dialogue with the West only to geopolitical and geoeconomic interests, it will continue to stagnate. Moreover, the Russian system of personalized power will scarcely allow Moscow to preserve Russia in its current geographical format. Only by accepting Western standards can Russia expect its relationship with the West to help guarantee not only its prosperity but also to protect its territorial integrity.

For the time being, both sides—Russia and the West—must regrettably build their relationship on two outdated sacred cows, "common interests" and "engagement."

ANDREW: Both of these terms are banal and devoid of concrete meaning. They also play into the idea of two separate blocs, which is misleading, though dear to a number of theorists who are haunted by the past. Perhaps we should once again raise our glasses to Peace and Friendship.

LILIA: Indeed! Both premises come from the Cold War period. Then, they were useful. The West and the Soviet Union had certain mutual interests (though not many), and they cooperated, above all, in the security area. Engagement was crucial for preserving the world order. However, the old understanding of these premises does not work today; in fact, it encourages dangerous illusions. With regard to "common interests," these do indeed exist: Russian society is as interested in prosperity and stability as Western society. The Russian elite, however, have their own unique understanding of "common interests." Contrary to official Western and Russian statements, both sides hold different views on terrorism, nuclear nonproliferation, missile defense, European security, Iran, and energy security. This does not mean that their positions must clash all the time. On occasion, they align temporarily, as they did with the New START treaty, but even this temporary alignment touches on difficult points of contention (missile defense being the hardest among them). And what is more, if the interests between the West and Russia are indeed common, then why should the two sides be forced to make tradeoffs when addressing these interests?

ANDREW: The whole trouble with this general approach is that the categories so piously invoked are so vague as to have no content. I am reminded of a Hollywood film of some years ago about an FBI agent who posed as a contestant in a beauty pageant to conduct her investigation. Naturally, she finished as first runner-up, but in the last round, which was supposed to test intelligence, she was asked what she wanted most in all the world. She began to reply that she would like all criminals locked up and the keys to be thrown away, but realized that this was not the right way forward, so turned like all the other contestants to say with her prettiest smile, "World Peace." Who could be against that? And what could it possibly mean?

The real problem with "common interests" is that no country has defined interests. Those proclaimed by the foreign policy establishment of Russia are based on assumptions as to what Russia's position in the world ought to be rather than what it actually is, let alone what the best interests of its people would be. I don't see why the rest of us, including those who live in Russia's desired area of privileged interest, should share the Moscow foreign policy establishment's perception that such a sphere is justified.

In short, you can only proceed by looking at concrete instances of policymaking. The same goes for the parallel idea of engagement. The Soviet Union was after all engaged in 1939 to 1945 with Nazi Germany as ally, enemy, and victor, which would seem to cover most categories of engagement.

But of course one does not have to go to quite such lengths to make the point that engagement is a necessary and ongoing process, particularly within Europe. The question is what sort of engagement, with whom, and about what. If you look across all European societies, then you see we are all closely engaged across most fields of life, and a good thing, too. Politically, however, things are more narrowly focused, and different countries have different outlooks. It is a distortion to my mind that Russia's leaders fixate on their relationship with the United States.

LILIA: Definitely. We should ask ourselves several questions: What is engagement supposed to be? Is it a goal in itself? Or is it a means to achieve an agenda? I think that for both of us "engagement" has to achieve definite goals.

If that is so, then we are faced with a new question: What kind of goals? Do we want to preserve the status quo or to push things in another direction? And which direction, exactly? For my part, I would say that we Russians should look to see whether or not a particular foreign policy agenda helps Russia to transform itself. Do, for instance, New START, cooperation on Iran, Gazprom pipelines to Europe, Medvedev's security initiative, and so forth help Russia to build a more prosperous and just society? If we look at things this way, we might well come to a variety of conclusions about engagement.

I assume that Western leaders are also capable of viewing cooperation with Russia from both short-term and long-term perspectives.

ANDREW: Undoubtedly. We have quite good short-term cooperation now, after a very bad period a couple of years ago. There are many in the West who hope, and because of that are tempted to believe, that this will transform Russia's relationship with the West on a long-term basis. It would be wise to see this as working in a pattern that goes beyond Russia. There are quite a lot of "known unknowns" that would have to go right for us to break out of the usual pattern of cyclical change coupled with increasing but often unremarked-upon interdependence.

LILIA: You've noticed, of course, that "engagement" is often understood in a technocratic way—that is, as the need to create as many channels of interaction as possible, such as commissions, joint groups, and so forth. The technocratic approach is especially popular in Russia. Officials here love to set up commissions. The West and Russia have already established dozens of joint commissions along the lines of the Gore-Chernomyrdin Commission of the 1990s to address immediate issues. But these commissions failed to prevent the crisis in relations between Russia and the West in 2008.

What we end up with is a situation in which politicians and experts spend a huge amount of time trying to intensify cooperation with Russia in various areas like security, economic cooperation, and civil society. They meet, draft reports, and make recommendations. If we look closely at these recommendations, we see that they differ little from the numerous recommendations of the 1990s, which failed to guarantee stable cooperation.

I am not saying that we should not talk, but it is time to realize that cooperation based on the old principles—namely, talking only about what brings us closer together and leaving aside what sets us apart—is a waste of time.

ANDREW: I have always been glad not to have served on these bodies. I do not have the patience. Multilateral diplomacy is necessary but enormously tedious. But the true dialogue between nations is more complex than that. I have faith, too, in what escapes governments.

LILIA: I believe that, if the West were suddenly to acquire the collective will, then it would be perfectly capable of pursuing multiple lines simultaneously: stressing interests, offering a values-based approach, trying to contain Russian traditionalists, and supporting liberalization. Now, both sides prefer the easy way. Kissinger should be happy since realpolitik is just as alive today as it was twenty years ago! This says something important about the political world and its tendency to respond to new challenges with old solutions.

ANDREW: Yes, but it is not just in relation to Russia that old suppositions outlive their validity. I remember saying earlier in our discussion that Western countries often failed to understand Russia properly. I added at some stage, or meant to add, that Russia was also often mistaken in projecting onto the West its own assumptions about what makes countries and their leaders tick. One result is that there is often a time lag before the truth dawns, by which time, if you like, the truth has moved on. Realpolitik is often founded on a rather static interpretation of what is happening in the country, countries, or area to which it is applied. Its purpose is to reach lasting bargains. It is not well suited in its cruder forms to dealing with countries in or approaching development crises like, it seems to me, Russia. Anyway, even if that assessment is wrong, as far as Russia is concerned, the present Cold War–inherited and traditional approach will not last.

LILIA: Meanwhile, the realists are trying to revamp their doctrine. Twenty years ago, they didn't use the "disentanglement" principle to brush aside domestic developments in the countries they were dealing with. They simply separated cooperation from the ideological struggle. Thus Reagan sought ways to cooperate with the Soviet Union even as he pressed America's ideological offensive forward. The new realists act as if domestic policy doesn't even exist. Moreover, they totally cleanse the foreign policy agenda of any unpleasant and inconvenient linkages.

ANDREW: That is very unrealistic of them, and I suppose they would not admit to it.

LILIA: Look, Western leaders talk about arms control, European security, and energy security while ignoring the consequences of the Russian-Georgian War, as if that episode was just a bad dream. Meanwhile, in the real world of interdependency, all of these issues are linked. Ensuring the security of oil and gas supplies out of the Caspian Sea region is of a piece with guaranteeing stability in Georgia. Stability in Georgia depends on the resolution of all outstanding issues with regard to Georgian territorial integrity and instability in the Russian Northern Caucasus. These two issues, in turn, are directly tied to Russian domestic developments. Economic cooperation with Russia can't move forward without there being a positive environment for foreign investments, and achieving this would require doing away with the fusion of power and property in Russia. In sum, enhancing European security depends on the Russian elite's rejecting the "besieged fortress" paradigm. One cannot avoid the domestic dimension!

The paradox (one of many) is that those who believe in the need to "untie" foreign policy from the internal situation argue that "engagement" would positively influence domestic developments! But how can this be true if the initial premise is to "de-link" the domestic and international areas?

ANDREW: Foreign policies do not develop in a vacuum, and diplomacy is not a chess game. It follows that, if you do not know what is going on in a country, you are acting blind. It also follows that, although you have to be careful, at least in the sense that you should not go beyond what may be effective, you will want to influence the internal situation in your partner's country. People arguing for greater engagement with Russia also tend to interpret the main obstacle to this as being a lack of trust—as if this were a major discovery or a concrete matter to be resolved by goodwill alone. I find this attitude exasperating. Anyway, in the end it goes to your point, that domestic and foreign policies are intimately linked. As we all know, Reagan was right to say, "Trust, but verify."

A November 29, 2010, article in *Vlast* usefully summarized how closely the Soviet and Russian periods of rapprochement with the West coincided with periods of internal economic difficulty for Moscow, and how quickly they were reversed when the internal situation eased. The oil price was high when the Soviet Union invaded Afghanistan; troops were withdrawn at a time of Soviet economic collapse. Most of the Yeltsin period was one of Russian-Western warmth, with NATO's action over Kosovo being the exception that proves the rule; Putin's terms saw a close relationship when oil was $18–24 per barrel and changed to hostility as the price rose to $80. And then, in 2008, when oil was $147 per barrel, there was military action against Georgia.

This is not to say that the price of oil, the present-day determinant of the Russian economy, is the sole reason for the current degree of re-evaluation in Moscow of its attitude toward the West, but the pattern is suggestive. And it is certainly proof, if proof were needed, that internal and external policies are cut from a single cloth.

LILIA: Andrew, this is the point that you've emphasized all along. I support it without hesitation.

As for realpolitik, it is a decidedly unrealistic policy. Allow me to quote Robert Kagan, who says that realism "does not fit reality." Here is what he argues:

> The nature of a country's regime does matter: not only as a moral issue, but also as a strategic one. That's because ideology is often decisive in shaping the foreign policies of other nations. Ideology determines their ambitions. It is through an ideological lens that countries determine who their friends are. Even a government's perception of its interests is shaped by the nature of the regime.

ANDREW: This is so obviously true that it ought not to need saying, though I suppose that Kagan is using the word *ideology* flexibly. It is also a central theme of Kissinger's most recent book *On China*, in which he examines that country's inner nature and what that means for other countries in managing their relationships, good or bad, with Beijing.

LILIA: Both sides tried in 2010–2011 to broaden the notion of "reset." In principle, the intention was noble. We know, however, that the best of intentions often bring unexpected results.

ANDREW: "The best-laid schemes o' mice an' men gang aft agley." It was popular to quote Robert Burns in Soviet times so I do it again now. But I suppose that it was natural for the Americans at any rate to try to find out if the reset could be developed to embody their wider hopes. In practice it has amounted to little more than clearing away some accumulated tensions, with the hopes of greater achievement remaining unrealized.

LILIA: I would like to mention in this context the idea of a "Strategic Union" between Russia and Europe that has been lobbied for by Sergei Karaganov and Igor Yurgens, who called for the creation of an energy union, and then for a single Russia-EU market. One could get behind this idea, if not for one very important detail. What would the basis of such a "union" be if Russia does not change its standards?

Another idea was to expand NATO-Russia strategic cooperation, up to the point of partial integration, or even endorsement, of Russia's NATO membership. A number of German authors have proposed this idea. The latest interpretation of "NATO-Russia dating" was Oksana Antonenko and Igor Yurgens's suggestion of a "NATO-Russia strategic concept," along with a list of "confidence-building measures." I guess attempts to lay plans for some form of dating or even marriage will multiply so long as we are in the "reset" mood.

Andrew, I know that you have followed these initiatives. What is your take?

ANDREW: All these ideas leap from the presently available to a general proposition based on extrapolating from current realities to a Bright Future. A free trade arrangement with the European Union has been on offer to Russia for decades. The obstacles to it are or ought to be obvious, including the impact it would have on a Russia that is already importing heavily because of domestic economic weakness. Let us see what happens when (fingers crossed) Russia finally dares to enter the World Trade Organization and adjusts during its transition period. An energy union would be a union of opposites. While nothing is to be excluded by way of political foolishness, the European Union would be unwise to hook up even more closely to a controlling, expensive, and opaque monopoly like Gazprom. Germany's decision after the Japanese disaster at Fukushima to close its nuclear power stations may of course increase its dependence on Russian gas, despite French nuclear power being a reserve for Germany.

NATO is an alliance of democratic states. Russia is ruled by a narrow and secretive group. There is a long way to go before strategic cooperation between two such entities could work, if we mean something significant by those portentous words. There is no way around this without deep political change in Russia, including change in its attitude toward its neighbors.

The November 2010 NATO-Russia Summit in Lisbon has been described as (another) breakthrough. Its atmospherics were good, but its concrete achievements were less than the rhetoric implied. The summit produced a list of areas where further cooperation should be pursued; these areas were, for the most part, familiar. The exception was the idea of working together on an anti-ballistic missile system, which would be an attractive, perhaps even transforming, project if it could be made to work. However, Medvedev put a condition on it, as Russia has with all other issues coming under a NATO-Russia umbrella. The condition sounds at first hearing quite plausible:

> Our participation should be absolutely that of equals.... We either participate in full, exchange information, and are responsible for solving this or that problem, or we don't participate at all. But if we don't participate at all, then we for obvious reasons will be forced to protect ourselves.

It is hard to interpret this as anything other than a demand for a veto—a demand that makes full cooperation impractical.

NATO and Russia are also far apart in agreeing on what they mean by a joint anti-ballistic missile policy. The Russian side offers a so-called sectoral principle, in which each side would be responsible for covering one direction or another. Russia, as I understand it, would cover missiles transiting its territory and the territory of several East European countries, some of them NATO members. That would make the West reliant on protection from a country that might or might not wish to provide it, and in any case is at present incapable of doing so. Russia still chooses to see a NATO anti-ballistic missile system in Europe covering NATO countries as an inherent threat to its security. Numbers and geography point the other way, but Moscow is not to be persuaded.

At Lisbon, Medvedev also demanded deep technological exchanges. It seems unlikely that the United States, or the West as a whole, for that matter, would lightly transfer valuable secrets to Russia, knowing that the return for such generosity would be meager at best. Russia has refused to withdraw its assertion that NATO represents an imminent threat. NATO for its part has had no problem declaring that it does not see Russia as an enemy.

So I think that the schemes drawn up by a number of people are fanciful, absent true modernization in Russia. This includes those schemes describing poles of various length and credibility. Russia is one country among many, for all its ambitions to the contrary. Both the West and Russia have a tendency to look at it as though it were still the Soviet

Union, a tendency that distorts our thinking. One step at a time is the way to go, not rearranging an imaginary chessboard.

LILIA: Two credible observers take a similar view to yours on the NATO-Russia partnership. James Sherr thought that the Lisbon attempts were "unlikely to transform the relationship" and that Russia "remains unreconciled to NATO's place in Europe and the world." Alexander Goltz wrote that "with Russia refusing in principle to retract its assertion that NATO represents an imminent threat, Moscow's cooperation with the Alliance is doomed to be limited in scope."

I have to admit that, while reading optimistic assertions that joint anti-ballistic missile and other security cooperation instruments can lead to "friendship" between Russia and NATO, I often find it hard to avoid the impression that I've either missed something important or I'm living in a different universe! How could Russia and NATO build a joint missile defense when Russia and the United States still exist under a regime of mutually assured destruction? As leading Russian analyst Alexei Arbatov says, Russian air and space defense is viewed by the Kremlin not as a deterrent but as a means "to prepare for a major war against the main powers and alliances in the world"(!). It's as if they were planning to bed down together with each one's hands at the other's throat. The latter action makes the former sound less than pleasant.

I want to remind us that the Russian ruling tandem stubbornly shoots itself in the foot while it attempts to pursue "realism with a smiling face." Neither Putin nor Medvedev misses an opportunity to threaten Russia's Western partners, saying that if the West does not accept Russia's proposals, Russia will return to a containment policy. I will quote one of Putin's relentless warnings:

> If there are only negative reactions to all of our proposals [on ABM, on European security], and if a threat emerges on our borders in the form of a new incarnation if the Third Site programme, Russia will just have to protect itself using various means, including the deployment of new systems to counter the new threats and the development of new nuclear-missile technology.

These warnings prove that "reset with a smiling face" isn't sustainable unless the West gives in to the Russian demands. The problem is that even if the West accepts Russia's demands, there will inevitably be new ones. The Kremlin can't afford to be agreeable; if it were, it would lose a pretext to make further demands and get angry when those are rejected. This is one of the key factors defining Russia's traditional consolidation.

ANDREW: There are some who take these sorts of outbursts from both Medvedev and Putin as mere posturing to placate internal critics. After all, they reason, Russia is in no position to start a new arms race, and the country's leaders know that perfectly well. I suppose that in their less emotional moments they also realize that the United States, let alone its European partners in NATO, has neither interest nor reason to take this guff about a new arms race seriously. The same goes for the wholly artificial fuss about NATO having plans to defend the Baltic states if need be, talked up immediately after the Lisbon Summit in November 2010 by Dmitri Rogozin (the Russian representative to NATO), Lavrov, and some Russian military figures, along with demands that they be repudiated or revoked. What else would you expect? The Baltic states are NATO members. In any case these contingency plans have been in place for some time, and publicly mentioned, too, including by President Obama.

However, I do not think that posturing is a sufficient explanation, though it is a plausible one. If comments like these are needed to reassure hostile domestic critics, then that in itself is a fact worth remembering. One must conclude in that case that either the famous power vertical is not in good order or that it wants to hedge its bets by threatening the very Western partners with which it claims to want a new relationship. As with Putin's interview with Larry King, which we have already noted, it shows an ingrained feeling in Moscow against the West in general and the United States in particular. Medvedev spoke in similar, if less direct, terms when he was in Vladikavkaz in February 2011 talking about how "they" had plans to split up Russia and so on. He talked about the "disintegration" of the Arab states and he concluded, "We have to confront the truth. They (!) had prepared such a scenario for us even earlier. And today they (!) will continue trying to implement it." On the face of it, this is so absurd as to suggest that he, or Putin, for that matter, cannot really mean what he is saying. However, I suspect that there is more to it than that. Russian spokespeople have continued to bang the logically unconvincing drum of Western ABM plans being a threat to Russia, coupled with claims that these will provoke a significant response from Moscow. We seem to be living in a parallel universe on this. The West has no military designs on Russia, none of the ideas for ABM systems would in reality affect Russian military potential even if the West had such ideas, and yet senior Russians seem still to feel the amputated limb of a confrontation that spluttered to its end in 1989.

LILIA: Without any doubt, "they" in Russian parlance means the West and first of all America. Well, yes—and it was interesting how quickly Putin began to press the anti-American button after Western countries, with support from the Arab world, set up the UN-endorsed no-fly zone for Libya. His references to U.S. aggression—"crusaders"(!) are becoming a persistent tic. Quite a few observers in the West saw Putin's references to Kosovo, Iraq, and Afghanistan as preludes to Libya as putting him at odds with Medvedev, who argued that using words like "crusader" was wrong. In Moscow most people saw all of this as moves in their habitual dance without drawing much of a conclusion about how power was or was not shifting between them. After all, dealing with the Libyan issue presented difficulties for Moscow, so mixed messages had their uses. Both Putin and Medvedev had an interest in looking cooperative in the eyes of the West, or at least not totally obstructionist, while also promoting their domestic agendas by appealing to anti-Western sentiment at home. They will also have had an eye on preserving a relationship with Qaddafi in case the colonel wins, while protecting a Russian presence in Libya in case he loses. This is all but one more example of tactics—and rather transparent ones at that—trumping strategy. Moscow's later refusal to support the French-British resolution on Syria only proved that the Russian tandem's willingness to be cooperative with the West has its limits.

ANDREW: This story still has some time to run, but I agree that Russia's approach has been ambivalent, raising questions as to how far Moscow really wants to engage with Western countries. They cannot like it that NATO has taken on a formal role in implementing UN Resolution 1973 for Libya.

LILIA: I want to bring to your attention another "engagement" effort. I have in mind a report of the European Council of Foreign Relations entitled "The Spectre of a Multipolar Europe." It is not untypical of its genre, but worth singling out because it illustrates two problems with a general way of thinking. First, it shows how some ideas that look appealing at first sight lack real substance when considered more deeply against present and likely future realities. And second because its underlying assumptions can lead prominent figures unwittingly to argue in favor of what would in practice turn out to be an anti-Western paradigm.

The authors suggest as the basis of "multipolar Europe" the strategic triangle of Europe-Russia-Turkey, with Russia becoming one of the "poles." What does becoming a "pole" mean? It means creating a political galaxy, with the pole as the center of gravity and the dependent states as satellites orbiting around the center. Or perhaps there is another meaning of "pole"? If not, and if my first definition has it right, then this is a new incarnation of the Russian traditionalists' dream to have "areas of influence." We have already discussed that such "areas" will mean the preservation of personalized power in Russia. Is it what the architects of the "triangle" really want?

The idea of the "strategic triangle" is based on a belief that the West should "take advantage of a political opening created by Moscow's desire to modernize." But what if official Moscow has no desire "to modernize"?

By raising these questions, one can easily get labeled a Cold War throwback. This is why I hasten to add that the Russian liberals who highlight these issues are not masochists who long to return to a time when supporting Western ideas made one a "traitor to the state." We have to discuss the plausibility of such seemingly positive ideas and what they could bring in order to prevent the inevitable mutual frustration and its typical political repercussions.

As always, "accommodationist" projects are full of inconsistencies. You can't help but smile when you see something like this: the authors of the new "multipolarity" admit that Russia has "revisionist tendencies," but this does not stop them from arguing that it has to be a "pole." What an invention! A "revisionist pole"! Yevgeny Primakov, the former Russian premier and minister of foreign affairs, guru of Russian statists, and an active promoter of the idea of "multipolarity," has to be jealous of this new variation on his beloved "multipolarity." He would never have had the courage or imagination to go so far.... By the way, the Kremlin would love this idea and could perhaps borrow it to support Medvedev's security initiative.

ANDREW: I have probably been dismissive enough about these things already, but then I have never been educated in international relations, so maybe I am biased. I took history at Cambridge and spent most of my career in the British diplomatic service instead. So the patterns I look for are ones of probable or possible evolutionary trends rather than systemic constructs.

LILIA: I've been educated in international relations, which hasn't prevented me from being, shall we say, politically incorrect.

I think it is time to mention that the Russian elite believe that the Western political establishment has either accepted some of the Kremlin's conditions or is pretending to accept them, perhaps temporarily at least. Or the Russian authorities interpret Western political circles' behavior as acceptance of the Kremlin's conditions.

This is the way the Russian elite perceive the West's position. Sergei Karaganov, for example, has said many times that, "although the USA publicly denies the fact, it has essentially recognized a Russian sphere of interest in the former Soviet area and has stopped attempting to prevent Russia from strengthening its position in this region." We've already discussed the fact that Western leaders try to close their eyes to what is happening inside Russia, which the Russian elite also take as a sign of the West's being ready to find it acceptable.

Andrew, perhaps you can tell us whether we are interpreting Western behavior correctly in this case.

ANDREW: I understand why Karaganov says that, and why he is not alone in believing it. But there are a couple of assumptions here that are questionable. The first reflects the idea that the former Soviet states are the subject of a contest between Russia and the West. That is a bedrock assumption in many Russian minds. It is wrong. Russia can strengthen its position where it likes, provided that it does so with the genuine and revocable consent of the countries affected. Moscow's forcing its policies on others is a different matter entirely. Its rights in this are no different from the rights of the United Kingdom to build up its relationships with other countries. And of course it follows that ex-Soviet countries are entitled to change their minds about Russia and to choose to develop their systems and attitudes in whatever way they wish, subject to international law. I repeat: Russia has no greater rights than other states. "Great Power" has no modern meaning.

Second, while it is the case that Ukraine has recently evolved in a way that is more pleasing to official Russia, that Georgia has been cowed, and that Western countries have to live with those facts, it does not follow that this will always be so, or that these outcomes are in the interest of a Russia that wishes to modernize.

LILIA: For a Russian liberal, it would be encouraging to hear that. Another question: I have the impression that there is a growing desire among various elites in both the West and Russia to believe that we are now living in a world better suited to the pursuit of short-term goals and pragmatism than longer-term ideals. If this is so, then perhaps we need a new crisis to force them to understand that we need to "think big" in order to respond to the new challenges. What do you think about the key mood?

ANDREW: I am rather averse to thinking big, as opposed to having steady attitudes, as you will have realized. The European Union thinks big, sometimes with poor results. I am merely English. Short-term goals can be valuable and, if achieved, they can alter the long-term context. Paying in advance in the hope of a big reward later can, equally, be a big mistake. Besides, for now Russia is in a somewhat short-term situation. To that degree, we have to wait and see what happens next.

However, I would not want that to be understood in a purely passive way. We have to hang on to the principal objective of securing the future of all of us in the transatlantic area, including Russia, which cannot depend only on unenforceable commitments not to fight each other, such as, for instance, those proposed by Medvedev for a new security architecture in Europe. There is absolutely no reason for us to be at real odds, and if there were, such treaties would be worth precisely nothing. But it is equally naïve to think that a patchwork approach between NATO and Russia such as is now under consideration can somehow transform itself into a merger between the Alliance and Russia. Bilateral negotiations do not work like that, if only because their very nature is to preserve the identity of two separate sides—and in this case we have got some way by brushing over the differences between the two sides, which in turn makes future cooperation less certain as and when they re-emerge. We have to get away from the familiar, essentially Cold War idea, of two balancing entities in favor of a flexible and variable approach. That is why true modernization in Russia is in all of our interests, and why the great-power delusion is so dangerous.

I do not know what term to give this general idea. A lot of old brands have been discredited: "Neocons," "liberal interventionists," "democracy advocates," "realists." I do not believe that we are trying to coin a new "term," nor would I begin to claim that my general approach is at all original. Both of us, I think, would agree that we ought to abjure inherited or acquired illusions and to avoid creating a new mythology. However, you cannot have constructive realism tempered by regular questioning unless it is based on standards and norms. This is not a problem of definition but of substance. I perhaps am more inclined than you, Lilia, to argue for the pragmatic end of the policy spectrum within this overall approach; you seem to place more emphasis on the normative dimension. Of course, I have the luxury of living in a society more at ease with itself and its place in the world than yours. But we both support one axiom: foreign policy may have its own instruments, but its nature for each participant is to reflect the internal realities and preoccupations of that country. There is no way round this, and to treat international affairs as a separate and defined activity is delusional.

LILIA: I accept your arguments and I am quite happy with the policy of "constructive realism based on standards and norms." It resembles Francis Fukuyama's "Realistic Wilsonianism." I agree with you: we are not coining new "terms"; we are trying to unwrap new myths.

MYTHS
WHY DO PEOPLE BELIEVE THEM?

LILIA: There is another problem that has taken on a personal dimension for me: mass-scale involvement by Russian experts and intellectuals in creating illusions, empty stereotypes, and clichés about Russia that only confuse people, distort the real situation, and in this way help to legitimize the current system. Not everyone has taken part in this process, but all too many have.

The reason why so many Russian intellectuals agree to serve the authorities is a separate issue that requires a lengthy discussion of its own. The Russian experts who have placed their talents in the service of the personalized power system understand what they are doing of course. No doubt about that! The question is why are they doing this? Apparently, they do not believe that change is possible. Or perhaps they even fear that change will bring an uncertain future (for them), and they aspire to a comfortable life. These are all powerful incentives for taking part in the creation of myths about Russia. A conformist attitude has become an integral part of Russian life. It is hard to resist, especially when such conformism is well compensated. Indeed, the authorities have spared no expense to co-opt Russia's experts and intellectuals.

What is harder to understand is why Western politicians and experts are willing to help spread the myths the Russian elite and its intellectual entourage create. As I said, this issue has taken on a personal dimension for me, because in raising it I have lost some friends and irritated some of my colleagues, who have tried to persuade me not to spoil the amiable mood among the pundit class. Many suppose that efforts to make the normative dimension a part of political analysis are either a sign of radicalism, political incorrectness, or human rights activism, none of which have anything in common with objective academic or policy analysis. I am convinced, however, that we cannot understand the Russian situation and its main trends without a series of coordinates as a reference point. Only value-based norms can provide this scale.

ANDREW: I cannot be sure how I would behave if I were a Russian analyst or bureaucrat today, so I shall not try to judge, but I suppose there is a range of motives. Some will hope to work from within, as it were, by mixing advice, even liberal advice, into the sugarcoating of conformity. That would not be dishonorable in itself, though it may often be futile. Others will of course have a career to build and money to earn. But everyone is bound by what they have said before, by what others expect of them, and by the desire to be heard and understood correctly. The latter means adjusting the tone of what you say to what you think may be acceptable enough to get through. It is hard to change course. And the more stringent the criticism, the easier it is to dismiss it as disruptive, prejudiced, or impractical.

LILIA: The authorities' liberal rhetoric allows conformists to get through without too much damage to their reputation. Let's come back to the "intellectual product" they disseminate. I will list a few of the myths about Russia that my Russian colleagues have created and then spread in the West. I will repeat some of the main ones that I've been fighting for several years already, without much success:

"Russia is not ready for democracy." To be sure, quite a few Russians still have a vague understanding of democracy. However, significant numbers of Russians are capable of moving toward a freer society. Another cliché: "Democracy will come to Russia after capitalism, which is the determining factor." In fact, in Russia, economic growth and capitalist development have gone hand-in-hand with an anti-democratic drift. And what kind of capitalism is it when the economy is so closely tied to the regime? Here is one more cliché: "Russia is a unique country." Does this mean authoritarianism is inevitable there? This cliché became a conviction held by Western politicians: "Relations with Russia should be built on interests, not ideas." You've been commenting on that, and I will leave it to you to respond.

ANDREW: There is a children's arcade game called "Swat the Mole," where you have to hammer back the moles that pop up out of the machine faster and faster as the game goes on. I was very tempted to take my hammer to some of your quotations. But we could be here forever at that rate and never win entirely. There are a lot more people in the West who think they know about Russia than actually do know about it, and you have mentioned some of the widespread propositions that are regularly repeated as if they were revealed truths. This is intellectual laziness, and condescension, too. If I believed in these ideas, I would be a Russophobe.

However, I can't resist taking a couple of swipes. The argument that interests, not ideas, should determine policies is meaningless, for interests *are* ideas, not obvious, known, unchanging, and unquestionable entities. Yes, democracy took a long time and much upheaval to reach its current Western form, but so did the market economy. Is Russia to wait for both, or is it to learn from others? No one would deny that change will be difficult, but preventing it creates its own problems, too. If India can be a democracy, why not Russia? The argument that you have to have capitalism first has no historical or theoretical basis.

LILIA: Other popular views would include:

- "Russia made great progress under Putin, especially compared to Yeltsin's chaos."
- "Russia remains one of the most attractive emerging markets."
- "Russia can be modernized only through reform from above."
- "The current Russian regime is as good as it gets."
- "The liberalization of Russia will lead to anarchy or dictatorship."
- "Russians have exchanged freedom for prosperity."

And so on and so forth. I will stop here. We've already commented on some of these assertions.

Why are the Western politicians and commentators parroting clichés straight from the Kremlin's propaganda handbook? What do you think their motivations are? Is it because of an inability to believe that Russian society can function in a system of liberal democracy? Or is it really fear of seeming Russophobic, or apprehension that being critical toward the Russian system will encourage a return to Cold War sentiments? Or perhaps their ignorance of Russian society?

John Kenneth Galbraith coined the term "conventional wisdom," understanding it as a means of avoiding "unwelcome dislocation of life." Stereotypes of Russia sound like tenets of a "conventional wisdom" that could indeed be the product of inertia and complacency.

ANDREW: There is a never-ending supply of these sorts of lazy assertions. I find the one about exchanging freedom for prosperity particularly galling. If it were so, why aren't prosperous nations clamoring for dictators so as to become still more wealthy? Are authoritarian regimes wiser than others? Obviously not, or if that is not clear, let's hear a cheer for Burma. The only one of your points with a grain of truth in it is about the risks of liberalization—and that is only true if the "strong men" hang on too long.

But that is not what you asked. You asked why there is so much parroting of official Russian banalities. I can't answer that very well, since it depends who is doing the talking. But what these views have in common is their hope that nothing bad will happen in Russia, as well as the evasion that accepting current realities rather than challenging them will turn out better for everyone. There will always be a number of people who will prefer such an unexamined hope to the possibility of disruption. I do not think, incidentally, that anyone who is not a salesman for Russian equities or enterprises sincerely believes that Russia remains an attractive long-term investment market. If it is, where is the money?

I have a cautionary tale taken from an account of a visit by a cultural delegation to China in 1954, retold in Patrick Wright's *Passport to Peking: A Very British Mission to Mao's China*. One of the delegates was a prominent intellectual of the day, Hugh Casson. Casson recognized that to show respect for his hosts, he had to "accept," among other things, "the distortion of truth, the insistence upon official infallibility, the mutual suspicion and informing, the need for the accused to prove his innocence and not the accusers his guilt." He remarked on his return that the group had not been asked a single political question in China: "Was not that a bit odd? Well, they were hosts; we were guests. No, we did not ask a single political question either—perhaps that was a little bit odd, too."

LILIA: It would have been nearly the same story of mutual politeness in Russia! With one exception, however: The Russian hosts would believe that there is not much difference between them and the Western guests and, hence, that there would be no need for unpleasant questions.

It is regrettable that even the most sensitive and intelligent people in the West sometimes get confused looking at Russia; the pitfalls of well-wishing often reminds us of the ambivalence of good intentions! I have to admit I was really unhappy, even depressed, to read an article by Walter Laqueur in *Foreign Affairs*. You know Walter Laqueur: He is a great person and author of *The Dream That Failed: Reflections on the Soviet Union* and other thoughtful books on the USSR. But in this particular *Foreign Affairs* piece, he wrote that he believes that "the Russian people prefer stability to democracy." I would retort: part of society, yes. But not all Russians! Look at what advice Laqueur offers the West, apparently on the basis of his understanding of what Russians prefer:

> Perhaps the West should not even press for it [democratization] given that the majority of the Russian leadership and the Russian people seem not to favor it. But will it be possible … to have fair trials and legal protection only for foreign enterprises—something much like the concessions to foreigners China made 100 years ago?

After reading this, I could only say, "Oh!"

I understand that even astute observers can be disappointed in Russia, but here Laqueur seems to be suggesting the creation in Russia of special zones for foreigners, because only in such zones can they have "fair trials and legal protection." This is Medvedev's idea of Skolkovo and of special legal treatment there. Need I remind you that those zones have to be surrounded by barbed fences and be isolated from the natives, as they were in China? This is hardly the way to promote Western standards in Russia; it's a recipe for making Russians loathe the West and its "fair trials." One has to remember how the Chinese viewed foreigners in the times of concessions and how those times ended.

ANDREW: Special zones and privileges for foreigners seem to me to be wrong. Why should foreigners want to go to such prisons anyway? The whole point of coming to Russia is to work with Russians. Huge parts of existing investment in, for instance, the energy, agricultural, manufacturing, or retail sectors would be impossible to act upon from little islands of special treatment. And as you point out, ordinary Russians would be right to see this as contemptible. The only people who might profit from such zones would be those working in Customs, who make enough as it is.

There is bound to be a range of attitudes, some of which will be irritating. Observers often want to be actors and slant their ideas so as to exert influence or be regarded as influential. Money enters into this, too. But it would be unfair to be too cynical. Without a scale of values, expectations built on the knowledge of political and economic systems, and a sense of history, no opinion is likely to prove realistic. Foreigners should study Khodorkovsky's November 2, 2010, statement, which brought together at the end of his latest trial a whole set of principled themes that ought to impress for their clarity—even if you would prefer not to listen to them, or to condemn them as hypocritical. Some of them, of course, have been said by Russia's president, though in a different context....

LILIA: Let me emphasize what you've just said about Khodorkovsky. I attended his second trial, which was a disgrace for Russia. His final statement was one of the most powerful expressions of Russian reality: "The state that ruins its best companies that are ready to become world leaders; the state that harasses and despises its citizens; the state that trusts only its bureaucrats and special services is a sick state." Khodorkovsky demolished the Potemkin village that the Kremlin elite have been trying to present as the image of the "new Russia" and revealed the ugly face of the Russian system. After reading this speech, one has problems believing or defending the stereotypes of Russia that we've mentioned.

ANDREW: That ought to be so, but humankind "cannot bear too much reality." Understanding Russia is not too easy, or at any rate it is said not to be that simple, and Russians love to play up to that—not least with the aid of Tyutchev's poem about Russia not being accessible to the mind, only to the heart. I remember telling the then-minister of defense that I regarded this as a professional insult, after which he had the grace to laugh. But if you think that Russia is a riddle wrapped in an enigma and so on (another overworked quotation, sanctified for the British by coming from Churchill), then why bother to try to interpret it seriously?

Mind you, if understanding of Russia is not widespread in the West, the same is true in reverse. Not many Russians are good at catching on to Western realities.

LILIA: Oh, not at all! We prefer to follow our own stereotypes with respect to the West. No wonder our interactions are dogged by misunderstanding.

Things are however beginning to change in the Russian expert and intellectual community—not with regard to the West, but with regard to Russia. There are signs that people are beginning to feel that supporting the authorities, especially Putin, is not … proper, and is in bad taste, even vulgar and a tad imprudent. The authorities are behaving so shamelessly that those who work for them risk injuring their sense of self-worth and dignity. Russian journals have started to publish the names of Kremlin "loyalists" and their adoring statements so that they may become a laughing stock for the broader public. There are more and more intellectuals and experts who only yesterday were proud to work for the Kremlin but today downplay that fact, for fear that their past work may stain their current reputations.

The Internet has emerged as a powerful tool. The blogger community, and a large proportion of Russians who actively use the Internet, has turned into a factor shaping public opinion and influencing society's moods. It is from the Internet that the most sober and shrewd views on events in Russia are emerging, and it is from there that the most devastating reviews of Russian experts' and intellectuals' reputations are coming. Many of them now think twice before supporting the Kremlin slogans, knowing that doing so will bring them under immediate fire from the blogger community.

My impression is that at least some former loyalists are now looking for ways to distance themselves from the authorities.

ANDREW: It seems that there is a combination of resignation and resentment that the choice for 2012 should be restricted to two men from the same small cabal, and that the decision of who it should be is intended to be hammered out between the two of them. I agree with you that it is, however, also the case that the outlines of change desired by many, in Russia's major cities in particular, are liberal rather than in favor of more centralization. The distrust of the state and its agents is proof of that, whatever the public approval ratings of the president and prime minister.

LILIA: People feel a growing need for frank discussions of what is happening in Russia, and this is a breath of fresh air. This development has not yet achieved large-scale success, as it did in the late 1980s, when the public mood was embodied in the slogan "We can't live this way!" But even people who took part in yesterday's "Putin consensus" are now beginning to say: "It's time to end the arbitrariness and corruption!"

ANDREW: We spoke earlier about modernization, and the various ways it could be brought about. On February 18, 2011, Finance Minister Kudrin said in Krasnoyarsk that transparent and honest elections were essential to Russia's future development. The INSOR proposals of mid-March 2011 for progress toward a desirable future for Russia (as judged by the Institute, of course) said in the preface to the report that two conditions are essential: First, unlocking Russia's potential for modernization can only be achieved through combining resolute leadership by the president with a concrete program agreed on by the authorities and society as a whole; and second, the president should be elected by transparent and honest due process. The foundation document produced by Mau and Kuzminov for Putin, which has been remitted to the group now chaired by Shuvalov to consider a program to be implemented from 2012 onward, makes a very similar point when it refers to the need for proper public discussion and endorsement of a modernization effort. It seems to me that this goes very much to your point that slogans from on high are no longer enough. But the electoral underpinning for such renewal seems to me to be in question. The regional and municipal elections of March 2011 were not really more convincing in this regard than those of 2010.

LILIA: No, the March elections seemed more like a dress rehearsal for the authorities' management of the Duma elections later in 2011 and, as necessary, the presidential contest in 2012. There was blatant manipulation of the process and results, and the clear purpose of the elections was to guarantee a decisive victory for the pro-regime United Russia Party in all twelve regional legislatures and the contested municipal offices. The authorities purged their most critical rivals from the list of candidates: 60 percent of the candidates from other parties and 40 percent of the independent candidates were not allowed to register their candidacies. During the campaign, the candidates were not allowed to rent venues to meet their voters, and they were often harassed or even beaten. Media outlets refused to run their ads, their posters were torn down, and voters were bribed to vote for the Kremlin party. But even this shameless campaign didn't help to mask the truth entirely: United Russia received 20 percent fewer votes than usual. That means that the authorities will have to use even more dirty tricks to manipulate the vote in the next elections. About 43 percent of respondents viewed these elections as "unfair," and 49 percent said that there were manipulations and distortions.

ANDREW: If that is so, then it will be all the harder to get full backing for whatever strategy the next government and president wish to pursue—whether it is conservative or in some way innovative. Moreover, the report submitted by the Center for Strategic Decisions warned about the "delegitimizing role" of rigged elections.

LILIA: The report of the government's Center for Strategic Decisions was desperate in its diagnosis and forecast.

ANDREW: Yes, I quote their message:

> The country has entered deep crisis.... It is reflected in the fall of support for Putin and Medvedev, in the diminished electorate for the "United Russia" party, and in growing criticism of the political system.... Sooner or later this crisis will evolve towards its open stage.

LILIA: The gloomy tone of the reports and of statements issued by the think tanks close to the authorities is revealing. It tells us that experts who have been incorporated into the system do not believe it will survive. Set against all of these facts, the Western tendency to view the Russian system and leadership in a benevolent way, or at least as non-threatening either for the West or for Russia, looks odd.

ANDREW: You can certainly hear a good deal of placatory noises about Russia, along with calls for patient understanding. We should all be for patient understanding, of course, if by that we mean understanding of the needs and evolution of Russia as a whole and not just of its present rulers. The reset mantra is a perfect excuse for putting forward complacency as a desirable policy, but calls not to rock the Russian boat and so on reflect concern about the future, too. It does not take too much prodding to show the extent of that in the West, particularly among those who have regular dealings with Russian realities.

But it seems to me that this is a case of Western understanding of what is happening in and to Russia being out of key with what Russians themselves believe, rather than a Western wish to go easy in expressing concern because of a wish not to offend.

LILIA: Patience is a good quality but hardly useful when the rot has set in. The old saying that "patience is a form of despair" strikes me as appropriate here.

ANDREW: You speak of fresh air, and it is there, no doubt. But there is foul air to be talked of, too. Russians—from the president and prime minister to Khodorkovsky, from the governors to ordinary citizens—condemn it, but corruption remains the lifeblood flowing throughout the ailing body politic. Corruption in Russia is the sign of a rotten core.

Western businesspeople are more and more shocked by its extent. It is one thing to read about it but another to be asked to add another 30–40 percent to one's bid (to cover payoffs), to endure a tax raid, or to know that if you do not contribute to a favored local project your business will suffer. It does not take long to know that one must avoid asking certain questions and to learn to give praise even when it is not due. And so on. I have yet to meet anyone, Western or Russian, who thinks that this evil is abating—on the contrary. Talk of modernization or liberalization does not stack up against this reality.

Corruption in Russia is far more than the passing of money in envelopes. It is a way of life, a system that grows when the laws, however good they sometimes look on paper, are either elastic enough to allow the right people to get around them or can be simply ignored if you are important enough. It is a system in which the rule of "understandings" prevails, when property is given or taken away by various levels of leadership, when farcical allegations that signatures are invalid are used to eliminate political parties, when threats are to be believed because you know they can be carried out without reprisal, and so on. Corruption, in brief, touches all, pervades all. Its very lack of definition makes it powerful and hard to attack. "You know it when you see it" is true but inadequate. The funeral of a major criminal is as public an event as the funeral of former prime minister Chernomyrdin.

No country is perfect, but this is a terrible disease, and the cure is not obvious. In my darker moments, I wonder if there is one. We spoke earlier about the importance of the societal assumptions that underpin democracy. If the prevailing assumption is that the government machine is staffed by thieves and robbers, then it follows that you might be wise to become a thief or robber yourself. When you help to stuff ballots, you know that the result is illegitimate, and that the chosen authorities have no standing. And so on.

LILIA: Do you think we can stop being serious for a minute? Here's a recent joke: "Russian citizens will face a difficult choice in the presidential elections of 2012: Putin, Putin, or Putin?"

ANDREW: I don't get to listen to Radio Armenia in London, but the revival of political jokes recalls the Beatles' "Back in the USSR."

WHY IS THE WEST READY TO PRETEND?

LILIA: The Russian liberal community is convinced that the West understands quite well what is afoot in Russia, but that Western political and intellectual figures prefer to turn a blind eye to it. Those who carried out the August 1991 coup against Gorbachev arranged for Swan Lake to be played non-stop on all television channels as a distraction while they tried to restore lost Soviet verities. For many Russians it is as though many in the West prefer to watch symbols of the past like Swan Lake in place of today's realities. Of course it is the Russian political class and Russian intellectuals who bear full responsibility for what is happening in Russia. But because the Russian ruling elite depends to a degree on the placatory positions of Western politicians and experts in order to sustain the current system, those Western figures also to some degree share responsibility for the present order of things in Russia.

ANDREW: Sorry to interrupt, but I am not so sure about how far to take this. I do not think it right to pin on the Russian groups you have mentioned the entire portion of blame for the failures of political development in Russia. Nor do I suppose that the fact that there are sympathizers in the West for the present state of affairs can be taken as a generalized fault of a definable section of the various countries of the West. But I agree that Western attitudes can affect Russian outcomes, and you are of course right to say that plenty of intelligent and well-informed Russians think that all too many influential people in the

West are all too easily, and in some cases willingly, fooled by the Russian authorities.

LILIA: I accept your clarification of the "political class." Apparently, I sound too Marxist! I am referring here to the way Western colleagues (not a "class" anymore!) allow themselves to be drawn into the Kremlin's games. Some of them do not hide their willingness to take part in these games.

ANDREW: I am glad you say "some of them."

LILIA: Oh, I am no adherent of "collective responsibility."

You already know where I would like to go, but I have to explain it to those who may read this account.

I have in mind the Valdai Club and the Yaroslavl Forum—two of the most successful Kremlin public relations campaigns inviting the participation of foreign (not just Western) guests. Valdai has become a platform for Putin to talk to a foreign audience, although Medvedev initially took part in it, too. The Yaroslavl Forum is Medvedev's principal platform now.

The main "dish" on the Valdai menu is either lunch or dinner with the Russian leaders. I think that all participants in the Valdai discussions know what sort of show they are taking part in. I could understand their interest in participation if these meetings actually gave them the chance to learn something new about Russia or to take part in real and honest discussions with the Russian leaders, but this is not the role they get to play. They get to ask the Russian leaders questions that for the most part have been approved in advance. Do they learn anything there that they couldn't learn by reading the official Russian newspapers?

I think I should stop here and calm down. We need to hear your reasonable views.

ANDREW: Putin is very good at this sort of thing and rarely breaks out on such occasions into street language. Participants in the Valdai meetings are usually impressed by his grasp of detail. And if they do not in truth get much in the way of new information, they can return home with the claim that they have heard it direct and, in that sense, fresh. This is a currency among experts, journalists, and others who need to demonstrate that they have access to the highest circles.

I do not suppose that that will calm you much but it is a reality.

LILIA: Perhaps it's hard to withstand the temptation to glimpse the object of one's study at least once. This human curiosity is fully understandable. But is one glimpse really not enough?

If only the Western guests offered an objective analysis of the Kremlin show on their return home. But no, more often than not, we hear from them smooth-sounding words that lean toward admiration. This is understandable: Say something you shouldn't, and you won't get invited again.

True, some Valdai members gradually become more critical of the Russian leaders. In 2004, respected American expert Fiona Hill published an article in the *New York Times* titled "Stop Blaming Putin and Start Helping Him," which called for all to accept Putin's explanation of the Kremlin's policy in the Northern Caucasus. More recently, however, Hill wrote thoughtful and candid comments based on her Valdai meeting that challenged the Kremlin's interpretation of the event and its modernization agenda. Still, I wonder whether it was necessary to take part in the event to understand the bogus nature of Medvedev's modernization and liberalization agenda.

Regrettably, some farsighted and shrewd people who have always promoted a values-based vision sometimes unconsciously slide into legitimizing the Russian system. When the great historian Richard Pipes, for example, argued at Valdai that there are "historic reasons for the Russian predilection for autocracy," including the enormous size of its territory, the role of the church, and the fact that "the majority of Russians are not socialized and politicized," he apparently could not anticipate what a great help he was being to Russian supporters of the "iron hand." When Pipes praised the "freedom of discussion" at Valdai, he was doing exactly what the Kremlin organizers of this show expected from its respected participants—to give them "the stamp of approval."

ANDREW: These are of course in some part shows, and foreign guests will have differing reasons for submitting themselves to the prospect of being exhibited. Some of them will come as believers in what they already know they will hear. There is a long Western tradition of individuals who tend to express sympathy for the Kremlin line of the day, and the Russian organizers of these events will naturally want to have a good selection of such people to invite. But there are also the skeptics, and the fact is that those who do not live in Russia as you do feel the need from time to time to get a sense of its atmosphere. It is not so much that they expect to learn a great deal that cannot be understood from outside as that they feel the lack of personal and emotional contact. Okay, perhaps they should go beyond such meetings, but there is force to this argument. And as you say, it is good to be one of the crowd, too.

It will be interesting to see how Valdai does in the future. These things have a shelf life. People also go, for instance, to the St. Petersburg Economic Forum, but my impression is that they do this increasingly because they feel that they have to be seen there rather than because they really want to spend that time there in June. That forum has maybe more in common with the Yaroslavl gathering than with Valdai. At any rate, Yaroslavl is more for political figures, past as much as present, and business representatives. It is an opportunity for Medvedev to present himself as a man of the future and to respond to different needs. It is instinctive for such an audience to hear such a message with built-in optimism, and to look around at the rest of the company and be reassured by being there with similarly talented colleagues.

LILIA: I see your point: There are so many people, including some of our good friends, who follow this "it's good to be part of the crowd" philosophy. In some cases it may be a waste of time but not harmful. In the Russian case, I am afraid, this philosophy means something different: it means consenting to be used. Besides, if they need "personal and emotional contact," why look for it from the person perhaps least suited for that: Putin?

Meanwhile, the Kremlin displays considerable imagination in preparing the various Valdai meetings, inviting genuinely respected liberal figures. Among those invited to Valdai 2010 was Adam Michnik, a well-known Polish dissident and chief editor of *Gazeta Wyborcza*, Poland's most influential newspaper, and an icon for Russia's democrats. Adam is a good friend of mine, and I, like his other friends in Moscow, was disappointed that he accepted the invitation.

True, Adam put some tough questions to Putin, in particular on Khodorkovsky. But did he learn anything new about Putin's position on Khodorkovsky? Later he wrote of the "revulsion" he felt at seeing the prepared questions other participants put to Putin.

Between what he wrote about Valdai in his newspaper and his comments on Putin's "steely eyes" and the way Putin treats the opposition, he seems to have no illusions about the Russian regime. But is it really necessary to go to Valdai to reach these conclusions? I think that Adam Michnik satisfied his curiosity and will be unlikely to accept a second invitation to play the Valdai game.

ANDREW: It is for Michnik, not me, to comment on this.

LILIA: I have an urge to comment, too, on Medvedev's event, the Yaroslavl Forum, which has also become an annual event. It is more ambitious in scope, seeking to discuss global issues and above all issues concerning democracy. Take the name given to the 2010 forum: "The Contemporary State: Standards of Democracy and Criteria of Effectiveness"(!). Doesn't that sound impressive indeed?

Participants in the two forums held so far include French Prime Minister Francois Fillon, Spanish Prime Minister Jose Luis Zapatero, Italian Prime Minister Silvio Berlusconi, and South Korean President Lee Myung-bak, as well as former NATO secretary general Lord Robertson and Obama's adviser Michael McFaul. Prominent intellectual gurus such as Alvin Toffler, Immanuel Wallerstein, and Fareed Zakaria have also taken part. Is this a Russian Bilderberg Group?

They listened without objection to Medvedev's declaration that Russia is a democracy and preferred during the discussions to keep to reflections on the need for democracy and what democracy and modernization signify.

ANDREW: Well, I suppose it was always unlikely that anyone so distinguished would rise to that sort of challenge, as it would have been rude and disruptive to call the president a liar. Maybe Medvedev does think that Russia is a sort of democracy, or that it is his duty to pretend that it is one. The account he gave last time of what democracy in Russia might entail seemed to me to be more about decent administration, a good thing to aim at and certainly very necessary in Russia, as Medvedev himself has pointed out—but not at all the same thing as having a government that is answerable to the people, subject to the law, and replaced by the people when it is reckoned to have failed.

LILIA: My former colleague from Carnegie, Michael McFaul, who became Obama's Russia adviser, argued at the latest Yaroslavl Forum that democracy is one of the most important driving forces for economic development. His speech was emotional and convincing, and he was entirely correct to conclude that dictatorship can help to carry out the industrialization stage of development, as was the case in Soviet history, but at a higher level of development it is "hard to find any evidence that an authoritarian regime can guarantee economic growth." All of this is right.

ANDREW: Sorry to interrupt, but I do not believe that it is in fact right. Stalin did a rush job, that's true. But it was also one that stored up immense problems for the future by its scale and inflexibility—the usual legacy of tyrants.

LILIA: Thank you for the correction: The price of the Russian industrialization was enormous indeed, and its longer-term results mixed. But despite what McFaul said, Russian officials were more than happy in the end. The level of abstraction and the fact that McFaul did not criticize today's Russia made it possible for the Kremlin to interpret his speech (and the other speeches) as developing Medvedev's own ideas! After all, neither Medvedev, nor any of the other official Kremlin representatives, said that they preferred authoritarianism or wanted to follow the Chinese model. They spoke the language of Michael McFaul.

I know I'm drawing out our dialogue, but I wanted to quote the Russian magazine *Itogi*'s view about Michael's speech (September 20, 2010): "Some political analysts expected that Michael McFaul would come to Yaroslavl to lecture the Kremlin, but their expectations were not fulfilled.... The speaker almost word for word repeated the Russian president's main arguments. Thus the issue of differences in values in Russia and the West that complicated our relations can be considered closed." Such was the conclusion of the forum's hosts.

ANDREW: Westerners can be misunderstood by being courteous. We all know how it feels when we suppose that what are intended to be wounding criticisms are too tightly wrapped up in well-meaning words to be taken to heart by our intended audience. But go on.

LILIA: "Being courteous"... This could be the case. Russian authorities apparently do not always get the depth of polite criticism, or they don't understand political correctness. However, I can offer another explanation of the Russian reaction in this particular case: The Russian authorities did not care what the Westerners would say. Words do not matter for the Russian elite; symbols do. The fact that Western officials attend the forum for the Kremlin is a symbolic endorsement of the Russian reality.

Some of the Western participants, Immanuel Wallerstein, for example, did not seem to realize that the theoretical reflections they propose (What is the "people"? What is democracy?) are exactly what the Russian authorities need for their imitation of democracy.

Other participants at the previous forums openly acted as Kremlin propagandists—not consciously, I hope. Here are a few examples of their comments, taken from *Russkiy Zhurnal* magazine, a pro-Kremlin source: Lord Robert Skidelsky: "Medvedev realizes the need for democracy," unlike Putin. (How can he be so sure?) John Nesbit: "Russia is putting its effort into creating what will later become its unique form of democracy." Does he really not understand that the "Russian form of democracy" is the complete opposite of real democracy?

Some Western intellectuals seemed happy (and some even ecstatic!) to play the game the Kremlin's way, not forgetting, for example, to mention that civil liberties are restricted all around the world, including in the United States and other countries, as a result of "rising geopolitical tension." This was exactly how the Kremlin justified clamping down on democracy in Russia right from the start. "You talk about restrictions on freedom, look at Guantánamo! You talk about corruption—look at the West! You talk about manipulating elections—how was Bush elected? And Blair named his own successor, Brown!" In other words, what is happening in Russia is no different than what goes on in the West.

ANDREW: Lord Skidelsky is of course an authoritative biographer of Keynes, and his views on Russia are published in the Russian media.

LILIA: Yes, he is overrepresented in the Russian media, usually bearing a message that suits the official line. There would not be so much of him otherwise. There is a known recipe for getting quoted in the Russian media.

ANDREW: It is always risky to say what others really believe, even when they are frequent speakers, like Medvedev. But he and the others must speak for themselves, and only for themselves. It is of course such a well-established and inherited Soviet tradition of political discourse to point to some spurious parallel with the West. It has even become a joke: "... and what about lynching in the South?"

The proper question to ask oneself about Medvedev is what has he actually done? Nice sentiments are one thing; concrete action another. I do not mean this as an attack on Medvedev but more as an illustration of how the same matters are seen one way in the West and another in Russia. It is premature, at best, to see Medvedev as a committed liberal, though that is what many in the West already do.

LILIA: We in Russia have lived to see that he is nothing of the sort—just a chameleon that can take on any color.

Yet Medvedev still fascinates the West and has its ear! Western pundits at meetings with the Russian president ask Medvedev things like, "In your view, what role can Russia play in establishing democracy throughout the world?" Such was the question that Professor Shapiro from Yale University put to the Russian president at the 2010 meeting. But maybe he was being sarcastic, and if so, Bravo Mr. Shapiro! You left Medvedev, who has become a master at praising Russia's progress without blushing, at a loss for words. True, he gave himself over to illusion in the end, declaring, "Russia must become an example of a successful country, where … democracy will radiate in all its fullness." The plane crash in Yaroslavl carrying one of the top Russian professional hockey teams during the 2011 Forum became a sad reminder of the true Russian "success" story….

ANDREW: I suspect that Putin still carries more weight in Western minds, but Medvedev has been the story until recently, at least. We love to speculate about what we know least about.

LILIA: I will tell you another story that appears anecdotal. At a meeting with leaders of American student associations, Surkov, the chief Kremlin ideologist, was discussing the "spread of democratic procedures" internationally as the U.S. audience enthusiastically nodded along with him. Surkov is a shrewd person, and I can only imagine how he must have enjoyed promoting "Russian democracy" before an attentive American audience.

I emphasize Western colleagues' involvement in the Kremlin's game not in order to display my critical acumen; Kremlin propagandists themselves are quite open about their project. Gleb Pavlovsky, for instance, has said: "In Yaroslavl we tested the 'Skolkovo' principle."

What this means is that the Kremlin is not just trying to create a new image of the Russian authorities as supposedly liberal and ready for dialogue with the West in order to help it get hold of Western technology. This is the small goal. The bigger goal is to draw the West into a discussion of strategic global development issues (from democracy to security) in an attempt to force the West, which in the Russian elite's view is going through a crisis (and I agree with this in part), to accept the Kremlin's vision for a new world order. The Kremlin wants to impose on the West its vision of democracy, modernization, economic progress, and European and global security.

What the Russian elite hear from Western participants at Valdai and Yaroslavl gives them confidence that their new project just might succeed.

ANDREW: And they are of course backing this up with money to think tanks, universities, Western media, and so on. They have rather more wind in their sails at present than I would wish, but I doubt that will last if there is no substance to back it.

LILIA: No, it will not last, at least not for long. But imagine the damage that Western accommodation (I am trying to use a softer word) inflicts not only on Russia but also on the Western community itself. The rot could spread far beyond Russia.

Western policy is based largely on how Western experts interpret Russian reality and what signals they send to political circles. A significant portion of Western observers, among them several influential ones, is still trying to paint an optimistic picture of an "advancing Russia." They talk about Russia emerging from the crisis, rising living standards, and a growing middle class. One Western Russia hand, a good friend of mine, enthusiastically compared Russia to the "Speeding Troika": "However one defines modernization, it seems incontrovertible that it is taking place in Russia." Where does my colleague see signs of modernization? Apparently, being tired of gloom and doom, Western colleagues have desperately been trying to find a pretext for optimism—again out of the best of intentions. However, wishful thinking hardly helps one understand what is really going on.

The Russian reality is different: the unbridled rise in corruption you have described; the growing gap between rich and poor; and the loss of faith in the future. Let me show you just a few numbers that reveal the real situation. The richest 10 percent of Russians make 23 times more than the poorest 10 percent. Russia's GDP per capita is $15,300—ahead of Romania and Ukraine at $11,700 and $6,400, respectively. Only 15 percent of respondents believe that the future will definitely be better than the present. And what can we tell from the fact that the rich do not want to keep their money in Russia?

ANDREW: Capital flight as you earlier mentioned reached $60 billion between September 2010 and May 2011.

LILIA: Thank you. Further indicators of how much faith rich Russians have in their country's future are the "Russian weeks" at the venerable London auction houses, Sotheby's and Christie's, at which wealthy

Russians invest the money they have expatriated. The unprecedented rise in prices at these auctions is a sign that Russians have little confidence in their own country's future.

ANDREW: I don't want to cap your Sotheby's and Christie's points—and I am grateful for these Russian contributions to Britain's GDP—but I cannot resist passing on the answer to a question I recently put to a London vintner about, forgive me, that very British passion, vintage port. The vintner had said that a significant Chinese market was developing for this wine, which must be held for decades for it to reach its maturity. I asked why not Russia? Because, he said, rich Russians do not know where they will be next year, let alone in twenty.

LILIA: This is the best indicator of modernization's "progress"! Let me add that if in 2003 Russia spent 1.23 percent of GDP for innovation, in 2011 it spends only 1.03 percent.

ANDREW: Western visitors to Russia are often rightly impressed by the quality of the young people they meet. And so they should be. But the key question is what sort of young Russians do they get to know? More than 70 percent of young people want to leave the country, according to recent polls. I have met successful and educated Russian parents who are much troubled by their children's reluctance to come home to Russia. And there are a number of young Russians that foreigners are scarcely aware of. The spate of riots in Moscow in December 2010, and the extensive precautions taken by the authorities to combat them, certainly showed the dangers of ethnic violence getting out of hand.

LILIA: Andrew, please, explain which riots you have in mind.

ANDREW: On December 2010, up to 15,000 young people of Slavic origin gathered on one of the main Moscow squares, Manezh Square, and began beating up any passers-by who had non-Slavic faces. The images of the brutality and the sounds of nationalist slogans chanted by thugs only steps away from the Kremlin walls dominated television broadcasts.

This violence began following an everyday conflict between two small groups of young people over a taxi. One of the groups consisted of young people from the North Caucasus and the other of Russian fans of a Moscow football club. A fan, an ethnic Russian, was murdered after a confrontation between the two groups turned violent.

The following day, back on Manezh Square, beside the Tomb of the Unknown Soldier, a huge swastika appeared. It was not the first time such things have happened in either Russia or Moscow. In 2002, Moscow's authorities set up huge television screens on Manezh Square to broadcast a World Cup match between Russia and Japan. Tens of thousands of young fans came to the square, many of them drunk. When the match ended with a 1–0 victory for Japan, the infuriated crowd burst into spontaneous rioting. From what I know, however, Russia has never seen such violent mass ethnic rioting as occurred in downtown Moscow in December 2010. It was its scale and its unexpected nature that was so shocking.

LILIA: Right, it was a new phenomenon that apparently shocked both Russian society and the authorities. Along with my Carnegie colleagues I watched the wild crowds of teenagers walking to Manezh past our office on Tverskaya street. When I took the subway that evening I saw with dismay scenes of hundreds of young, agitated thugs searching the trains for non-Slavs and beating them. The police were either in hiding or looking on with tacit approval.

ANDREW: The number of young hooligans taking part was distressing. But it seems to me that this was not just about ethnic tensions or the sheer enjoyment to be had from a good bust-up. There was also a strain of despair about the country's future. It was, I fear, significant that the violence was triggered by the allegation that those accused of murdering the Russian fan had been released thanks to a bribe to the police. The point is not that this was true. I have no evidence for that one way or the other. The point is that the allegation was instantly believed. And that showed, once more, the depth of public cynicism as to the real nature and purposes of the forces of law and order in Russia. This is a dangerous cancer.

If I were in the Kremlin, I would be troubled by these outbreaks. Will there be fewer of them come 2018, when Moscow will have done the United Kingdom a great favor in deciding to spend at least $50 billion to host the World Cup? Many observers have noted links between nationalist groups and parts of officialdom, pointing out that hard-liners within the government support the nationalists to justify tight Kremlin controls and fend off efforts to open up Russia's political system.

LILIA: You are right to be troubled. While Russian police quickly, intentionally, and brutally disperse peaceful protests by anti-Kremlin activists demanding respect for human rights and the constitution, nationalist groups, including neo-Nazis, have been allowed to hold their rallies freely in recent years. It's widely known that pro-Kremlin youth organizations created and sponsored by the authorities often hire soccer hooligans and ultranationalists to carry out attacks on critics of the Kremlin. Actually, the authorities' Young Guards youth movement was clearly inspired by the Chinese Red Guards, which had been used by Mao to fight his opponents during the Cultural Revolution.

You know, the formation of pro-Kremlin youth movements began after the Orange Revolution in Ukraine. Frightened by the possibility of a color revolution breaking out in Russia, the Kremlin invested enormous resources in loyal youth movements with two aims: to control street political activity and to prepare brigades for a future struggle that might include more than just ballot rigging against political opponents.

ANDREW: This is peculiarly dangerous. The appetites of those who give in to such temptations grows with the feeding. The mob also has impulses beyond the calculations of those who hope to exploit it.

LILIA: Exactly! But this sort of activity is now a Kremlin staple. The authorities build up these "muscles" in order to flex them against critics and opponents.

Special youth brigades fostered by the Kremlin regularly beat up opposition activists. They especially target liberals and anti-fascist youth (who call themselves "Antifa"). If perchance the police detain members of the Kremlin young guards, a telephone call from the presidential administration follows, and the detainees are released. That is why the police fail to take any action against rioting young thugs. In December 2010, despite the fact that this time the Kremlin was panic-stricken at the severity of the disturbances, the police were confused as to how they were supposed to react.

What started as a Kremlin initiative has now acquired a new dimension. There is a whole new generation of "network" nationalists who recruit and organize over the Internet. In other words, one can never be too sure what they're up to. They have become an independent force. This is a completely new development in Russian society.

Clearly, the Kremlin's flirtation with hard-core xenophobes has led to serious social and political destabilization. In a society characterized by a weakened immunity to extremism and an utterly dysfunctional government, the authorities are playing with fire.

ANDREW: Fire warms, but it also consumes.

LILIA: Ethnic violence points to the state's failure to address social problems. In Russia, such problems easily acquire an ethnic and racist hue, especially when the Kremlin intentionally uses the "nationalist" card. The security organs and the ruling elite have no clue how to address mass riots with an ethnic and racist dimension. Russian politicians like to claim that the country has been hit by youth or ethnic protests just like other European states. Students have, they note, taken to the streets in Paris and London, for example, and others have protested migration in France and Germany. The Russian case is different from these European examples, however. The regime's only solutions to such unrest is repression, or to channel social dissatisfaction into ethnic tensions, preferring these to frustration with the regime. However, ethnic provocation always backfires, and it brings bloody consequences—especially because there is a permanent state of civil war in one of its regions, the Northern Caucasus. I feel that the authorities understand the gravity of the situation but have no solution….

ANDREW: There is a spectrum of views in the West, and a time lag between events in Russia and the evolution of those views. Western observers are charitably reluctant to take on board the dark side of Russian reality. It is discouraging to think how quickly opinion has shifted in some countries and within some groups after the lessons of the gas crises, Ukraine, Georgia, the deaths inside and outside Russia, and the speed with which these seem to have been forgotten or put to one side. Obama attracted a number of American experts on Russia who had felt sidelined by Bush, and, as we have agreed, the reset has achieved some results. The danger, however, has been in attempting to extrapolate these beyond their present viability, and from the modish attempts by others to have their own resets, too. We should all tally up our concrete results but also be careful of what we can count on in the future.

If the wicked West, as so many Russians suppose, is determined and organized to bring Russia down, then why does it react with such credulity to anyone in Moscow who seems to be offering cooperation and friendship? Come to think of it, that is a foolish question: Such Russians may suppose that this is just another instance of Western cunning, and their ill-wishers are trying to damage Russia by false pretenses or by supporting a Russian president who may well be weak and easily manipulated.

LILIA: The second option is quite possible—even more than possible, perhaps!

I will share another thought with you. It seems to me there are various motifs in Western political and intellectual circles' approaches to Russia, from pragmatic to idealistic. One popular motif seems to be the belief in the evolutionary nature of global development. The logic this motif follows assumes that liberal democracies developed their institutions gradually, that it took their peoples a long time to learn to live within a framework of ever-increasing freedom. Russia will travel this same road, following the West's experience, and sooner or later it will arrive at the same destination, liberal democracy. Meanwhile, there is no hurry. Is my reading wrong?

ANDREW: I do not think that any serious historian or political theorist could possibly believe this, except maybe over such a long run that it would be a useless insight in practical terms. Nice work if you can get it, perhaps, but not a weighty argument. Keynes, as Lord Skidelsky is probably fed up with having to hear, remarked that in the long run we are all dead. And the run to democracy can be very long indeed. I see nothing automatic about it.

LILIA: I enjoyed your comment! You are graciously dumping transitology that seeks to prove that we are all inexorably moving toward a happy future. I'm bringing up this "evolutionary approach" (Democracy will come at some point—not to worry!) because it justifies taking a wait-and-see approach, both for Russians and Westerners.

ANDREW: Naturally, one can shorten the road by learning from others. But democracy is not just about voting. That, too, has to be tolerably honest, and its results accepted by the losers. India has achieved it. So could Russia. But what democracy cannot, and ought not, achieve is a preordained result that will please those currently in power. It is hard to argue that the Russian political class, if by that one means those currently charged with deciding the country's fate, should include their departure as a permissible mark of modernization on the way to convergence with Western norms.

LILIA: Indeed, democracy is not just about voting. Fareed Zakaria was right to speak of "illiberal democracies" that allow elections but have no rule of law.

I am concerned by the fact that many view the rather high degree of Russia's openness to the world as a guarantee of its future liberalization. Western observers point out how many Russians live in the West, study in Western universities, and do business with the West. They note, too, that Russia is asking for the West's help in building a modern economy. "We have to help the Russians," they say. "We've got to eliminate the negative and accentuate the positive," goes their refrain, as if a technological and cultural injection would do the trick.

ANDREW: The fact that there is so much interaction across so many spheres of life is a good and welcome thing, as we have already agreed. It helps Russians, Russia, and the rest of us, too. And in principle, if we can work together better, that would also be a good thing. But it is a leap from that to say that we should ignore the negative and stress only the positive. That is to distort one's judgment. Within the case you report, there is a hidden assumption that it is "Russia" that has sought our help in creating a contemporary economy. But has it really? The Soviet daily *Pravda* often used the headline "In Whose Interests?"—usually with a cartoon featuring a top-hatted capitalist—to slam some Western idea. The question is nonetheless a good one here. We are perhaps being asked to help the present ruling group and its business interests, but Russia is more than that, as I keep saying. Real modernization cannot just be about propping up existing structures.

LILIA: Yes, Russia is definitely more than the Kremlin.

But outside observers, even astute ones, are sometimes carried away by the Kremlin's performances, which are skilled, I have to admit. For instance, there are Western observers who are not happy with what is going in Russia domestically, but they say that Russian foreign policy has once again returned to constructive cooperation. This change should be supported in every way possible, in the hope that a foreign policy softening could begin a domestic thaw as well.

I don't want to imply that a cold relationship would be better. But I believe it is prudent to understand the limits of and motivations behind the Kremlin's charm offensive.

I was even more surprised by Zbigniew Brzezinski's words at the Munich Security Conference's Core Group meeting in Moscow in the fall of 2010. At the meeting with Medvedev, Brzezinski said,

> People admire you in America, especially because you say so frankly and convincingly that Russia's modernization must go together with democratization. These two processes go hand in hand, and this has touched hearts in America. It is inspiring to talk with a young Russian president who is creating historic opportunities.

Russian journalists wrote that these words sounded like "a declaration of love."

Even Brzezinski has given in, I thought to myself mournfully. Has even he fallen for Medvedev's tales? Maybe he hasn't. Maybe he, like the others, has decided that Russia's evolution is a lengthy affair, and that today Americans need to worry about American interests first and thus should support any positive signals coming from the Kremlin, regardless of what else is happening inside the country. It's the new realpolitik!

ANDREW: If your judgment is fair, it describes a mood that will not last. There is no separating domestic from foreign policies, especially in Russia. It may be easier than before to turn a blind eye to this because of how Ukraine is slipping back into primitive political habits, which masks the central question of what Russia's great-power ambitions imply. But there is no masking the link between modernization as a mere technological band-aid and modernization as true renewal, and the way that will determine Russia's attitudes or options in relation to the rest of the world.

LILIA: There is something else I want to draw your attention to. In today's Russia, words either have no meaning or they mean something else. Russian citizens who have lived in this "through the looking glass" world for a long time and who still remember the communist time, when one always had to read between the lines, have learned to interpret the real meaning behind the government's words. But Western observers sometimes take its declarations at face value.

Consider Medvedev: The more he speaks, the more people in Russia see him as just a "talking head" parroting meaningless words. But a significant portion of the Western political community treats Medvedev, or makes an effort to treat him, as the Russian leader who wants to pursue change.

The Western media like to mention that Medvedev is on Twitter, and they present him as a very modern, tech-savvy guy, all of which sounds promising. But his Tweeting and tech-foolery are in reality a sign of his estrangement from the outside world and his pathetic impotence when it comes to the real decisionmaking process in Russia.

ANDREW: Twitter is full of foolishness, and the web is, too. If the president of Russia spends much time on either he may not have enough of weight to do.

LILIA: You can imagine what ordinary Russians who lack the basic necessities of life think about a president who shows off his computer skills during his television appearances. Houses burn, dams collapse, pensioners go on strike, planes crash, terrorists blow up trains, subways, planes, and airports—and the president is blissfully engaged in playing with his computer. It's as if he and reality follow two completely different orbits!

Anyway, inhabitants of the Kremlin know how to seduce the West. Or Western observers often hear only what they want to hear. They hear Medvedev talk about the need to work together on the "common European agenda" and this sounds markedly different from the way Putin talked only a few years ago. But they're failing to hear the message that really matters: Having spoken the magic words that soothe Western ears, Medvedev adds, "But this does not mean that our priorities have changed."

Words like these are always the main point of the speech! Medvedev is telling us directly that he and Putin have the same priorities, one of which is to keep the old system in place and not make any concessions to the West. Thus what is the admiration that Zbigniew Brzezinski, one of few Western politicians who has always had a deep understanding of the Russian reality, expressed for Medvedev based on?

ANDREW: Perhaps Brzezinski is flattering to deceive? That would be one possibility. Or maybe Medvedev is not entirely sure about what he wants or what he can deliver.

WHY THE WEST WON'T POKE THE BEAR

LILIA: You should go to the Russian liberal websites and read the comments there. You'll find severe criticism of the political West by the Russian liberal pro-Western wing. This is something new in our history.

Andrew, you helped me to understand the logic of Western policy, but I would still argue that, whatever the logic that underpins its policy, the West really prefers to live with the status quo rather than taking up the challenge of formulating a collective and strategically focused course of action. This may be of some help in solving the West's domestic problems but I am not sure how short-term pragmatism can help liberal democracies in the long run. What I am sure of is that it dooms Russia. Russia can't make it alone!

Western politicians and commentators typically wield two arguments when they attempt to argue that the West can't influence Russia's transformation. Here's the first: "The West cannot transform Russia and bring it into the West. This is a task for Russian liberals." True, Russia has to reform itself. Russian liberals don't want the West to save Russia. What they can't understand is why the West insists on openly supporting what is going on in Russia and treating the denizens of the Kremlin as bosom buddies.

ANDREW: You have every right to your feelings, and it would be a shame to hide them in a dialogue like this. But it is a mistake, for me at least, to push the blame game too far. First, Russian liberals are not a group able on their own "to transform Russia and bring it into the West." And second, the West, too, is varied in its views. While I agree with you that the West is preoccupied with itself at present and therefore less liable to have an active, let alone transformational, agenda, this may not always be the case. And both Western governments and societies, on the one hand, and the people of Russia, on the other, are taking part in what can only be an ongoing process. I believe that as and when Russia moves in a liberalizing direction the West will respond positively.

We do not know how Russia will change, how the European Union will develop, or what will happen in Russia's immediate neighborhood. The passage of time matters. Changing realities will continue to exert their pressures. We have discussed how the ground has shifted in the recent past, and liberals in the narrow sense have played their part in that, along with a wider group of people who share in generally liberal sentiments. It seems to me that there has already been a significant shift in the consensus in Russia, and that the combination of a sclerotic power structure and a changing dynamic in the social and economic life of the society it rules cannot over time be stable. The fact that Medvedev has attracted sympathy in the West for his liberal-flavored talk shows that the West would react positively to such a trend.

LILIA: Thank you for believing in our (as we joke among ourselves) "hopeless" cause.

ANDREW: I was struck by the conclusion drawn by the well-known historian and political analyst Dmitri Furman in his recent book comparing the Russian political system with its analogues. He said that there were two converging tendencies in Russia today:

> On the one hand, there is the ritualization of elections, and the crumbling of the democratic "façade" of the system, which is becoming more and more obvious. We have on the other hand society's evolution, and the direction of that makes it harder and harder for that façade to deceive the public. At some point these two streams will collide, and make it impossible for the system of imitation democracy to survive.

(My translation may not be elegant, but there it is.)

This of course does not tell us when such a change may occur, and you do not have to agree with Furman's belief that it is inevitable, but it does make the point that there needs to be a shift in general sentiment before liberal change can take stronger root.

LILIA: Dmitri Furman is right! "Imitation democracy" will not survive. But it's still unclear whether the Russian system will start to unravel before or after the liberal alternative is formed. By "liberal alternative," I mean not only the program but also a consolidated opposition that would win the support of the population and thus have the political mandate to implement that program.

ANDREW: Western representatives can also argue that they have to deal with existing facts, but I certainly agree with you that their tone is important and that they should pay close attention to Russia's conversation with itself.

LILIA: I hope that the Western community at least understands the nature of this conversation.

The second Western argument is, "We have no levers of influence on Russia." This is simply not true. Western civilization has plenty of levers. The Russian political class, in particular, is sensitive to pressure. This class lives in the West. It keeps its money there, buys equity and real estate there, takes its vacations there, has children there, and sends them to school there. The elite make money in Russia in order to support their lifestyle in the West. This elite desperately want to stay with (and in) the West. Hence their vulnerability to Western influence. The West, for instance, can influence the Russian elite by disciplining Western appetites for Russian energy resources and commodities and by creating incentives for the Russian elite gradually to adopt internationally accepted norms of behavior inside Russia.

Why hasn't the West taken advantage of these levers? Some in the West fear that any push will stoke the Kremlin's aggressive tendencies. Others fear the loss of Russia as an economic partner. Still others believe that Russia simply can't be changed, so better to deal with the elite on its own terms. Finally, some in the West are simply tired of Russia.

What would you say, Andrew?

ANDREW: The West is both a magnet and a threat for Russia—or even a rebuke. It always has been. I hope that this may be in decline, but it is there still and a force to be used inside Russia. I am less sure as to how Western countries can use the idea of the West to influence a Russian government. The present ruling elite has more often invoked the vision of the West as a threat to rally domestic support. But if one is speaking of the West in general terms, then what the West should try to do is to live up to its proclaimed principles as best it can. Easier said than done, of course, but better to be called a hypocrite than not to try at all.

Sticking with the general points you make for now, yes, there are those in the West who believe that Russia will not change, and that it will in any case not do so under Western pressure, and, yes, Russia is a constant problem. Many would go on to say that it is not the West's business to democratize Russia. But I do not believe that it follows that this will always be the case, or that "dealing with the Russian elite on their own terms" is a permanent attitude, if one assumes that the elite you have in mind is the present one. There are, for a start, a number of areas where Western interests and the interests of individual Western states clash with the aims of the present elite in Moscow. And that elite is not there forever, with the same power over Russia. So I think it best to view the relationship as something in constant evolution, and Western policies and attitudes as part of that process of evolution. I would add, again, that the West is not a collective, except maybe when it comes under real threat, but a group of individual countries with their own attitudes and changing priorities.

LILIA: To be sure, the current Russian elite will not be there forever, but they can still demoralize the society beyond repair and bring Russia down in flames. With regard to the Western political community, I believe that this is our role—the role of intellectuals—to help it change its priorities, or at least to understand what the degradation of Russia would mean for the outside world.

ANDREW: I also need to speak about the individual ideas you mentioned as possible levers.

First, the Russian elite and the West: I accept that there are many members of the dominant sectors of Russian society who want to stay in and with the West, and that they are vulnerable to Western influence. This is a good thing—and good for Russia, too, in my opinion. However, it does not follow that this community constitutes a lever on the ruling cabal in Moscow that can be used for direct policy purposes by Western governments, even if one assumed, which I do not, that Western governments could agree on united action of this nature. I would prefer to see these individuals used as a channel for encouraging Russia's integration into general European value systems than as a group of potential hostages. Incidentally, in describing these value systems as "European," I do so as shorthand: These values are universally applicable.

Second, energy. Western appetites for Russian energy have been curbed, and oil and gas are not the levers some in Moscow had hoped. Some European countries are more dependent on Russian gas than others, true. And it is true that Russian definitions of energy security imply the extension as far as possible of Gazprom's monopoly into Western Europe. That would be bad for Russia, as well as for the rest of us. I trust that the European Union and its members will not be so foolish as to allow it. The pressures in favor of that are less than they were.

I should enter an obvious caveat here: Things change. Putin has argued that the present unrest in the Middle East underlines the worth of Russia as a reliable energy partner and, if I were he, I would argue that as well. But it is fanciful, if tempting to analysts, to extrapolate too far into the future from present events and to conclude that the end result will be a permanent shift in the pattern of energy supplies to Europe, or to the United States, for that matter. That seems unlikely to me.

Third, the business relationship. Yes, there are individuals, some of them powerful, who warn against any criticism of the Russian leadership, who suggest that the "stability" they find in Russia is lasting and productive, and, yes, who argue that business and politics do not mix. But if you adopt a broader view, then both Russian and Western business interests want a better-structured, more predictable, and more independent economic system. To that extent, they are in the liberal camp. So while there are Nervous Nellies, I would not write off business as a whole. On the contrary.

LILIA: Let me comment on one of your thoughts. I think there are ways to influence the members of the "ruling cabal" in the Kremlin. A lot of its members have families living in Europe. As Deputy Premier Shuvalov said to the participants of Valdai, he has an apartment in London, meaning that he or his family live there. I don't think he rents this apartment or has it for fun. I am sure the rest of the Kremlin cabal have houses in London, Paris, Rome. That means that they would love to be treated as respected residents of these states. But don't you think that the British, French, or Italian authorities could make them understand that respected citizens should behave in a dignified way outside of their countries? That would really help Russia to integrate into Europe. At the moment, Shuvalov and the rest are integrated into Europe on a personal basis.

There are even more persuasive ways to remind the Russian elite about the rules. I remember the shocked and fearful reaction of the Moscow establishment to George W. Bush's cancellation of the visa of one of the most powerful Russian oligarchs, Oleg Deripaska (who is, by the way, a member of Yeltsin's family). They took it as the severest possible punishment, and a sharp warning. You should have seen how they panicked!

The United Kingdom, for its part, has more leverage than any other state, more than the United States, even. The Russian elite have chosen the United Kingdom as their escape haven. Ironically, the godfathers of the Russian system like Berezovsky, Abramovich, and now even Luzhkov have chosen to live in the United Kingdom, and you should expect another tide of Russian VIPs. Can you imagine how many of them will arrive if Russia were truly to awaken? This means that London has a great deal of leverage. I would bet that representatives of the Russian elite would behave better if they knew that they might not be welcome in London or, say, Vienna.

ANDREW: "Give me your rich, your sated, yearning to breathe safe," is it? I am not sure how this can be used as a lever in advance. The United Kingdom is not going to say that unless you do thus-and-such before you come, we shall not let you in to stay, nor would our courts promise to refuse extradition if it were legally justified. It is good that Russians have confidence in our judicial system, and perhaps that has some beneficial effect. But I ought to admit that I cannot be sure of my judgment on this. Maybe the possibility of coming freely to the West and living there is a more powerful magnet than I imagine.

LILIA: There is at least one beneficial effect so far. The fact that Russians in the United Kingdom and other Western states follow the rule of law shows that Russians are not genetically doomed to be lawless!

But back to the key line. There are various reasons for Western pragmatism in policy toward Russia. They include a desire to avoid being associated in any way with the American "neocons." The West's short political cycle also plays a role; Western political leaders have to achieve measurable results over the course of their brief terms. A values-based approach, however, will only yield results in the long term. Having no time and readiness to get strategically engaged, the Western powers are allowing the Kremlin to force them to return to the old geopolitical reality. The West certainly understands this trap but prefers to embrace Russia, fearing that an isolated Russia will start smashing windows—something that is quite possible. For all its provocations, the Russian elite is trying not to cross a line that would force the West to consolidate against Russia. The Kremlin sees the red line!

ANDREW: I agree that we are in a short-term cycle, given the imminence of the next Russian election cycle, Russia's desire to attract Western resources, and its diminished fears about Ukraine. I would add that this lull will very likely prove temporary because the situation in Russia itself is so uncertain. This would not be the first time that the cycle has changed its rhythm. I suppose, though I am not entirely sure that the European Union will one way or another get through its present crisis, and that the U.S. economy will recover. None of us can know who in the West will then be in office but perhaps they will prove to be effective leaders who will have the time, interest, and need to look with fresh eyes at the way forward on Russia.

LILIA: While the developed democracies are coping with their agenda, Russia, despite the Kremlin's modernist rhetoric, is moving in the opposite direction. I will be blunt: Russia's current system has no internal incentives for self-reform, and in its current state it could become a threat to Western civilization. I don't mean by this the threat of military confrontation; the Russian elite do not want military conflict with the West. I have in mind, rather, the destructive consequences of Russia's decay: instability, social turmoil, collapsing infrastructure, lawlessness, endemic corruption, and uncertainty in the Russian "backyard."

ANDREW: This is a very important point. I assume that what you have in mind is the problem of a self-contained elite at the top being incapable of generating or, for that matter, surviving real change. We have been here before, but the Soviet Union had a more developed infrastructure. The rigidity of the present setup is a critical weakness compounded by what seems to be the increasing unreliability of the instruments that underpin it.

LILIA: You've coined an axiom: "rigidity produces weakness." I have another axiom about Russia. The more the Russian leadership tries to prolong the life of the personalized system, the more it speeds its decay. Due to Russia's geography, its role in the world order, its elite's integration into Western society and the influence it exerts on various segments of the Western establishment, this decay will affect the outside world.

We've been discussing the leadership and the traps it faces. We have to look at Russian society as well. Russian society is in a much worse moral and political state than it was during the Soviet Union's final years. People back then had hope that freedom and pluralism would lead them to prosperity and a normal life. But twenty years of rot, disarray, and confusion disguised by liberal slogans have left some of them disillusioned with liberal democracy. The West's cooperation with the corrupt Russian state has increased the people's frustration with the West. The inevitable failure of "modernization from the top," supported by Western governments, could make Russia more anti-Western and more anti-liberal.

I don't want to draw conclusions that are too far-reaching. At the moment, a significant part of Russian society still is capable of moving toward liberal standards. This fact is amazing in itself: For years the Kremlin has tried to discredit liberalism and democracy, and yet many still want to believe in it! However, I have to admit that the longer the Yeltsin-Putin-Medvedev system, or, for that matter, any political regime with a "personalizer" in place, the deeper the degradation of society will be and the more difficult its transformation. Ironically, the Soviet system did not prevent people from embracing democracy and believing in its ideals, whereas the postcommunist Russian system of imitating democracy has put society in a destructive, nihilistic mood.

ANDREW: I recognize the truth of your saying that the Western model has lost by its association with past failures in Russia, and that Western courtship of Russian leaders has contributed to that, too. But I am loath to accept that this means that Russians would see a more brutal form of governance as a better outcome in the event of a crisis. There may be doubt as to either Medvedev's desire to deliver on his liberal-sounding agenda or his ability to do so even if he does want it. Yet his words seem to have gained some purchase in Russia anyway, which surely argues that liberal democracy in some form retains its attractions.

LILIA: Andrew, liberal democracy is still an attractive project for many Russians. This is not thanks to Medvedev and other talking heads at the top, but in spite of them! Or maybe I should rephrase that: The model itself is attractive. It is Western policy toward Russia and some trends within the Western political world that disappoint Russians or make them suspicious.

ANDREW: We should take this warning very seriously in the West. The alternatives to the emergence of liberal democracy in Russia are repellent. If Russians perceive that the West is indifferent to what goes on there, or is unprepared to be true to its own declared standards, then that would increase the threat of the repulsive becoming the reality.

LILIA: With respect to one "repulsive" option—the "iron hand," with its anti-Western agenda—I am afraid it is a possibility. A regime that is losing control could attempt to hold on by turning to violence. This scenario may only accelerate the downfall and implosion of the state. The Russian authorities have increased their use of scare tactics and repressive mechanisms. Not yet ready to turn to true mass violence, they employ selective intimidation. Gennady Gudkov, the Duma deputy and retired FSB colonel, explained this tactic. "The authorities have invented a new mechanism. They hire certain 'unidentified' folks who have 'to deal' with people. [Gudkov is referring to human rights activists, journalists, and opposition members as those to be 'dealt with.'] This is the way to intimidate and to harass opponents." He further explained that "dealing" with people means beating and murdering them. This is only one of many Kremlin intimidation "gimmicks."

Over the past five years (2005–2010), 41 Russian journalists have been killed and 344 severely injured. I don't want to imply that they were all killed on the direct orders of the authorities. But the political atmosphere—the total disrespect for law, freedom, and independent views cultivated by the ruling elite, their harassment of the opposition, and the fact that political murders go unpunished—establishes fertile soil for further violence. Scare tactics and the selective use of repression (executed not just by law enforcement structures but also by criminal gangs linked to these structures) reflects the emergence of a quasi-repressive regime, which might be more successful than blatant dictatorship and still be able to use liberal rhetoric. I believe that our goal is to prove that imitation and half-truths concealing ruthless arbitrary ways can be more dangerous than open authoritarianism, which, at least by its nature, discourages illusions. If this quasi-repressive regime fails to defend itself, it can morph into a truly repressive one.

ANDREW: We described late 2003 and early 2004 as a climacteric, because of the Yukos affair and the Orange Revolution in Ukraine. The turn of the year in 2010/2011 was ominous, too. The verdict against Khodorkovsky and Lebedev after their second "trial," whose reading began on December 27, 2010, was followed by authorized demonstrations in support of constitutional freedoms on December 31. The sentencing of, among others, opposition leader Boris Nemtsov to fifteen days in jail on charges of "insubordination" to police during those demonstrations in Moscow, and actions against those taking part in such gatherings elsewhere, had every appearance of being a preplanned government operation to intimidate vocal opponents of Putin. The authorities' message was clear: Think twice before you criticize Putinism. The authorities have continued to crack down on their opponents since then.

LILIA: Opposition representatives, especially Nemtsov, were detained in such a way as to humiliate them and demonstrate the Kremlin's readiness to be tough. They were detained on December 31, 2010, and had to spend New Year's Eve, one of the most important Russian holidays, in prison. Nemtsov, a former Russian deputy prime minister and one of the leaders of the liberal opposition, had been made to sleep for two nights on the concrete floor of a prison cell, and during his hearing the judge denied him a chair, forcing him to stand for five hours. As Nemtsov discovered later, a special official from the presidential administration had given orders to the police and court about how to humiliate him. Moreover, the pro-Kremlin movements were ordered to stage provocations inside and outside courtrooms where opposition leaders' trials were held. These facts demonstrated the Russian ruling team's crude methods. Putin certainly knew the details of these persecutions, and perhaps even took some pleasure in inventing them. "Liberal" Medvedev was nowhere in sight during this crackdown or during other police and court "performances." He usually vanishes from the scene when unpleasant events occur and then re-emerges as if nothing had happened. Even as the president tries to persuade the world that "freedom is better than non-freedom," the Russian regime has begun to employ methods that resemble those of Lukashenko in Belarus. Humiliating and repressing the opposition has now become common practice in Russia, especially in the regions.

This time, the political West was forced to express its concern, although the wording of these expressions was rather cautious and mild. Western civil society groups reacted in a much stronger way. Amnesty International, the human rights watchdog, declared Nemtsov and four other detainees (Ilya Yashin, Konstantin Kosyakin, Eduard Limonov, and Kirill Manulin) as "prisoners of conscience."

Open harassment of opposition spokespeople became a key element of the new election campaign of 2011–2012. The tough Kremlin approach reflected its growing insecurity.

ANDREW: Earlier, Freedom House, in its annual *Freedom in the World* report, also expressed concern over worsening human rights conditions in Russia. The report ranked Russia among the so-called "not free" countries, in which human rights are widely and systematically violated.

LILIA: So far, however, the major part of the Western political establishment has preferred not to notice the strengthening of the Kremlin's repressive syndrome. Let me again urge our readers to consider this paradox: Relations between Russia and the West have warmed and at the same time the Russian authorities have increased coercion over Russian society and the opposition. What does this say about Western governments? How can they justify their resets? How many representatives of the Russian opposition will be detained and persecuted, how many Russian journalists beaten and killed, before Western capitals decide to find ways to persuade the Kremlin that they are truly serious when they express their concerns?

I admit that the Kremlin understands that it has to think about its image and not overdo the "iron fist." Thus the Kremlin's "dual-track" policy: On the one hand, repression and open violence, on the other, co-optation of all those who are ready to serve the system by creating new "forums" for dialogue, with the agenda set by the Kremlin team.

ANDREW: I suppose you are thinking of the All-Russia People's Front (ONF), which Putin launched on May 6, 2011? There are also a lot of councils and other consulting bodies that sprang up at the initiative of the authorities that include popular personalities....

LILIA: Exactly! By the way, the emergence of Putin's Front was a clear sign that he wanted to return to the Kremlin. The very name, "Front," also showed that he was going to fight for his power!

There are still a lot of people who are ready, albeit only grudgingly, to be "co-opted" into those councils you've mentioned. The Presidential Council on the Development of Civil Society and Human Rights, in which the president discusses human rights abuses, is one of them. This policy of co-optation allows the Western establishment to pursue a "soft approach" to Russia, dismissing the crackdowns as "exceptions."

ANDREW: While we are talking, the Russian election campaign proceeds. We and the Russian population, of course, know the intended outcomes—the pro-Kremlin Front with United Russia as its core is to have a solid majority in the new Duma and a Putin appointee or very likely Putin himself is to settle down in the Kremlin for the next six years. As Stalin once said, the most important thing is not how many ballots were cast but how they are counted. Previous Russian elections have proved that the Russian Electoral Commission knows how to count votes.

But the sudden activity of the authorities is curious: Fronts are formed, new movements emerge, old parties are diminished. There is even a pro-Putin women's movement called "We Are the Best" (*Otlichnitsy*). The forgotten pro-Kremlin "liberal" party Right Choice was first reshaped by the Kremlin against the instincts of its existing leadership and then eviscerated because the Kremlin's new appointee, oligarch Mikhail Prokhorov, was deluded enough to imagine that he could lead an independent party. Just Russia is radically diminished, having failed the Kremlin. So much noise and gold for nothing!

LILIA: This election campaign will soon be over. But you are right: We need at least to mention its circus-like nature. We also have to put on record the fact that this merry-go-round of multilayered activity—repression–seduction–co-optation–bribery—means only one thing: Putin's team is not sure of its future and is not even sure whether it can manipulate the election. The fact that it has to cheat, harass, bribe, and rig more than it ever did before will have only one result—a lack of legitimacy for its power in the eyes of the population.

ANDREW: But outside observers may think otherwise because reformist talk by both Putin and Medvedev and modernization plans being drawn up by various experts look like signs of change to come.

LILIA: Thank you for reminding us about the continuing "reform talk." My hunch is that after the election Putin and his team will try to undertake some reforms in the economic area. But how will they succeed in stimulating growth while rejecting market competition and preserving the fusion between power and property?

I would argue that the most likely scenario for Russia is that of a determined authoritarian regime, which can put on soft gloves as necessary, presiding over continuing decline. This scenario will hold true even with some economic growth. After all, the economic successes of Putin's "Bonanza" presidency did not prevent crisis in the economic model that had supposedly flourished so vigorously from 2000 to 2008.

ANDREW: That last point may be true, but there are plenty who would prefer to think that the 2008–2009 crisis was the fault of others, and who would turn a blind eye to the fact that Russia suffered more than its peers because of its underlying problems. This is the key issue. Outsiders can and no doubt will think what they like. Some of them will continue to be seduced by the idea that Russia needs a "strong hand." Some of them will continue to listen to the traditional chorus of Russian claims to privileged victimhood. But what if a "strong man" is returned to office and his strength is confined to repression? Can one be strong in this narrow sense if one has no idea of what to do beyond sitting on the throne?

LILIA: You've raised rhetorical questions. A "strong man" with only a repressive agenda is the sign of a weak and ineffective system.

More and more Russians have started to understand that the Russian system is the core problem. The system is the source of the decay of a huge country with nuclear weapons and a demoralized population—decay that could have serious repercussions. Stagnation at any moment can turn into an ugly and violent struggle of various clans. Western leaders and experts are still "reading the old book" and reflecting on threats already familiar. Meanwhile, Russia's disintegration could mean a nightmare that could make the Yugoslav collapse look like a walk in the park. We have to understand that a Russian state that still seeks to base its identity on imperial ambitions is not sustainable in the long run.

Is the world ready to see Russia unravel, to see the emergence of new states or quasi-states on its territory, or even to see it devolve into a lawless, turbulent space? The process of disintegration has already begun. Vassal regimes subsidized by the Russian budget but independent from Moscow have already emerged in the North Caucasus. These are sultanates built on a foundation of militarism with elements of Wahhabi Islam. I'm referring to Chechnya, of course, as well as to other North Caucasus republics that are following its example. The emergence of anti-constitutional and alien elements within the Russian state in the North Caucasus has been eating away at it like a cancer.

ANDREW: The world is not ready for this, but it does have a hazy idea of the possibility. There is little objective reporting about the North Caucasus, and Russia restricts access by independent journalists. We know more perhaps about the situation in other parts of the Russian Federation. However, I have yet to see a convincing scenario as to how this nightmare might develop. It would be dangerous for us all. When I was in Belgrade at the end of the 1980s, it was hard enough to warn Western countries about what might happen, and hard for them to plan for it. But at least the possibility of a fresh breakdown in Russia needs to be on our minds. I think it is an element, if only as a suppressed fear, in Western attitudes already.

LILIA: This scenario has to become a hot topic for debate. Russia's existence as a country imitating the West and its co-opting of the Western political class already pose a threat to the Western community. You've mentioned earlier that Khodorkovsky was the first person in Russia to talk about this when he spoke about how Russia "exports corruption." He bitterly summed it up:

> My country is a huge exporter of two kinds of commodities. The first export is hydrocarbons, crude oil or natural gas. The second is corruption. In years past, certain European and American political leaders became victims of Russia's exported corruption.

In order to export a "commodity" like corruption, one must of course have a consumer!

A huge and prospering industry has emerged in the West. This industry includes law firms, banks, consulting firms, image makers, research centers, people in the arts, and former and acting politicians. The purpose of this industry is to serve the interests of the Russian elite directly or indirectly. Unable to modernize Russia, its elite have shown exceptional ingenuity when it comes to co-opting the West to sustain themselves and influencing Western policies.

ANDREW: Yes, but with mixed results.

LILIA: We need to recognize that Russian domestic problems could begin commanding international attention sooner than anyone realizes. The most exquisite makeup will not conceal these ugly blemishes.

Respected Russian economists estimate that the Russian authorities have enough economic and financial resources to get them through 2014–2015. The Kremlin can prop up these resources by raising taxes. This would mean that business will gradually move "into the gray" or leave the country. The authorities would then start borrowing from the West. The moment would inevitably come when the Russian state would have nothing left with which to pay them back. The economy would have exhausted its internal growth sources and be unable to develop under the burden of a corrupt bureaucracy and lack of transparency. Actually, even government economists recognize this unpleasant truth—though not always openly.

The authorities would then be obliged to start looking once again for an "enemy" to blame for their problems, and the West would be the ideal candidate. Thus the risk of a new "Cold Peace" is very real indeed for the foreseeable future.

ANDREW: There are other daunting problems. Russia's internal security is once again a matter of deep concern. Putin's promise when he came to power in 1999 was, above all, to ensure it. But twelve years later, things look worse, not better. Terrorism continues unabated. The most dramatic and distressing incidents include the following: in 2002, the "Nord Ost terrorist act," in which 916 people were taken hostage during a theater performance and 174 killed during the ensuing rescue effort; in 2004, two airliners were blown up in mid-flight by suicide bombers, killing 89 passengers and crew; again in 2004, a suicide bomber killed ten people in Moscow's metro; in 2004, 334 hostages died in the Beslan attack; in 2009, a bomb blasted the Moscow-St. Petersburg express, killing 26; in 2010, suicide bombers killed 40 people in an attack on Moscow's metro stations; and in 2011, a blast at Moscow's Domodedovo airport killed 35 and left more than 100 severely wounded.

LILIA: Let me add to this list hundreds of terrorist acts in the North Caucasus and southern Russia that never made the headlines or primetime news broadcasts. During Putin's presidency, the number of terrorist acts has increased sixfold. Terrorism has become an everyday fact of life in Russia. According to the general prosecutor's office, the number of terrorist acts in the North Caucasus doubled during 2010, with over 900 terrorist acts taking place in Russia's southern regions.

ANDREW: There is another criterion of domestic security: the crime rate. A total of three million crimes were registered nationwide in Russia in 2009, according to official statistics. However, a report by a research group attached to the general prosecutor's office says that the real number of crimes committed that year, including unreported ones, stood at 26 million and will reach 30 million by 2020. One can question such statistics, of course, but it seems that there is a trend here, with the crime rate increasing by some 2 percent a year or more, with millions of wrongdoings going unreported.

LILIA: Russia's murder rate is even more shocking. General Vladimir Ovchinski, former chief of the Russian Interpol Office, has admitted that the authorities hide the real numbers. Official statistics say that in 2009 only (only!) 18,200 people were murdered. According to Ovchinski, the real rate could be as high as 46,200.

The murder rate is rising 2.4 percent annually. Even the tally of officially registered murders ranks Russia as the third most violent country in the world, with 14.2 murders per 100,000 people, putting it behind South Africa (36.5 per 100,000) and Brazil (22 murders per 100,000). Russia is the only European nation to appear among the countries with the highest murder rates, falling between Namibia and Surinam.

ANDREW: The "Kushchevskaya murder" (Kushchevskaya is a small town in southern Russia) in November 2010 of a large family, including children, by a gang connected to local authorities that had been terrorizing the region for twenty years, struck a deep chord in Russia. This tragedy showed that links between organized crime and officials are an everyday feature of life in Russia. There are persuasive indications of organized groups within the federal bodies responsible for maintaining law and order themselves acting as criminal and predatory enterprises. This dangerous phenomenon appears to be on the increase.

LILIA: We are dealing with a situation in which essential parts of the state apparatus, from the bottom up, behave like criminal gangs. The key mobsters could be deputies or prosecutors, and they could use both thugs or the police to kill and rape. They appear in some cases to have ties to regional governors' offices, and some apparently even to the federal authorities in Moscow.

The Russian state has been extremely successful in guaranteeing the security of its ruling elite, however. In fact, Russian law enforcement organs have only one mission beyond their key task of taking care of the authorities: to grab assets, harass businesses, and persecute the opposition. Even Russia's leaders recognize that the corruption of the "power" structures is overwhelming. The new police structures introduced on March 1, 2011, are reckoned, according to Levada Center polling, by 63 percent of Russians to be no more than window-dressing reform, and by a further 13 percent as likely to have the effect of increasing police brutality and license.

As for terrorism, unfortunately, Russia is doomed to suffer another wave of attacks, not only because the Russian law enforcement organs are helpless and unable to conduct proper investigations, but even more important, because the situation in the North Caucasus is fueling terrorism among the younger generation that was born amid the brutality of the two Chechen wars. Observers report that five years ago, Islamist radicals had problems finding candidates for suicide bombings; now people are eagerly queuing up to do the job. We can see the beginnings of a vicious cycle at work. Rising Russian ethnic nationalism provokes a North Caucasian response, which in turn triggers more animosity among the Slavic population.

ANDREW: Several observers have commented on an unwritten pact concluded between Putin's team and society: political stability, security, and economic growth in return for the emasculation of political freedom and civil society. The formula worked for some time, as it did in North Africa. But today….

LILIA: This "pact" is finished, and the outward appearance of calm throughout Russia does not mean that society is ready for another "pact" with the Kremlin.

ANDREW: The next Russian president will certainly have some formidable problems to confront, and budgetary pressures will be one of them. The temptation to blame difficulties on outsiders will always be there. And while Russian politicians have plenty of company in doing that, their habit of pointing the finger at outside "enemies" is more deeply rooted than most.

LILIA: You're right. Russia will have enormous problems to confront; indeed it already has them. This is why Russia's normative transformation is so important; without it, Russia will present the darker side of its face to the world.

There is, however, a formidable obstacle on the Russian path to transformation. At the beginning of the twentieth century, the obstacle was an archaic society that was unprepared for freedom and competition. Today, the obstacle is a Russian elite that combine power and property and do not want any change. This elite will never begin Russia's liberalization of its own free will. Even a domestic crisis may not be enough to force it to change the rules. Pressure from below plus external influence could make this elite consider change, or at least get out of its way. Such pressure could well up at any moment after the state exhausts its capacity to bribe the population. As I've mentioned, the bubble could burst in the next four or five years.

ANDREW: Russia's rulers have been unsettled more than once by unexpected crises in other countries, with their own "power verticals" proving vulnerable. The temptation to put upheavals in former Soviet states down to foreign plotting was strong—so strong that they needed no evidence to assume that it was true. There are, of course, differences between Russia, Ukraine, and Georgia, and those countries in the Middle East that are presently experiencing difficulties. But there are enough similarities to trouble minds in Russia, it seems.

LILIA: There is definitely a common logic in the evolution of closed systems: When they lose their legitimacy, they implode. The official Russian reaction to the turmoil in the Arab world has been an odd mixture of unease and euphoria. The authorities know that they, too, have built a personalized regime and fear that it might not be any more resilient than those that have suffered in the Middle East. The Kremlin has stridently insisted that there are differences between itself and those other regimes. That seems to me to point to a degree of concern. The rise in the price of oil, which has come about because of the troubles in the Middle East, on the other hand, suits Russia's rulers and blunts the case for economic reform. No doubt they can sleep easier for that. But complacency can only accelerate their demise.

Sometimes systemic collapse can take a less obvious form: The rot "eats" away the system and the state, and society gradually decays. This scenario is the most dreadful, even compared to going down in flames or revolution, because it leaves such little hope for revival. One can detect strong elements of decay in both the system and society in Russia. People lose hope in the future. Those who still have energy emigrate. Indeed, there is a new wave of emigration from Russia today. According to independent sources, about 2 million Russians, first of all intellectuals and businesspeople, have left the country over the past two years. They are not so much fleeing a country as fleeing a system.

ANDREW: The government attempt to increase military conscription because of demographic pressures will only trigger further emigration of the able young.

LILIA: Of course! The question is, when will the West realize that Russia is moving down a disastrous path that could eventually present a grave challenge to it?

ANDREW: There can be no doubt that Russia's trajectory is of critical importance to the West, perhaps especially if that trajectory is one of increasing weakness. The West has nothing to fear from a strong and prosperous Russia, not least because such a Russia would be properly integrated into the international community. I do not see how an imperialist great power can be either prosperous or a valid partner for others.

You are right, too, to distinguish between the interests of Russia as a whole and the perceived interests of its ruling elite. The West should not confuse the two, though it frequently does. Government-to-government dealings are needed, however, and the tactical case for keeping them polite often gets in the way of telling hard truths, or even seeing them. Political leaders are inclined to see others in the same light as themselves, which is only human. It took Bush time to conclude, as he recalls in his memoirs, that the man who was by then Russia's prime minister was cold-hearted.

LILIA: Belief in appearances is an old and universal tradition.

ANDREW: I also agree that it is the West's duty to hold Russia to its freely accepted obligations as best it can, and to take note when it does not live up to them. You are right, as well, to say that the West's involvement is essential to Russia's transformation. I would only add that Russia has to earn that involvement. Western involvement cannot be conducted just by means of governments, but through the voluntary and, if you will, self-interested investment of the assets, whether financial or personal, of Western societies.

LILIA: In the meantime, Russia is approaching a moment when it will be not so much leaders or the elite as society at large that will determine Russia's destiny. No, I am not going to exaggerate society's readiness to reform itself. Russians have lost their constitutional right to choose their authorities by free and fair ballot and have returned to their accustomed lethargy. They've been watching passively and helplessly as their other rights (civil, social, and economic) have been taken from them. Having no opportunity or desire to express what they think and want through legal channels (such as independent parties, media, and parliament), they may well be reduced to speaking out through the only channel left to them, that is, by taking to the streets. As it always has been for us, we Russians are left with the worst possible option. Yet even as we speak, society has started to stir. Deep down, you can feel the formation of an angry and resentful tide. People are still reluctant to let their voices be heard openly, but emotions are burning inside—not because of Russians' world-renowned patience, but because they don't see a viable alternative. But too many factors have started to undermine the current stability. The only real debate left is whether the current order is fragile or brittle.

There is a lot of evidence that society and the system are drifting in opposite directions. The last time that happened, the Soviet Union collapsed. Revolutions can happen when just 1 percent of the population is prepared to take to the streets. In Russia nearly 30 percent of the population is ready to take part in protests. About 55 percent of Russians polled in spring 2011 believed that Russia needed adequately expressed political opposition, while only 16 percent thought otherwise.

ANDREW: The Levada polls reveal trends that ought to dismay the "power vertical." Fifty percent of respondents in the poll you have mentioned did not believe that the government could cope with inflation or prevent incomes from falling, and 32 percent said that the government could not ensure security or guarantee employment. About 74 percent said that the government couldn't make things "better." Only 23 percent still believed it could.

The parallel fact, much credited in the West, that both Putin and Medvedev get high approval ratings, rests, as you have said, on the fact that there is no alternative structure in place. The public fears that if they go down, the country may very well go down with them. Otherwise it is hard to explain that, despite this apparent confidence in the top leadership, only 40 percent of respondents reportedly felt in March 2011 that Russia was moving in the right direction, while 42 percent believed that it was moving the wrong way, with the remaining 18 percent uncertain. The polls showed, too, that 48 percent had no faith in Medvedev's anti-corruption program.

Polls shift, of course, but these figures were part of a downward trend.

LILIA: Frustration and disappointment do not mean that Russia will rise up tomorrow. The lull can continue for some time yet. The tide of wrath rises only slowly. We don't know exactly when or how it will happen. What might detonate an explosion? Economic collapse? A technological or climate disaster? A price hike? Pensioners' anger? A student movement? Official ruthlessness and corruption? A new terrorist attack? Or a government official's car hitting a child on the highway? It's not clear who, or what social or political group, will become the driving force of the inevitable dissent, but it is clear that it is coming. Government manipulation of the coming elections is playing with fire. It will only add to the erosion of the authorities' legitimacy. The apparent apathy and indifference of the Russian population are deceptive.

Moreover, there are systemic factors that have recently worked to support the Russian system, and now they are slowly but surely working to undermine docility. Corruption, for instance, helped both the elite and society to solve their problems through informal trade-offs and bribery. Today corruption has grown unbearable even for some segments of the elite. Corruption amounts to at least $300 billion annually and has become one of the key factors driving decay. Defense funds, according to an official estimate, are embezzled at one-fifth of the total. Or consider another factor: the "power vertical." Until recently, top-down governance helped the elite to guarantee their omnipotence. Today, it forces people to take to the streets to make their demands heard. Moreover, a breakdown in any branch of Russia's centralized system will cause the paralysis of the entire system, since all its elements exist in a pyramid of nominal subordination but uncertain control.

ANDREW: This is a dangerous situation. My guess—and it can be no more than a guess—is that the most senior members of the elite, very probably including Putin, are conscious of it but uncertain of how to deal with its risks. It is conceivable that the existing but hollowed-out constitutional structures could be revived to allow a turn toward constructive participation by a wider public in Russia's political life. That is what happened under Gorbachev, after all. However, it is also conceivable that frustration will grow, and that the ruling elite will refuse to acknowledge the right of the frustrated to be heard in time to prevent what the chairman of the Constitutional Court has warned could turn into a cry for dictatorship. Zorkin didn't refer to revenge, but a search for the guilty would be one implication of such a course. Zorkin has been accommodating toward the interests of the ruling elite in his rulings, which makes his December 2010 remarks in *Rossiyskaya Gazeta* worth summarizing. He warned that the interpenetration of crime and officialdom has reached such a pitch in Russia that it not only puts modernization into question but threatens the constitutional system, too. "Criminals take over major functions of the state and civil society and the consequences are not just alarming, but terrifying," Zorkin said. "A state which is incapable of defending its citizens from massive violence by bandits and corrupted officials is doomed to degradation. I stress degradation, not stagnation."

I very much hope that Zorkin's warning is premature, and that the liberal and constitutionally aware parts of the Russian body politic may be able to help channel things in a healthy direction.

LILIA: I would like to hope so, too. There are some numbers that could give us grounds for optimism. In early 2011, 56 percent of respondents said that they preferred "order," and 23 percent preferred "democracy." But at the same time, 36 percent were convinced that one couldn't exist without the other. And here is one more exciting number: 46 percent of Russians believed that people had the right to fight for their rights, even if those rights ran counter to the interests of the state. And another 16 percent said that the rights of one person were "higher" than the interests of the state. Around 48 percent of Russians said that Russia "needs more than anything that power should be placed under control of society."

Around a third of Russians constitute a frustrated "swamp" that would have to be awakened and convinced of the need for a new trajectory if change were to come about. This "swamp" has been deeply demoralized during Putin's time, but these people are not lost completely. Even as we speak (and I doubt this trend will have changed by the time our readers see this), about 40 percent of Russians believe that Russia needs radical change in some unspecified direction. The last time this mood held sway was 1991! Apparently some from deep within the "swamp" have awoken. The archaic part of the population that longs for the status quo constitutes 27–30 percent. That is Putin's base.

ANDREW: I do not want to be the wet blanket here but we should remember that change is difficult, and that a fair number of people would lose if it came about, and not just the powerful. Short-term pain for long-term gain is a difficult sell. Organized liberal opinion is not widespread, though the constituency for change is stronger in the major cities than in the country as a whole, and particularly I would guess in the heart of political Russia, that is, Moscow.

LILIA: You are right about that, but what is really amazing is the fact that Russia is not a traditionalist society anymore. It is a country with an atomized society that has lost its adherence to the old norms and standards, meaning that the secure base for political traditionalism is now very narrow. At the same time, atomization has not prompted Russians—or at least not yet—to consolidate around new rules of the game. Even so, Russian experts argue that Russians are more ready for risk and innovation than are many other nations. The problem is that Russians, not having strong normative regulatory mechanisms, are more inclined to become anarchic in their behavior than others. However, there are no insurmountable barriers preventing Russian society from learning new norms, as hundreds of thousands of Russians living in London or Silicon Valley have done. The key problem is the ruling elite, and not even the whole elite but only its upper echelon. Plus, of course, the bureaucracy. Yet polls in 2008 showed that 45.5 percent of the second echelon of the Russian elite were ready for freedom and competition—only they didn't want to fight for it. Thus the picture still is fluid, but there are some hopeful trends.

But I have to return to this warning: a society that has been demoralized as the result of deliberate government policy could become quite nasty. In an extreme situation aggressiveness and revenge could prove dominant emotions!

Consider just this one example: After twelve years of Putinism, the number of Russians who believe that Russia has enemies continues to increase. In March 2011, 70 percent of Russians said that they believe

Russia is threatened (only 19 percent think that Russia has no enemies). Who are these enemies? About 48 percent of respondents name the Chechen terrorists, 40 percent say the United States, 32 percent say NATO, and 30 percent say "certain forces in the West." This "enemy-haunted" mentality thrives even during a time of "reset"! About 63 percent said that Russia is threatened by NATO members!

Andrew, you come to Russia pretty often, and you therefore have some sense of the evolution of the public mood in Russia. What do you see?

ANDREW: There is a present malaise and a disconnect between the rulers and the ruled. There is no sense as far as I can tell of how, or by whom, this feeling that Russia is headed in a wrong direction may be addressed. The ruling group has, on the other hand, a more complacent idea of their future than others, and a continuing overall but maybe less assured belief in their ability effectively to manage the development of Russia. That said, there are divisions at the top as the next presidential cycle approaches and as, from time to time, troubling but not threatening public discontent surfaces, usually in response to local issues. Or so it seems to me, from my inevitably limited and largely Moscow-based experience. Russia is, as it were, looking for a fresh theme, and that is difficult for familiar faces to provide.

I said when we began this conversation that I was uneasy with the implication that the Yeltsin succession led necessarily to the power vertical established by Putin and defended by Medvedev. Personalities matter, and that could be significant over the next decade, too. The hardest thing to see is a structured outcome. I am sorry to come to such an unclear conclusion, but it is the best I can do in the first half of 2011. The smell of danger is in the air, but to me, no more than that.

Another point I made at the start was that the word "state," when applied to Russia, had a different sense from what a Western audience would understand by it. That observation has its bearing here when you think of possible futures for Russia. Let me use the change in Moscow to introduce a thought experiment about that. The removal of Moscow mayor Yuri Luzhkov in October 2010 took place in a controlled atmosphere, in the sense that the federal government and the Kremlin were there to prevent anything from getting out of hand. But even so, there was a pattern to the process that resulted. First, Luzhkov's departure, once it had happened, looked like no more than an incident to be forgotten quickly. The old mayor did not disappear without protest, but it was quickly obvious that he was powerless to do anything about the situation. His former colleagues and supporters did little more than turn to the new mayor, offer their services, and attempt to show that they, too, had always thought Luzhkov had been overly powerful. Those a bit lower down the scale showed zeal in anticipating what the new mayor Sobyanin wanted even before he had really asked for it, for instance, by clearing so many of the kiosks that he seemed to dislike without having clear instructions to do so. Or at least so it was said. And pressures for the redistribution of property and property rights rapidly grew, threatening the wealth built up by Luzhkov and his wife, Baturina.

Now for the thought experiment: Moscow was a mini power vertical. If the lynchpin of the Russian vertical were removed or diminished, would the bureaucrats not look first to ingratiate themselves with a new boss, if they could identify one, and do so by competitive denunciation and excessive zeal in putting into action what they supposed the boss wanted? Would they refrain from attacking the owners of assets that might be vulnerable, justifiably or not, to the charge of corruption? The various security forces would surely look for a master. To whom would the governors attach themselves? Would Ramzan Kadyrov, for example, attach himself to anyone? And so on. The picture is clear I suppose. But remember that in this case, unlike that of Moscow, there would be no outside controlling force to prevent a chain reaction. The conclusion is twofold: Any loser of power is likely to be forgotten quickly and is likely to lose more than just power; and unless a changeover is quick, the results of a struggle will be destabilizing. Those presently in power know all this very well. Controlled liberalization is institutionally improbable in a Russia that lacks the structure of a state in the Western sense.

LILIA: I would go even further. Real liberalization of the Russian state from within and from the top is impossible, because liberalization will trigger its collapse. The elite and the leadership know that. The Russian matrix can survive only as personalized power. However, this matrix is doomed but its collapse will be ugly and dreadful.

Andrew, you've raised several troubling issues. I will comment on one: what will happen if centralized power starts to unravel? The short answer would be: I don't know. We remember what happened after Gorbachev started to lose control at the end of the 1980s and the very beginning of the 1990s. Elite groups started to grab property and tried to wrest as much independence from the center as they could; the national republics ran away; and society was left to seek its own means of survival. We observed complete state failure. Thus we can expect to see the same today if the Kremlin vertical breaks its "spine." Centrifugal trends will restart, and the struggle for power and property will be renewed. The question is how bloody this struggle will be, given that there are new political forces in the game, for example the law enforcement structures—the FSB, the Interior Ministry, and the prosecutor's office. They could add terrible violence to the cycle, especially if the liberally minded opposition is not consolidated and if moderate pragmatists from the political class fail to support the idea of transformation. The nightmarish prospect that the system may unravel before a constructive alternative is formed haunts me. We can already observe signs of systemic paralysis. I can only guess at what this process might bring.

The unraveling of a top-down system based on repressive institutions cannot help but be painful, even at its best. But if that system continues to metastasize, the results will be even more cataclysmic.

WHAT CAN THE WEST DO?

ANDREW: So what is the answer? I will give my view of how the West should act and ask for your comments and reflections on the Russian point of view. I have usually found that the Russians I speak with argue that there is rather little Western countries can do directly to encourage liberal change in their country. I've also found that those who consider that Moscow's present course is the right one say that the West ought to redeem itself by accepting the premises of that course, notably Russia's right to be the dominant actor in the former Soviet space. Both groups, however, say that, difficult though it may be, the West has a duty to understand what is really going on in their country. I could not agree more with that.

LILIA: Liberals do not belong to either of these groups. But we also hope that the West will understand Russia.

ANDREW: Analyzing Russia will be an ongoing task with ever-changing answers. Different points of view within the European Union, United States, and former Soviet countries—which are also owed the respectful attention to be accorded to Russia—will persist, along with the interests of the various countries involved.

Grand schemes like the one that pictures the European Union, Russia, and the United States as three legs of a security stool are flawed. Russia is in no fit state to prove a reliable leg. Nor is the European Union. Better to look at the concrete possibilities before scheming.

LILIA: I agree with you on the "grand schemes" that Russians and some Westerners enjoy all too much. Things that receive the title "grand" usually do so to compensate for a lack of vision, confusion, or to hide vested interests. Soviet leaders loved "grand designs," and the whole communist myth was based on the idea of greatness that constantly retreated from you, like the horizon.

ANDREW: The West attaches too much importance to individual figures. It should lift its gaze to the wider picture. We have discussed the role of business and mentioned the need to take into account the various audiences that make up the whole of Russia, not just the leaders of the day. The West is an idea as well as a set of countries for Russians, and how it addresses them matters. We agreed that the West had been tainted by its close association with Yeltsin. The lesson is obvious, or ought to be, today.

LILIA: It seems that the Western community has been even more tainted by its association with the current ruling tandem.

ANDREW: So I would advocate a piecemeal approach, concentrating on concrete possibilities. Russia is one of many European countries, not a singular power with overarching rights. Its entry into the World Trade Organization has been held up not by opposition to Russia as a political entity, but by the difficulties of negotiating with Moscow on particular issues. If Russia decides to join and implement the necessary agreements, then that has every chance of becoming a liberalizing force within Russia and a major step toward the further integration of the country into the global economy, very much including that of Europe. Russia's integration into the world economy has been proceeding, bump by bump, to be sure, for many years now. We can take heart from that.

I hope this is enough to describe a general attitude. What is your advice?

LILIA: I accept your framework. Here is my "inside" perspective.

For starters, there is a legitimate issue to consider: To what extent can foreign policy be an instrument of leverage on domestic developments if the country does not intend (and it does not at the moment) to join the European Union or NATO and voluntarily limit its sovereignty?

In this era of interconnectedness, even U.S. sovereignty is limited. Upon joining the Council of Europe and signing the Universal Declaration of Human Rights, Russia affirmed that it agrees that its domestic affairs are not solely its own private concern. Therefore Europe should pay attention to what is happening in Russian society, and it should pay special attention to the state of human rights and democracy. For Europe not to be worried about what is going on in Russia would constitute a violation of its own principles.

ANDREW: Yes indeed. You touched on a central point when you referred to the limitations on sovereignty inherent in membership in multilateral bodies. Russia has great difficulty in accepting that. Great powers, as Moscow sees it, make their own rules and can change them as they will, just as the rulers of great powers are not bound by the laws they expect their subjects to obey. You may see that statement as too highly colored. But I believe that it illustrates a real attitude that affects the current regime's approach to both internal and external affairs. We have spoken of the possibilities of major change in Russia, as have for that matter both Putin and Medvedev. Until that happens, it seems inevitable that the interaction between Russia and all her neighbors will be less effective than it ought to be, and that relations between the West and Russia will in practice be governed by short-term tactical shifts rather than solid commitments. It is essential that the West does all it can to hold Moscow to its word, for instance, in the Council of Europe, which you referred to, and I hope, in due course the World Trade Organization.

LILIA: Agreed. As for Western influence, in my view there are two approaches to take.

The minimalist approach could be called "Practice what you preach." The West should try to restore the role it once played in the eyes of Russian society, as an attractive alternative to Russian personalized power. Earlier you expressed the same view. It bears repeating.

One would hope that Western leaders would also follow Western standards when they deal with the Russian elite. For now, they still consider "personal chemistry" with the Russian authorities as the secret to success with Russia. What does "following Western standards" mean in practice? First of all, it means a more reticent and dignified way of dealing with the Russian elite and leadership. In other words, don't behave like Berlusconi or Sarkozy!

Western politicians must also stop making informal trade-offs with representatives of the Russian ruling team. A change in style and rhetoric, a switch to businesslike cooperation without attempts to please and hug the Russian leaders, would constitute a real contribution to Russia's transformation.

The maximalist agenda is tougher. It is all about creating incentives for change. The problem is that one has to decide whether conditions are ripe for such an approach. Ripened conditions would include the maturation of Russian society and the emergence of an opposition prepared to pursue liberal aims. I would also add to this list evidence that the continuation of personalized power is threatening to foment a crisis in Russia that might have international spillover effects. Finally, I would look for some clarity in realizing that an accommodating policy toward authoritarian Russia will bring more negative consequences than would attempts to create a "transformational environment."

Several of the conditions mentioned above are already in place. The rest could be the subject for discussion.

ANDREW: I have great sympathy for your points. Your conditions for a maximalist approach come, however, in two different sets. The first paired set is based on a benign evolution in Russia and the second pair on the reverse. Western policies are at present based on varying degrees of hope that the first will come true.

LILIA: The problem is that the second pair of premises will be understood and accepted too late. I believe the West must urgently understand that Russia continues to be a factor that influences not only Western (and especially European) security, but also the principles on which the West is based. This brings us to the next two steps: an admission of the existence of a causal link between domestic evolution and foreign policy and the creation of a benevolent environment for Russian reforms.

ANDREW: Yes, certainly.

LILIA: Indeed, any external incentive for Russian transformation will require a common and coherent Western strategy toward Russia.

The West should also introduce a conditionality mechanism into its dialogue with Moscow. It has many ways of showing the Russian elite that its ability to prosper in the West and its behavior inside Russia are intimately connected. Of course, the West needs to be sure that its salvos fall on target. The Russian public should not suffer from a Western attempt to find a way to civilize the Russian elite. The West must therefore learn to distinguish between the regime and the people, and to understand that the interests of the two do not coincide. This is what you, Andrew, have stressed in our conversation.

Finally, Europe could make an indirect contribution to reforming Russia by supporting reform in the newly independent states—above all in Ukraine, Georgia, and Moldova, where pro-European forces are more consolidated. A flourishing and democratic Ukraine or, of course and for the sake of argument, Belarus would make for a convincing argument that Russian society, too, needs to develop a new relationship with its regime. A stable and democratic belt around Russia would thereby become an important factor in its renewal. This is also something the Russian elite fears much more than the West's direct influence on Russian society.

Do you think this approach is too idealistic?

ANDREW: No, I think you are absolutely right. The difficulty will continue to be in reaching sufficient agreement on where Russia is headed, not least in Europe. I doubt that the European Union will soon in reality have a Common Foreign and Security Policy (to use its official title) to make this as effective as it might be.

LILIA: Even an attempt to move in this direction would be an achievement. Measures proposed in Congress to target particular Russian officials accused of complicity in the brutal treatment of detained Russian citizens, notably the lawyer Sergei Magnitsky, who died in a Russian jail in 2009, have been echoed in Canada and the European Union.

Their effects in Moscow have been palpable. All of this proves that even individual European members of parliament and U.S. congresspersons can really stir the waters. In July 2011, the State Department placed Russian officials implicated in the death of Magnitsky on a visa blacklist. One has to admit that the State Department move looks like an attempt to save the "reset" from greater damage looming in a Senate bill that envisages much tougher and wider sanctions (it also includes asset freezes and would affect not only the 60 law enforcement officers accused in the Magnitsky case, but also the officials implicated in the killings of reporter Anna Politkovskaya and human rights worker Natalia Estemirova).

The Russian opposition has become more active in appealing to Western institutions, mainly legislatures. Mikhail Kasyanov, Boris Nemtsov, Vladimir Ryzhkov, and Vladimir Milov have addressed Western parliaments to demand an end to the policy of acquiescence toward the Kremlin. Boris Nemtsov suggested that Congress should adopt a bill supporting democracy in Russia, one that would slap sanctions on Russian officials, not on the country as such. While such initiatives are hardly in immediate prospect, the fact that they are raised by Russian opposition figures may act as a corrective on those in the West who persist in believing in rosy portraits of the Russian political regime. The Russian liberal opposition puts Western governments in an uncomfortable situation when their representatives come to Western capitals. It's also a sad irony that we, the liberals, sometimes provoke more irritation in official Western corridors than do Russian officials.

ANDREW: There are also Russian journalists who need support, for example. It would be difficult to arrive at a general policy to cover individual instances, but actions like these have their place.

LILIA: Even if the Western political community is not ready to think about how to combine situational pragmatism with the normative dimension, we should keep raising the issue. To be sure, this discussion would interrupt the Russo-Western waltz and thus would not be popular.

By the way, after Lukashenko rigged his presidential election in December 2010, sent goons to beat up the demonstrators, and arrested more than 600 people, including seven of the nine presidential candidates, the West reacted pretty harshly. The United States and the European Union condemned the repression and reimposed sanctions against the regime. However, I heard from Western observers and politicians a lot of reasons and excuses as to why the West can't take the same approach with Russia. Those excuses didn't persuade me. I continue to believe that a selective approach to principles undermines both those principles and those individuals who would counsel such a course.

ANDREW: You are right, in principle, but tactics get in the way of purity. And of course it is easier to be strict with Lukashenko, the ruler of a small power who has few if any friends, than it is to be strict with Russia, a bigger power with a more ambivalently perceived political profile.

I don't see why becoming unpopular by raising awkward issues, which you mentioned just a little earlier, should deter us. We have been discussing the possibility of Russia's evolution getting out of control. The results would be grim if that happened. If there is any way that the West can legitimately and effectively support the emergence of an alternative and more liberal structure in Russia, and one that might be able either to direct frustrations into constructive channels or encourage existing power holders to devolve authority into such channels, then the West should seize the opportunity. That would mean taking your warnings to heart first. We should obey the ancient injunction to be strong and of a good courage.

EPILOGUE: DREAM OR NIGHTMARE?
A CONCLUDING LETTER TO THE READER

We've come to the end of our conversation, for now. It would be good if the coming years proved our anxieties about the future wrong. Nevertheless, it is clear that difficult times are ahead.

We have tried to establish, from both the liberal Russian and Western perspectives, a view of today's Russia and the West's past and future interaction with it. This "dual-track" approach helped us to clarify our initial assumptions and to reconcile them when they appeared at first to conflict. We hope that the resulting dialogue will prove useful to others in testing their own convictions. We've tried to act as devil's advocates for each other, and we hope to have done the same for you.

We have raised issues that we believe are important, even crucial, for a proper understanding of Russia and the nature of the Western agenda with respect to it. Others will have their own ideas about these topics. The manner in which Western beliefs about post-Soviet Russia have evolved—along, of course, with the parallel dynamic in Russia itself—has been crucial to the shifting attitudes of both parties. That will remain the case. Western society's ability to cope with what is now very much a post–Cold War legacy will rest on the constant and rigorous re-examination of underlying Russian realities. Thus, to a great extent, this discussion is about the Western democracies, the nature of their engagement with the illiberal world, and the way pro-Western observers view the West from the outside.

We retraced recent history and discussed whether there had been chances for other scenarios to prevail in postcommunist Russia. Here, we allowed ourselves to disagree, but we found common ground in the need to look back without emotion or undue prejudice, and to try to see past "windows of opportunity" so as to consider why what happened, happened. Our hope has been that this exercise may illuminate future political choices. We explored in particular how far the erosion of the potential for a better institutional framework and its replacement by a system of personal and therefore inherently arbitrary rule led to the dangers confronting Russia today, and why Western political and business leaders were reluctant at the time to foresee and then consider the likely consequences of these events.

We agreed to differ on the degree of inevitability in the transition from Boris Yeltsin to Vladimir Putin and his political regime, as well as on the West's degree of responsibility for Russia's trajectory. We offered different views on the Western role in Russia's transformation and on the nature of the West's preoccupations.

We came to similar conclusions on several things of importance to both of us. We are convinced that the Russian system of personalized power is not sustainable in the long run. An imitation democracy that helps this system to survive has now begun to lose its legitimacy. We are also convinced that, in the end, foreign policy is the servant and product of domestic imperatives. We agreed that realpolitik, especially in its simplistic edition, is a policy that will soon prove frustrating and may well surprise its advocates. Pragmatic gains from that policy may be at risk in the longer term.

We argue that the relationship between Russia and the West cannot be based on narrowly defined interests only. That approach is inadequate because it leaves out a fuller understanding of how the relationship is shifting and what tomorrow may bring. We are therefore convinced that liberal democracies cannot develop a proper strategic agenda if they limit their policies to short-term pragmatism. It is natural and right for preoccupied political leaders to focus on immediate and pressing priorities, but the real power of the West to aid Russia in its transformation into an effectively governed and liberal member of the transatlantic community resides in the power of Western ideas and standards.

The more we engaged in debate, the more challenges and loose ends we seemed to discover. Having reached the end of our ruminations, we find that we are confronted with a serious intellectual puzzle and political conundrum: A Russian civilization that reproduces archaic personalized power has been able to survive so far by imitating the leading paradigm—liberal democracy—and by co-opting its representatives. There are many political imitations in the world, but Russia's is unique. It is a state with certain elements of a superpower; it is alien to the West, rejecting the West internally but surviving by cooperating with and even partially integrating itself into the West. There is no doubt that this phenomenon has had an impact on the West.

How will the world's Cold War–era institutions cope with new challenges? Will the West solve the dilemma of developing a security partnership with Russia even as it co-exists with it under a regime of mutually assured destruction? Is the West simply too exhausted to think about a new normative engagement with the outside world? If not, can liberal democracies find more prudent ways to pursue their democratic ideals? Or will they continue to follow their self-interest? What will Western governments do when they discover that the Russian modernization and the reset are just another restart down a familiar road? Finally, what will the West and the rest do when Russia's current stability proves to be a myth? There will always be questions, but there are more than the usual number today, and they come at a particularly worrisome moment in the history of the new Russia.

Imagine yourself in the theater. The third act is over but the actors do not want to leave the scene. Some of them could have left it, but the director and the producer forced them to go on. Lights are shining, music is playing, and the actors have ceased to play any coherent part, but they nevertheless keep trying to win the attention of a weary and impatient audience. The latter is beginning to look for the exits. But the doors are closed, and the only way out is to tear them down. Indeed, some of them are already hammering on the doors....

We believe that this theater metaphor is suggestive for Russia today. The 2011–2012 electoral cycle is intended to keep the same play on the stage through yet another version of the same underlying script. The acclamation that greeted Medvedev's strained call at the United Russia gathering on September 24, 2011, for Putin to run for president again confirmed the bitter truth of this parable—that a regime that cannot renew itself is condemned to decay. Although more and more of their Russian audience is tired of that script, they lack the will or the faith to come together and demand that the players get off the stage or take a new direction. The playwright, producer, and their team still have a chance to continue the show, but not forever. Maybe not even for much longer….

Russia is entering a new stage in its development, in which it will try to find a civilized way to break out of its debilitating rut. Certainly, no insurmountable obstacles prevent Russia from fully joining the shared adventure of European civilization. But it could be that, as happened in 1991–1992, the present system will start to unravel before an institutionally robust alternative can be built to replace it. Such an alternative, if it could be established, would be founded on values that are as dear to the majority of Russians as they are to Westerners. As such, it would command the true assent of Russian society. The contrary risk of another false dawn would become a moment of truth for the West, for the rest of the former Soviet states, and for Russia itself. Mikhail Khodorkovsky's concluding words in his January 26, 2011, interview in the *New York Times*, among others, ought to trouble the consciences of all of us: "People are living for a long time these days. The current generation of Western politicians is going to hear the gratitude or the condemnation of its own descendants in its own lifetime." The West cannot treat Russia without having a care for its own soul.

INDEX

C

F

G

H

M

N

O

P

Q

R

S

T

U

V

W

Y

Z

ACKNOWLEDGMENTS

These conversations would have never been published without the support of a wonderful group of people. We are grateful to Jessica T. Mathews, president of the Carnegie Endowment for International Peace, for her unwavering encouragement. We also thank Executive Vice President Paul Balaran and Vice Presidents Thomas Carothers and Tom Carver for their support. We appreciate the insights of James F. Collins, director of the Russia and Eurasia program, and Dmitri Trenin, director of the Carnegie Moscow Center. Our thanks also to David Kramer, executive director of Freedom House, for his advice.

We are also grateful to Chatham House for its role in nurturing inquiry into the questions we've been debating. We profited greatly from a discussion of our ideas in fall 2010 with James Sherr, James Nixey, Bobo Lo, Craig Oliphant, Alex Nice, Andrew Monaghan, and Elisabeth Teague. We thank James Nixey for his comments on an initial account of our conversations.

It would be impossible fully to acknowledge all those who have, in one way or another, contributed to our dialogue. We have in the course of our conversations mentioned the names of some of those with whom we have agreed, or disagreed, both recently and over the years. But the list could never be complete, so instead we thank the people, whether Russian or not, who have talked, argued, and written about the seemingly eternal question of what Russia is and how the West should relate to it.

None of these of course takes the blame for our mistakes. Nor do those in Moscow, Warsaw, Paris, Washington, Berlin, London, or even Davos or Yaroslavl whose conversations or writing have fed our minds over the years.

We would also like to thank the great team who prepared this manuscript for publication.

Our thanks go to Ilonka Oszvald, senior publications manager at Carnegie, for her terrific help and for shepherding the book through the production process. We are also grateful to Daniel Kennelly, our editor, who gave the manuscript invaluable polishing. We appreciate the help of compositor Zeena Feldman, proofreader Carlotta Ribar, and cover designer Jocelyn Soly. We also appreciate the enthusiastic promotion of the book by the Carnegie team.

We are grateful to all, and to our families for their patience, support, and help.

CONTRIBUTORS

LILIA SHEVTSOVA is a senior associate at the Carnegie Moscow Center, where she chairs the Russian Domestic Politics and Political Institutions Program. She is also an associate fellow at the Royal Institute of International Affairs (Chatham House). Shevtsova is the author of *Yeltsin's Russia: Myths and Reality*; *Putin's Russia*; *Russia: Lost in Transition*; and *Lonely Power*.

ANDREW WOOD is an associate fellow at Chatham House and a consultant to a number of companies with an interest in Russia. He was British ambassador to Russia from 1995 to 2000.

CARNEGIE ENDOWMENT FOR INTERNATIONAL PEACE

The Carnegie Endowment for International Peace is a private, nonprofit organization dedicated to advancing cooperation between nations and promoting active international engagement by the United States. Founded in 1910, its work is nonpartisan and dedicated to achieving practical results.

As it celebrates its Centennial, the Carnegie Endowment is pioneering the first global think tank, with flourishing offices now in Washington, Moscow, Beijing, Beirut, and Brussels. These five locations include the centers of world governance and the places whose political evolution and international policies will most determine the near-term possibilities for international peace and economic advance.

OFFICERS

BOARD OF TRUSTEES

FSC
www.fsc.org